The Spider's Thread

The Spider's Thread

Metaphor in Mind, Brain, and Poetry

Keith J. Holyoak

The MIT Press
Cambridge, Massachusetts
London, England

This book was set in ITC Stone Serif Std by Toppan Best-set Premedia Limited. Printed and bound in the United States of America.

Library of Congress Cataloging-in-Publication Data

Names: Holyoak, Keith James, 1950- author.
Title: The spider's thread : metaphor in mind, brain, and poetry / Keith J. Holyoak.
Description: Cambridge, MA : MIT Press, 2019. | Includes bibliographical references and index.
Identifiers: LCCN 2018017618 | ISBN 9780262039222 (hardcover : alk. paper)
Subjects: LCSH: Poetry--Psychological aspects. | Psychology and literature. | Metaphor--Psychological aspects.
Classification: LCC PN1083.P74 .H65 2019 | DDC 808/.032--dc23 LC record available at https://lccn.loc.gov/2018017618

10   9   8   7   6   5   4   3   2   1

for Hongjing,
who after an eclipse renewed the light

Because You Asked about the Line Between Prose and Poetry

Sparrows were feeding in a freezing drizzle
That while you watched turned to pieces of snow
Riding a gradient invisible
From silver aslant to random, white, and slow.

There came a moment that you couldn't tell.
And then they clearly flew instead of fell.

Contents

Acknowledgments

So many people contributed to this book, in so many ways, that it's hard to know how to start thanking them all. My good friend Koon Woon, poet and critic, led me to appreciate the complexities of both metaphor in poetry and the process of poetic creation, and contributed his sensitive interpretations of several poems. Herbert Clark, who long ago taught me the importance of pragmatics in thinking and language, brought me up to date in his review of an early draft of the manuscript. The book also benefited from the careful reviews of Keith Oatley, who pointed me to connections with literary psychology, Adam Green, who helped refine my discussion of the neuroscience of creativity, and Dušan Stamenković, who guided me through the thorny thickets of the linguistic and psycholinguistic literatures on metaphor.

Many others came to my aid, sometimes unknowingly, by helping me think through hard questions that arose as I tried to grasp how the brain operates as an engine of creation (Mark Beeman, Mathias Benedek, John Kounios, Robert Morrison, Oshin Vartanian), how metaphor relates to analogy and conceptual combination (Zachary Estes, Sam Glucksberg, Boaz Keysar, Walter Kintsch, Patrick Plummer), why politeness is inherent in poetry (Peter Gordon), how to teach children what poetic symbols are (Joan Peskin), how personality impacts creativity (James Kaufman, Gerardo Ramirez), why consciousness remains a mystery (Hakwan Lau, Martin Monti), and how artificial intelligence relates to the natural variety (John Hummel, Hongjing Lu, Alan Yuille). I also thank my consultants from the next generation of Holyoaks, who advised me on art (Jim), music (Neil), and French literature and philosophy (Vanessa).

I'm especially grateful for the practical help Airom Bleicher provided in tracking down permissions to reprint poems and reproduce art works, and generally doing his best to keep the project organized. Finally, I thank my editor Philip Laughlin at MIT Press for encouraging me to weave the book from its first tentative thread into a completed web.

Preface

"A Red, Red Rose" by Robert Burns

O my Luve is like a red, red rose
  That's newly sprung in June;
O my Luve is like the melody
  That's sweetly played in tune.

So fair art thou, my bonnie lass,
  So deep in luve am I;
And I will luve thee still, my dear,
  Till a' the seas gang dry.

Till a' the seas gang dry, my dear,
  And the rocks melt wi' the sun;
I will luve thee still, my dear,
  While the sands o' life shall run.

And fare thee weel, my only Luve!
  And fare thee weel awhile!
And I will come again, my Luve,
  Though it were ten thousand mile.[1]

Since civilization began, people have yearned to grasp what it means to be human. For some that quest has led to religion and spirituality. For some it has led to the arts, including poetry, and for some to science, psychology in particular. A seeker may travel multiple paths. One of the founders of the Romantic movement in poetry, Samuel Taylor Coleridge, was proud to call himself a psychologist as well as a poet.

Indeed, there was a time when poetry and psychology were linked almost as closely as the legendary Eros and Psyche, love and the soul. As in Burns's "A Red, Red Rose," poetry has always embraced love and the emotions more generally. Meanwhile, *psychology* (from its Greek root) originally meant "the study of the soul." Only much later, with the rise of the modern discipline of psychology in the late nineteenth century, was the field reinvented as "the study of mind and behavior."

Since its modern inception, psychology has been a fragmented discipline. In the early decades of the twentieth century some of those fragments maintained a connection to poetry. A subfield of literary psychology developed, dominated by ideas brought to prominence by Freud and Jung and influenced by the methods of phenomenology. Long before psychoanalysis was invented, poets and writers had explored the antechamber of consciousness and the darker caverns of the unconscious mind.[2] Inner conflict and emotional confusion have provided rich fuel for poet and psychologist alike.

But as psychology blossomed through the twentieth century, its connections to literature (with some important exceptions) largely faded away. The behaviorist movement heaped ridicule on the very idea of consciousness, or even of mental events—as far as psychology was concerned, poetry had been dispatched to the scrap heap. Though behaviorism was largely passé by midcentury, the cognitive zeitgeist that replaced it favored the study of elementary mental processes in tightly controlled laboratory experiments. The guiding idea was to first focus on basic processes underlying perception, attention, and memory, on the assumption that more complex cognition would eventually be understood in terms of its elementary building blocks. As a practical matter, the poetic experience is not easily captured and held up for scrutiny in a laboratory. Within modern cognitive psychology, psycholinguistics (the psychology of language) has flourished, and the comprehension of metaphor has been viewed as fair game, but only after extracting it from the complexities of poetry.

The separation between poetry and psychology is a microcosm of the greater schism between the arts and sciences, which in 1959 the novelist and chemist C. P. Snow famously dubbed the "two cultures."[3] In the ensuing decades, heated debates have flared as to who's to blame. The favored culprits are either the soulless scientists, who arrogantly anticipate building a Theory of Everything, art included; or the scientifically illiterate intellectuals steeped in the humanities, who see science as just another subjective viewpoint pretending to be somehow special.

I toss this small book out as a filament—a spider's thread—in hopes of making a connection between the arts and sciences, and in particular between poetry and psychology. This filament is made of metaphor—a mysterious human capability that links thought and emotion with language. My aim, in part, is to suggest how literary psychology, now extended to include literary neuroscience, might be developed further based on recent work in cognitive science. This effort can be nurtured, I will argue, by bringing together ideas developed by poets, literary critics, philosophers, linguists, psycholinguists, cognitive psychologists, computer scientists, and neuroscientists.

But my hope is to do something more than encourage the scientific study of poetry. The experience of reading or writing poetry is not reducible to a scientific description, any more than the experience of watching a butterfly is reducible to theories of vision and entomology. In the sense I intend, literary psychology will keep is connection to the original Psyche— the symbol of the soul, which takes the butterfly as its emblem.

Why me? A fair question indeed. I'm a cognitive psychologist by training, with experience in the methods of computer simulation and cognitive neuroscience. Much of my research has been focused on understanding human thinking, and in particular thinking by analogy—a process intimately connected to metaphor. I'm also a poet and a translator of poetry (a risky endeavor with its own connection to analogy). Like many young people, I wrote poetry in my early years, but was swept away by cognitive psychology as soon as I entered the University of British Columbia as an undergraduate. Decades later, established as a professor of psychology at the University of California, Los Angeles, the poetry came back.

Fine—a psychologist and poet—a plausible base, perhaps, for trying to link the two fields. But scientists and poets (the latter especially) tend to make a fetish of "greatness," so perhaps my effort has been doomed from the outset—alas, I've failed to hit the exalted mark in either endeavor. I'm reminded how poor C. P. Snow was berated for daring to talk about the two cultures given that he was acclaimed neither a great novelist nor a great chemist.

I stand open to the analogous criticism. But let me offer my own analogy in defense. In chapter 6 we'll talk about a process called conceptual combination—merging two concepts to create a new one. Psychologists have noticed that in some cases it's hard to predict what will make the best example of the new concept, even if we can point to stellar examples of each of its constituents. Suppose we combine the concepts of *pet* and *fish* to form the concept of a *pet fish*.[4] Now, a cat is an example par excellence of a pet, yet it makes a terrible pet fish. And though a tuna is an impeccable fish, you wouldn't want one as a pet. A guppy, on the other hand, is not especially impressive as an example of either a pet *or* a fish—but as a pet fish it serves quite well, thank you. And so as psychologist poet, I (at the risk of immodesty) aspire to be the guppy.

In my case, the psychologist-poet combination did not gel immediately. For most of two decades I kept psychology on one side of my brain (metaphorically speaking) and poetry on the other, taking care not to let them bleed into one another. I took a passing interest in psychological studies of metaphor, but gleaned nothing that helped in writing poetry. Psychology, like science in general, takes the objective view of things from the outside. But poetry, like all the arts and (not coincidentally) like the life of a human being, requires the subjective view of the experiencer. It's all very well to take the first line of "A Red, Red Rose" and investigate why it makes such an effective simile. A more subjective but perhaps more important question is why I was moved to read Burns's poem at my mother's funeral, and what *that* felt like.

This book began when I finally let drop the mental curtain I had placed between poetry and psychology. Here I try to play both sides of the fence, combining the objective view of a psychologist with the subjective view of a poet. Regarding the latter, I don't mean to elevate my own introspections as special evidence (though I'll draw on remembered experiences from time to time). Rather, I've aimed to draw insights from poets and other humanists who've tried to convey their own inside views of how poetry is created and appreciated.

So, though this book is about the science of poetry, it's also about poetry. Its overarching theme is not metaphor, but metaphor in poetry. Along the way, we'll sometimes approach our theme via wide detours—as though trying to surround it and take it by surprise. But metaphor in poetry is the topic to which we will keep winding back. To guard against getting lost in the thickets of the mind and brain, each chapter (even this preface!) begins with a poem. Think of each as a homing beacon to guide us back on track. I try to heed the advice of the literary theorist Philip Wheelwright: "There is a danger here as in any other analytic approach, of spoiling the poetry by talking about it too much or too glibly, of imposing alien patterns on holy things. But the danger is minimized if, after the necessary theorizing has been done, we are wise enough to become silent and turn back with reverent attention to the poetry."[5]

As for that great gulf separating the arts and sciences, perhaps we can shrink it a little. Just remember that the opposite of art is not science, and the opposite of science is not art. The opposite of them both is barbarism.

1 The Space Within

"Tao Te Ching" (Chapter 11) by Laozi

Thirty spokes share the wheel's hub;
It is the center hole that makes it useful.
Shape clay into a vessel;
It is the space within that makes it useful.
Cut doors and windows for a room;
It is the holes which make it useful.
Therefore profit comes from what is there;
Usefulness from what is not there.[1]

This book is an extended conversation about poetic metaphor. The conversation began when a fellow poet and I each read a few of Robert Frost's essays on poetry. One passage in particular grabbed our attention: "Poetry is simply made of metaphor. So also is philosophy, and science, too. ... Every poem is a new metaphor inside or it is nothing."[2] I decided to take Frost's claim seriously, and follow where it might lead. You, the reader, are invited to join the conversation.

The tradition of bringing psychological insights to bear on literature began with Aristotle. Over the past century this tradition has been enriched by the contributions of scholars who have called attention to the ways stylistic devices in literature relate to the operation of the human mind.[3] Many who came before me—poets, psychologists, philosophers, neuroscientists, linguists, logicians, literary critics—contributed ideas that impacted this book. My aim has not been to rehearse the myriad academic controversies, but to focus on ideas that I anticipate will prove especially fruitful going forward.

Why focus on metaphor in *poetry*—why, in fact, turn the spotlight on poetry at all? After all, metaphors are found in prose as well (as this book will demonstrate repeatedly). And over the past couple of centuries prose has almost entirely displaced poetry in popular literature. Yet there are reasons to suspect that poetry has a special connection both to metaphor and to the human mind and brain. A first clue lies in the fact that poetry arose, often independently, in the oral and later written traditions of virtually all cultures and languages around the world. As I will discuss in chapters 9 and 10, poetry is a special form of language in which symbolic meaning is wedded to the rhythmic patterns of speech sounds. Or as the contemporary literary critic Harold Bloom succinctly defines it, "Poetry essentially is figurative language, concentrated so that its form is both expressive and evocative."[4] Metaphor is an especially important variety of figurative language. More generally, the language of poetry calls attention to itself—in the words of the Romantic poet John Keats, "Poetry should surprise by a fine excess"[5]—and in so doing casts an aura of "strangeness" over its subject matter.[6] Metaphors are certainly common in prose and everyday conversation, but (if Frost is right) they are particularly essential to poetry. In his "Defense of Poetry," another Romantic poet, Percy Bysshe Shelley, argued that as the richest source of new metaphors, poetry serves as an engine to generate new concepts—making poets (metaphorically) "the unacknowledged legislators of the world."[7]

The poet Frederick Turner and neuroscientist Ernst Pöppel called attention to the peculiar way rhythmic poetry triggers the joint activity of brain regions that support language, thinking, emotion, music, and internal reward.[8] In essence, an engaging poem brings the reader's entire brain into play. And the psychological impact of poetic engagement—what the poet and critic Dana Gioia, harking back to the origins of poetry in magic and shamanism, calls *enchantment*—can be profound.[9] Turner and Pöppel observed, "There is an awareness of one's own physical nature, of one's birth and death, and of a curious transcendence of them; and, often, a strong feeling of universal and particular love, and communal solidarity."

The scientific study of poetic engagement may therefore open a unique window on the mind and brain because poetry (to quote the neuroscientist Arthur Jacobs) "might be well suited to compactly demonstrate the complexities with which our brains construct the world in and around us, unifying thought, language, music, and images with play, pleasure, and emotion."[10] In this book I argue that the scientific investigation of literature, and specifically metaphor in poetry, occupies a rich borderland between the humanities and science that deserves to be explored more deeply. Poetry is not only of interest in its own right, but can also serve as a microcosm of human creativity more generally.

citir Aristotle?? . _____

A poetic metaphor is a kind of metaphor, and a metaphor is a kind of comparison.[11] A comparison elevates the number two—two things are considered in relation to one another. Breaking each down into aspects of some sort, we note points of commonality and points of difference. We make this effort, most often, for a reason. We want to learn something.

One particular comparison bears on the nature of this book—that between two modes of knowledge, the *objective* and the *subjective*, or what is sometimes termed the *outside view* and the *inside view*. As the philosopher Thomas Nagel has emphasized, the axis from the objective to the subjective is a continuum, not a clear categorical divide.[12] When we take the objective view of things, we act as spectators considering the world, including ourselves, as if from the outside. In the most refined and disciplined form of the objective view, humans take the stance of scientists, obtaining knowledge derived from shared, systematic, and verifiable observations of the world. At the subjective extreme, we each view the world from our unique inner vantage point. Any normal person (we presume, though each of us only has firsthand access to oneself) has an inner consciousness—sensations, perceptions, feelings, and thoughts. Though we can attempt to express our inside view to others, using words or other modes of communication, no one else directly shares our personal consciousness. There is an irreducible loneliness at the core of the human condition.

There are many ways to try to understand poetic metaphor, and these vary in objectivity. A psycholinguist might conduct experiments to try to answer questions such as these: How long does it take to understand a metaphor as compared to a literal statement? Are similes and metaphors processed differently? What factors lead people to judge different metaphors as more or less apt? A neuroscientist might investigate the neural circuitry activated when people process metaphors. A linguist might sample a body of poetry and tally the frequencies of specific metaphorical comparisons, perhaps comparing how these overlap with metaphors that occur in prose and everyday speech. A philosopher might consider in what way (if any) the meaning of a metaphor is truly distinct from that of literal language. A literary critic might analyze individual poems and evaluate the novelty and aptness of their metaphors, and trace links to the writings of earlier poets. And a poet (with a suitably analytic bent) might ponder the emotions and circumstances that spur him or her to write.

Objectivity seems to fall off as we move from the methods of science through those of the humanities, on down into the realm of subjective experience. Many assume that objective knowledge is the best, and perhaps only, form of knowledge. I prefer to take seriously a deep insight that permeates the poetry of William Butler Yeats: that "no one can choose absolutely between opposites."[13] In traditional western thinking it's natural to take dimensions of difference and break them into strict binary oppositions, as in figure 1.1.

But in eastern thinking, opposites are viewed very differently, as figure 1.2 suggests.

Figure 1.1

Figure 1.2

The latter figure shows the famous symbol for yin and yang. According to Chinese philosophy, two interdependent forces underlie everything that exists. Yin, represented by the dark portions of the circle, is the negative, passive, hidden, cold, wet, feminine force, associated with the earth. Yang, the white portions, is the positive, active, visible, hot, dry, masculine force, associated with the heavens. Neither of the two is elevated above the other; rather, everything depends on the balance between them. The vessel is only useful because of the empty space within it. As the curved boundaries suggest, the two forces are dynamic and their relative power varies (much like the shifting and cyclic seasons). And each embeds a small circle representing its opposite: within yin we find the seed of yang, within yang the seed of yin. They are opposites that complement each other, eternal and ever changing.

Returning to poetry, we need to balance and merge the inside and outside views, which interact as yin and yang. I take inspiration from the poet and critic T. S. Eliot, referring to a friend of his who helped mold modern views of metaphor: "Mr. I. A. Richards, who ought to know, if anyone does, what equipment the scientific critic needs, tells us that 'both a passionate knowledge of poetry and a capacity for dispassionate psychological analysis' are required."[14] I offer this book, in part, as an example of how passion and dispassion, humanism and science, can work together.

Building on the ideas of many forerunners, I will sketch a *neurocognitive* approach to metaphor as it works in poetry and explore what it means for literary criticism. I use the term *cognitive* very broadly, embracing not only cognition in the sense of the intellect, but also emotion and personality as these bear on creative cognition. The prefix *neuro-* is appended to emphasize that cognition and emotion are grounded in the operation of the brain.

The book is not meant to be exhaustive (or exhausting!) in its treatment of metaphor. The intended audience for the book spans C. P. Snow's two cultures. In fact, one key aim is simply to introduce the two cultures to one another, and perhaps get them on speaking terms. With this goal in mind I've tried to include enough background material to keep everyone on the same page (quite literally). My implicit rule of thumb is to include material I believe a poet and a cognitive neuroscientist would both need to know in order to strike up a meaningful conversation about metaphor in poetry. In general, I've tried to minimize linguistic formalisms, computer algorithms, neuroanatomy, and the like—indispensable tools for suitable experts, but too likely to be off-putting for the uninitiated (or even experts in allied disciplines). But while aiming to be accessible to a general audience, I've tried to avoid the pitfalls of superficiality. I delve into details whenever these seem especially important to understanding the neurocognitive approach to metaphor in poetry. Those interested in tracing scholarly sources and exploring further will find a great deal of background information in the notes section at the back of the book.

Each of the remaining chapters addresses a basic question that needs to be answered on the way to understanding the neurocognitive foundations of poetic metaphor:

—Chapter 2: How do people interpret a metaphorical poem?

—Chapter 3: How is metaphor related to literal meaning and to the basic organization of human language?

—Chapter 4: How have modern views of metaphor evolved from the insights of a peculiar forerunner—the poet (and psychologist) Samuel Taylor Coleridge?

—Chapter 5: How is metaphor related to inner experience—the core of human consciousness?

—Chapter 6: What have psychologists learned about two mechanisms that make it possible to grasp metaphors—analogical reasoning and conceptual combination?

—Chapter 7: How does the brain enable creative thinking, including the ability to create and grasp metaphors?

—Chapter 8: What roles do analogical reasoning and conceptual combination play in understanding metaphors?

—Chapter 9: How does metaphorical meaning relate to the sound patterns of poetry?

—Chapter 10: What are poetic symbols, and how have they been used in modern poetry?

—Chapter 11: How are poems actually used by people, and how is metaphor linked to a particular quality of poetry—politeness?

—Chapter 12: How do conscious and unconscious brain networks work together in writing poetry?

—Chapter 13: How is poetic creativity linked to personality traits and (sometimes) mental illness?

—Chapter 14: What makes poetry (or anything else) authentic—and could a computer create authentic poetry?

—Chapter 15: Can poetry teach critical thinking, imagination, and empathy?

My hope is that the approach advanced in this book will help give a sense of how poetic metaphor operates, even though the story is preliminary and leaves our understanding incomplete. Rather than presenting a finished theory, I aim to point the way forward—as more is learned about the mind and brain, more will be learned about the human capacity for metaphor. Given the choice, I would rather be approximately right than precisely wrong.[15] It has been claimed, after all, that it's impossible to talk about metaphor nonmetaphorically.[16] Indeed, the word *metaphor* itself originated as a metaphor in ancient Greek—its root implies a meaning that has been set in motion, a displacement carried over from one thing to something else quite different. I will freely use many metaphors for metaphor (starting with the book's title), and raise questions that lack ready answers. To follow Jorge Luis Borges, "It's enough that if I am rich in anything, it is in perplexities rather than in certainties."[17]

2 Launching the Filament

"A Noiseless Patient Spider" by Walt Whitman

A noiseless patient spider,
I mark'd where on a little promontory it stood isolated,
Mark'd how to explore the vacant vast surrounding,
It launch'd forth filament, filament, filament, out of itself,
Ever unreeling them, ever tirelessly speeding them.

And you O my soul where you stand,
Surrounded, detached, in measureless oceans of space,
Ceaselessly musing, venturing, throwing, seeking the spheres to connect them,
Till the bridge you will need be form'd, till the ductile anchor hold,
Till the gossamer thread you fling catch somewhere, O my soul.[1]

Let's begin by reading a poem together. The word *poetry* comes from a Greek root meaning "to make"—a poem is an act of creation. To be readers we need the help of another, a maker of poems (one of those the Scots, half a millennium ago, called a *makar*). A poet. Answering the call, Walt Whitman kindly lends us "A Noiseless Patient Spider," a poem he first published in 1868. Read it over—once to get the general sense of it, then again more closely. What does it mean to you? Ponder awhile, then read on.

What does the poem say? What shall *we* say? Perhaps something along these lines. ...

The poem is written in two parts—two stanzas—each five lines long. In line 1 the poet draws attention to a spider, working quietly ("noiseless") and steadily with a humanlike quality ("patient"). The poet also draws attention to his own presence in the scene ("I mark'd" in line 2). The spider is alone ("isolated") on a small space ("promontory") that abuts a chasm. From within this isolated space embedded in nature, the spider strives to make a connection to something, anything, out in the "vacant vast surrounding" by drawing forth its delicate inner substance. The spider aims, we suppose, to weave its web. But the first step is making a connection to something firm, and that goal requires painful, repetitive, lonely work—"It launch'd forth filament, filament, filament, out of itself." The spider does what spiders must do, but we sense this is no ordinary spider.

Rather, the spider and its labors provide a metaphor for the soul of the poet. The early cue to the personal human element, the "I" of line 2, becomes in the second stanza a direct address to the deepest part of the poet himself ("O my soul"). The spider (line 1) and the soul (line 6) are brought into immediate correspondence by virtue of being positioned in parallel lines (each in the first, shortest, line of their respective stanzas). Now we see how the spider's struggle to survive by making connections within the natural world is like the soul's struggle to build a bridge that can somehow bring it out of its own isolation. The soul, like the spider, is patient and persistent ("Ceaselessly musing, venturing, throwing") in drawing out its inner substance and seeking to form connections to something beyond itself. Just as we hope and guess the spider will eventually succeed in building its web, the poet ends with a note of hope that the soul's quest will be realized, that the threads of itself, thrown forth almost blindly into the "measureless oceans of space," will at last "catch somewhere."

Was your own reading of the poem similar? Is it possible to read the poem differently somehow? Suppose, for example, that we try to imagine what the poem may have meant to Walt Whitman himself.

A bit of biographical background may be helpful. Whitman is today revered as a founder of American poetry and of free verse, but during his early life and career he endured many defeats and rejections. He was almost certainly homosexual, in a social milieu where this form of sexuality was not accepted. He was fired from various jobs. His masterpiece, the poetry collection *Leaves of Grass*, was revised and republished multiple times over his lifetime. The first edition, self-published in 1855, contained just twelve untitled poems. Its critical reception ranged from tepid to cold (with the notable exception of Ralph Waldo Emerson, who became an early supporter). Some readers labeled the work obscene.

Even in midlife (he was in his late forties when he composed "A Noiseless Patient Spider"), Whitman may well have felt that neither he nor his poetry had found a stable connection to the social world around him. Whitman had been deeply affected by his experiences aiding the wounded in military hospitals during the American Civil War, a calamity that had ended in 1865 but left the nation with enduring divisions. Against this backdrop, then, what might the poem have meant to him?

An intriguing possibility is that Whitman chose the word *filament* in part because of its association with electricity, a form of energy that fascinated him.[2] He used the adjective *electric* in well over a dozen poems, most written after the Western Union Telegraph Company was formed in 1856. In the 1867 edition of *Leaves of Grass*, the first line and title of an early poem was changed to "I Sing the Body Electric." During the middle of the nineteenth century a number of inventors were struggling to develop an incandescent lightbulb, for which the filament was critical. Curiously, Thomas Edison, who in 1879 succeeded in creating a practical lightbulb, was also the inventor of the first commercial recording device (the wax cylinder), and around 1890 may have captured the voice of Whitman reading. In any case, electricity (and by extension the filament) for Whitman provided a symbol for the harnessing of powerful natural forces, including sexual energy.

The opening of the poem can be read as an appositive, a juxtaposition of two noun phrases that refer to the same individual: "A noiseless patient spider, / I mark'd. ..." The spider is thereby identified with "I"—the poet is himself the spider. "Mark'd" (an old-fashioned contraction of *marked*) simply means "noticed," but the word is also suggestive of making a mark, or writing on a page. The poet, though "isolated" in the world, endlessly sends forth his poems as "filaments" that might connect to others. And indeed, over the course of decades Whitman kept revising, expanding, and republishing *Leaves of Grass* (in which "A Noiseless Patient Spider" was eventually included).

In the second stanza, the "measureless oceans of space" perhaps symbolize America itself. The poet consoles himself with the hope of one day connecting to and linking the separate "spheres" of a nation recently divided by the Civil War. Perhaps (if the "filament" is metaphorically electrical), he imagines his fresh kind of poetry casting its light on the new land of America. Whitman the outsider dreams of becoming the spiritual leader of a new democracy.

The poet can surely be granted a personal connection with his own poem, but perhaps readers may as well. A friend of mine, a poet who has long struggled with mental illness, read the poem and was immediately struck by the word *patient*. Instead of reading it as an adjective, he took *patient* to be a noun modifying another noun, creating a conceptual combination—a noiseless "patient-spider." My friend identified the spider with himself and was reminded of his experiences long ago as a patient in a mental hospital. The first stanza conveyed the sense of a dungeonlike place where he, the spider, labors in the most meager light. He interpreted the verbs in lines 3–5 of the first stanza—*explore, launch'd*, and *unreeling*—as describing himself, doing the work of preparing to connect with something or somebody in the world beyond the hospital. Similarly, he read the second stanza as describing how the soul struggles to connect with something (the world, or some person) even in the flimsiest way. This reader, as a poet, felt a similar longing goading him to write poetry.

My friend had read a lot of poetry, especially on the themes of isolation and madness. For him, Whitman's poem resonated with others. For example, a Theodore Roethke poem, "In a Dark Time," includes the lines, "What's madness but nobility of soul / At odds with circumstance?"[3] Roethke seems to suggest that the soul itself is not fundamentally altered by madness. Through a chain of allusions, Whitman's poem about isolation and the quest to escape raises a deep ethical question—who gets to define madness, anyway? In "Counting the Mad," Donald Justice describes (in verses that echo the children's nursery rhyme "Three Little Pigs") the varying fates of the mentally ill—with the chorus "And this one cried No No No No / All day long."[4]

I suspect that my friend's interpretation of the Whitman poem is rather different from the one you formed initially. Is there any other way to read it? I had my own reaction. For days I was seeking a title for this book, before a line had been written, before having any clear idea of what I wanted to say. I felt I needed a working title to give myself some direction. I thought the title of a book about metaphor should be a metaphor—preferably, a metaphor for metaphor. I began googling and reading, meandering in search of something, not knowing what, unsure where to look. Perusing famous poems, I found "A Noiseless Patient Spider."

It struck me as a beautiful poem, expressing something about the struggle to connect the lonely realm of inner experience with the external world beyond. A few months earlier I had read a book by the philosopher Thomas Nagel, *The View from Nowhere*. Nagel raised a fundamental problem, with deep implications for the nature of mind, knowledge, morality, and freedom: "how to combine the perspective of a particular person inside the world with an objective view of that same world, *the person and his viewpoint included* (italics added).[5] I thought, is this not the heart of poetry, its very soul, the struggle to communicate inner experience to the outer world in which we live?

With these ideas evoked, I read Whitman's poem as a metaphor for metaphor. From the soul of inner experience, we draw filaments of language—strings of words that are more than mere words—and toss them out in hopes of connecting our subjective world to the objective realm in which communication is possible. If the first connections can be made, if "the ductile anchor hold," then we can begin to weave a metaphor that might recreate some image of our own inner experience inside the consciousness of another human being.

I first thought that the book's title could be *Gossamer Thread*, from the last line of the poem. But that seemed a bit too vague, obscure out of its context. Some days went by, and then I thought of *The Spider's Thread*.[6] To connect to metaphor, we need to start from the spider.

So, we have considered multiple interpretations of the poem. These include an interpretation guided by knowledge of the poet who wrote it (Whitman), another guided by the difficult personal history of a particular reader (my friend), and one guided by the current pragmatic concern of a further reader (myself). Each different—but not altogether so. In each reading, the spider's filaments provide a metaphorical source for understanding some struggle to form a basic human connection—of the soul, of the poet's offering, of a marginalized individual, of metaphor itself. The struggle persists in the face of uncertainty, even despair. Another reminding, this from the existential philosopher Kierkegaard: "When a spider plunges from a fixed point to its consequences, it always sees before it an empty space where it can never set foot, no matter how it wriggles."[7]

Working together as readers, have we gleaned all the allusions and possibilities suggested by the poem? Have we extracted the essence of its meaning? Alas, although our various interpretations may seem insightful, something seems missing. We might say that after our dissection, nothing has been lost but the poem itself.

What is poetic metaphor? What is it for? What does its nature tell us about the minds of those who write or read it? How does it relate to creativity and to madness? This book is an exploration of questions such as these.

3   I'm a Riddle

"Metaphors" by Sylvia Plath

I'm a riddle in nine syllables,
An elephant, a ponderous house,
A melon strolling on two tendrils.
O red fruit, ivory, fine timbers!
This loaf's big with its yeasty rising.
Money's new-minted in this fat purse.
I'm a means, a stage, a cow in calf.
I've eaten a bag of green apples,
Boarded the train there's no getting off.[1]

To use a metaphor, it is often said, is to say one thing to mean something else. How is this possible, and why do it? "I'm a riddle. ..."

Over the centuries, the use of metaphor has been admired as a mark of genius, most notably by Aristotle: "The greatest thing by far is to have a command of metaphor. This alone cannot be imparted by another; it is the mark of genius, for to make good metaphors implies an eye for resemblances."[2] But metaphor has also been disparaged as a mark of muddled thinking. One of the greatest psychologists of the twentieth century, Amos Tversky, was particularly dismissive: "Because metaphors are vivid and memorable, and because they are not readily subjected to critical analysis, they can have considerable impact on human judgment even when they are inappropriate, useless, or misleading. They replace genuine uncertainty about the world with semantic ambiguity. A metaphor is a cover-up."[3] Tversky's conclusion would be damning indeed—if it weren't a metaphor!

Ambiguity, of course, is generally disparaged. The philosopher Ludwig Wittgenstein admonished people to speak clearly or else keep silent.[4] But for better or worse, his advice is routinely ignored. Certainly, any decent computer language will define a fixed meaning for each symbol so as to avoid confusion in programming. But the natural human languages that we speak are spawning grounds for all manner of ambiguity and vagueness.[5] Take the simple word *line*. The mathematical definition is clear enough: a straight one-dimensional figure having no thickness and extending infinitely in both directions. But that is hardly the most common use of the term in everyday speech. A line can be a segment drawn with a pencil—noticeably thick, limited in length, and wiggly. It can be a length of cord, or part of a communication system, or a wire used to catch fish. It can be a bit of speech to be uttered by a character in a play, or a bus route, or a boundary between states or countries. A line can be the track on which a railway is built, or a dose of cocaine ready to be snorted through one's nose.

Those meanings are all for *line* used as a noun. But the same word can instead be a verb: people can line the streets, or line their pockets. These (and many other) meanings of *line* are literal enough to be listed in standard dictionaries, along with various conventional expressions rooted in metaphor: we can read between the lines, worry about it down the line, or put it all on the line.

These myriad ambiguities might seem to blur the line between metaphorical and literal language. And indeed, we might say that metaphor plays yin to the literal yang—not simple opposites, but interdependent forces. Still, creative metaphors have some special properties. Here is an example of the word *lines* embedded in a very metaphorical poem (line 12, highlighted by added italics).

"Sonnet 18" by William Shakespeare

Shall I compare thee to a summer's day?
Thou art more lovely and more temperate:
Rough winds do shake the darling buds of May,
And summer's lease hath all too short a date:
Sometime too hot the eye of heaven shines,
And often is his gold complexion dimm'd;
And every fair from fair sometime declines,
By chance, or nature's changing course, untrimm'd;
But thy eternal summer shall not fade
Nor lose possession of that fair thou ow'st;
Nor shall Death brag thou wander'st in his shade,
When in eternal lines to time thou grow'st;

So long as men can breathe or eyes can see,
So long lives this, and this gives life to thee.[6]

Line 12 would make little sense out of context, but its meaning grows organically within Shakespeare's poem. Line 1 starts the metaphors rolling—"Shall I compare thee …?" To introduce terms I will use throughout the book, what is being talked about (here the poet's lover) is the *target*, and the concept to which the target is compared is the *source*.[7] The first source introduced is a summer's day, relative to which the lover is more lovely and more temperate. Like summer, and like all mortals, she or he is threatened by time.[8] The shadow of Death looms over us all. And then line 12, the line about lines—not just any lines, but "eternal lines." The poet is talking about his own poem, bragging that it will be remembered forever. "Lines to time" emphasizes the songlike meter of the sonnet (words set "to time"). And the poem itself, once finished, is now consigned "to time." Yet another suggestion is that in this eternal poem, "thou" (the lover, or the reader, or perhaps anything beautiful) will continue to grow like a line (a lineage) extending across time, just as the poem resonates through the generations to come. So far, Shakespeare's bold promise of "eternal lines" has been kept—his poem is remembered after half a millennium, and counting.

In a poetic metaphor, we do not need to absolutely choose between different interpretations. In fact, it's best to let them resonate with one another—a metaphor acts as what Philip Wheelwright termed a *plurisign*, in which multiple meanings merge into a new unity.[9] Or as Paul Ricœur remarked, a "poetic reading, as opposed to that involved with scientific or technical discourse, is not obliged to choose between two meanings that are equally admissible in the context; what would be ambiguity in the one is honoured as the plenitude of the other."[10] A bit more formally: in a standard case of ambiguity, some X can mean A *exclusive-or B*, but it's not clear whether A or B is intended. In a plurisign, by contrast, X can mean A *and B*. The contrast between true ambiguity and a plurisign resonates with what the neurobiologist Semir Zeki has described as a continuum in neural activity in response to perceptual inputs.[11] Depending on the nature of the image cast on the retina, the brain sometimes constructs a single interpretation, sometimes shifts between multiple interpretations, and sometimes blends multiple interpretations. Zeki argued that this neural fluidity contributes to the aesthetic impact of visual art. Similarly, a metaphor talks about the target, but to some extent blends it with the source. The result is a plurisign that conveys a sensation akin to double vision.

Many metaphorical sources that arise from basic aspects of human experience and from frequent use have become conventional, both in poetry and in everyday communication. For example, metaphor can turn almost anything into a person, a transformation so commonplace it has its own term—*personification*. Death is seen as the Grim Reaper who harvests us; a floating cloud is identified with a human wanderer; a bead of dew falling from a flower becomes a teardrop. More generally, as Jorge Luis Borges observed a half century ago, many metaphors are woven from recurring connections between concepts, which manifest themselves in similar phrases.[12] Thus rivers flow, and so does time; eyes can look down on us, and so do stars; sleep brings rest, and so too perhaps does death.

Within modern cognitive science, the observation that conventional metaphors permeate everyday thought and communication became the defining hypothesis of a field known as *cognitive linguistics*. As initially articulated by George Lakoff and Mark Johnson, this view seemed to go so far as to deny any real distinction between the metaphorical and the literal.[13] (The philosopher Max Black had cautioned that "enthusiastic friends of metaphor are ... ready to see metaphor everywhere."[14]) Lakoff and Johnson suggested that metaphor pervades thought so completely that the meanings of almost all expressions (basic perceptual terms like *red* were excepted) are metaphorical. They claimed, for example, that a word like *depressed* is understood in terms of a conceptual correspondence or *mapping*, summarized by the slogan SAD IS DOWN. As a psychological claim, however, this extreme view failed experimental tests.[15]

A few years later, Lakoff and Mark Turner surveyed many examples of conventional metaphors that abound in poetry—life is a journey, its stages are the seasons of a year, death is a departure, and so on.[16] They characterized metaphoricity as a kind of continuum and accepted that some meanings (such as the ordinary sense of *dog*) are quite literal. In their more nuanced view, metaphors require grounding in source domains that are not themselves completely understood via metaphor. My own view (widely shared) is that a novel metaphor is a creation of the imagination built on the foundation of literal language. The metaphorical and the literal are interdependent: yin needs yang, and yang is not just yin in disguise.[17]

Metaphorical sources, especially those used in poetry, have strong ties to human perception, action, and emotion. Lakoff and Turner argued that metaphorical sources are often grounded in normal sensorimotor experience, but also acknowledged that some conceptual mappings, such as PEOPLE ARE PLANTS (underlying such metaphors as the youth in full bloom, the invalid wasting away), are not. Humans do not experience the life cycle of plants, but they do understand it and feel its emotional impact. As I will explore in chapter 10, poetic symbols (such as a rose as a symbol of love) are often sources that transfer emotions to a target with which they have become associated. A poetic symbol acts as a kind of plurisign—it refers simultaneously to something concrete, specific, and emotion-laden, and *also* to something more abstract or ethereal. Considered as a type of category, this dual character of a poetic symbol creates what the philosopher Hegel termed a *concrete universal*.[18] Unlike a logical universal, which refers to the characteristics of a class of individuals rather than to any particular instance, a concrete universal is not fully explicit. Instead, the universal remains tied to the individual entity that symbolizes it. Rather than separating itself to form an airy abstraction, the concrete universal inherits and keeps the emotional charge of the symbol.

Because metaphors based on especially powerful symbols remain productive, a new writer can potentially weave them into novel variations. Jean-Paul Sartre, playing with the perennial conception of time as a river, spoke of "time flowing softly, like an infusion warmed by the sun."[19] Writing a century and a half ago, Victor Hugo took darkness, the familiar symbol of ignorance and evil, and created a metaphor to project calm and caution: "Nations, like stars, are entitled to eclipse. All is well, provided the light returns and the eclipse does not become endless night."[20]

To help clarify the nature of poetic metaphor, it may be helpful to consider an example of language that is neither poetic nor metaphorical—just flat-out literal. On the afternoon of January 15, 2009, bird strikes caused both engines to fail on a jet that had just departed from New York's LaGuardia airport. About three minutes after his plane lost power, the pilot, Captain "Sully" Sullenberger, made an unpowered emergency water landing on the Hudson River. All 155 passengers and crew were safely evacuated. The incident was dubbed the "miracle on the Hudson." Here is the transcript of conversation between the air traffic controller and others in the first two minutes after power was lost.[21] "Cactus 1549" refers to the distressed aircraft (US Airways 1549), and "New York Tracon" is the air traffic control group. Teterboro is a nearby airport in New Jersey that was considered as an alternative to LaGuardia for a possible emergency landing. Each utterance is time-stamped (EST).

3:27:32 New York Tracon: "Cactus 1549, turn left heading 2-7-0."

3:27:36 Flight 1549: "Ah, this, uh, Cactus 1549. Hit birds, we lost thrust in both engines. We're turning back towards LaGuardia."

3:27:42 New York Tracon: "OK, yeah, you need to return to LaGuardia. Turn left heading of uh, 2-2-0."

3:27:46 Flight 1549: "2-2-0."

3:27:49 New York Tracon: "Tower, stop your departures. We got an emergency returning."

3:27:53 LaGuardia airport: "Who is it?"

3:27:54 New York Tracon: "It's 1549, he ah, bird strike. He lost all engines. He lost the thrust in the engines. He is returning immediately."

3:27:59 LaGuardia: "Cactus 1549, which engine?"

3:28:01 New York Tracon: "He lost thrust in both engines, he said."

3:28:03 LaGuardia: "Got it."

3:28:05 New York Tracon: "Cactus 1549, if we can get it to you, do you want to try to land runway 1-3?"

3:28:11 Flight 1549: "We're unable. We may end up in the Hudson."

3:28:17 New York Tracon: "Jet Link 2760, turn left 0-7-0."

3:28:19 Jet Link 2760: "Left turn, 0-7-0 Jet Link 2760."

3:28:31 New York Tracon: "All right Cactus 1549. It's going to be a left. Traffic to runway 3-1."

3:28:34 Flight 1549: "Unable."

3:28:36 New York Tracon: "OK, what do you need to land?"

3:28:46 New York Tracon: "Cactus 1549, runway four is available if you want to make left traffic to runway four."

3:28:50 Flight 1549: "I am not sure if we can make any runway. Oh, what's that over to our right? Anything in New Jersey, maybe Teterboro?"

3:28:55 New York Tracon: "OK yeah, off to your right is Teterboro airport."

3:29:02 New York Tracon: "Do you want to try and go to Teterboro?"

3:29:03 Flight 1549: "Yes."

3:29:05 New York Tracon: "Teterboro, uh, Empire actually. LaGuardia departure got an emergency inbound."

3:29:10 Teterboro airport: "Okay, go ahead."

3:29:11 New York Tracon: "Cactus 1549, over the George Washington bridge want to go to the airport right now."

3:29:14 Teterboro: "He wants to go to our airport check. Does he need any assistance?"

3:29:17 New York Tracon: "Ah, yes, he, ah, was a bird strike. Can I get him in for runway one?"

3:29:19 Teterboro: "Runway one, that's good."

3:29:21 New York Tracon: "Cactus 1549, turn right 2-8-0, you can land runway one at Teterboro."

3:29:25 Flight 1549: "We can't do it."

3:29:26 New York Tracon: "OK, which runway would you like at Teterboro?"

3:29:28 Flight 1549: "We're gonna be in the Hudson."

This multiway conversation offers nothing that smacks of Plath or Shakespeare—just crisp, direct, literal language. Everything is focused on the here and now. The emergency is stated, solutions proposed and discarded. Tracon gives Flight 1549 a new heading back to LaGuardia, which the pilot repeats back immediately. Another plane (Jet Link 2760) is told to change course, and in two seconds echoes back the instruction as acknowledgment. Within 40 seconds, Captain Sullenberger states his idea of a water landing; within two minutes the final emergency plan has been settled. There are no ambiguities, no multiple meanings, no comparisons, no metaphors. This is what it's like to say one thing and mean it. With 155 souls in imminent mortal danger, the power of literal language comes shining through.

Notice that the literalness of the communication masks astounding cognitive complexity. Each of the several speakers has an entirely different visual view of what is happening—their knowledge is necessarily fragmented. And yet over the course of their two-minute life-or-death interchange, each participant acquires enough shared understanding of the overall situation to determine what action is required of them. This is an example of what is known as *distributed cognition*.[22] Distributed cognition resembles metaphor—the individual participants in an activity (a bit like a source and target) elicit different pieces of knowledge not previously connected and integrate these pieces into something coherent, a kind of *schema* or rough mental sketch of the overall situation. But whereas metaphor connects very different domains, the schema formed by the participants in the lead-up to the miracle landing captured a single spatiotemporal situation: airports and a river at their various locations, airplanes in flight, one of them unpowered and in peril.

Literal language is an enormously complex story in its own right.[23] But this book is about metaphor, and I will simply take literal language and its affordances—the things we can do with it—for granted. Literal language depends on a conventional set of semantic categories: the Hudson is a river, a jet is an airplane, an airport is a place, which has a runway, which is a possible destination where an airplane can land, and on and on. The entire cognitive structure underlying literal language, including the conventional categories in which word meanings are rooted, constitutes the foundation for metaphor. The literal provides the yang against which the yin of metaphor is defined.

———

Let's return to Sylvia Plath's poem; it's time to consider the riddle more carefully. "I'm a riddle in nine syllables"—if you count the syllables in each line of the poem, you will find that each of the (nine) lines contains exactly nine syllables. So here is the first clue of many: the number nine, the number of months it takes for a woman to carry a fetus to full term. The poem is about pregnancy (the target). Of course, nowhere in the poem is pregnancy even mentioned in any direct way. Rather, we have a series of metaphors, which collectively form one grand metaphor expressed by the poem as a whole. "I'm ... an elephant"—the target is a pregnant woman (the speaker of the poem) and the source is an elephant, the largest land animal, a ponderous beast. In a metaphor, like this one, the source and target are drawn from different domains (humans versus other animals), freely transgressing the boundaries between conventional categories.

"A melon strolling on two tendrils"—now the same target is being compared to a large plump fruit as source. But there is more—this melon is "strolling" on its tendrils—did you ever see that? Not likely. This source is itself the target in an embedded metaphor, in which the humanlike verb serves to personify the fruit. The verb *stroll* relates a person to their legs, the part that generates locomotion. This is an example of analogy at work—a relation (strolling) creates a mapping between multiple entities (the melon corresponds to a person, its tendrils to a person's legs). Even inside this embedded metaphor, there is not really a single source and target, but rather an interwoven set of mappings between the two domains.

So, Plath uses the embedded metaphor to create an imagined melon—round, fat, and strolling (probably tottering) on its two "legs." Then she deftly makes *that* the source for describing the real target, the pregnant woman. And so it goes, metaphor upon metaphor, each adding something to our ideas and feelings about the woman and her pregnancy. Finally, the poet tells us she's "Boarded the train there's no getting off." Probably none of us have ever boarded such a train, though we might have seen something like that happen in a movie. Certainly we can imagine it. And feel how scary that would be. Once again, the poet does not simply take some well-known situation to use as the source—she *makes one up*. She creates a source that can be easily grasped even though it's unreal. For that's all that matters—we need a source that can be easily understood, not necessarily one that is familiar, or that even exists. A male reader is more likely to board a runaway train than carry a baby to term; for a female reader the odds likely reverse. The real-world probabilities aren't important. For readers of either gender, the metaphor helps to give a sense of what *that* would be like.

The interpretation of a poem will vary from one reader to another. A poet friend of mine gave me his own reactions. The opening, "I'm a riddle ...," might refer to the poem itself, but it could also of course refer to the *speaker* of the poem. Even without knowing the author was named Sylvia, it's obvious from the topic—pregnancy—that the speaker is a woman. My friend observed that men often say they don't understand women, and women often think men lack empathy for them—in particular, men don't grasp what it means to bear a child and give life. So, the speaker is saying that she herself—a woman, with all those maternal associations—is a riddle. Then in the last two lines of the poem, when the speaker says she has "eaten a bag of green apples," she may be alluding to the ancestral Eve in the Garden of Eden, where the eating of an apple signified knowledge of sin. In a mocking tone the speaker suggests that by becoming pregnant—by eating a whole bag of green apples—she has left herself open to the charge of ruining some mythical paradise. A sense of ambivalence toward the pregnancy pervades the poem. The expectant mother feels like she's simply being used: "I'm a means, a stage, a cow in calf." And now she's boarded that train from which there's no getting off—she must endure pregnancy and the birth of a child, and the responsibilities and loss of personal freedom that will follow. Moreover, her child will in turn share in the fate—certain mortality—that is the human lot.

You see, no doubt, that the poem is not really about elephants and houses and melons and money and runaway trains—sources, all of them. Plath has written a poem that lets the reader create a rich web of metaphors and allusions, the parts interrelated in complex ways, playing multiple roles, playing off of one another based in part on whatever associations each reader brings to bear on the poem. This is what I will term *analogical resonance*.[24] It is the heart of poetic metaphor.

———

I'll venture a few provisional definitions now, to be unpacked in the chapters to follow. A *poetic metaphor* is a metaphor that honors the constraints of a poem. A *metaphor* is a comparison in which the source and target cross conventional category boundaries (a cross-domain comparison). An *analogy* is a comparison between a source and target each considered as a system of relations among constituent elements.[25] An analogy is thus a particularly complex type of comparison—one that yields a set of correspondences (a *mapping*) between elements of the source and target, based in part on relations within each domain.[26] *Conceptual combination* is a process (less cognitively demanding than analogy) that uses the meaning of a source word to selectively modify the meaning of a target word.

Metaphors vary enormously in their sheer size—from a phrase to an entire poem. Adapting a term from Max Black (more on him in chapter 4), I will refer to brief metaphorical expressions as *focal* metaphors when a specific word or words (the focus) radically changes in meaning. In Plath's poem, "I'm ... an elephant" provides an example of a simple focal metaphor. Here *elephant* is the focal word. It does not refer to its conventional meaning of a large gray mammal with tusks. Rather, the word in this context means something like "very large or fat"—a predicate now applied to a woman at an advanced stage of pregnancy.

A more extended metaphor (such as the poem "Metaphors" considered as a whole) need not necessarily have a specific focal word. For example, in Whitman's "A Noiseless Patient Spider," the activities of the spider are juxtaposed with activities of the soul. The meanings of individual words are not radically unconventional (*spider* is of course an important word, but it is not a focus in Black's sense because it keeps its meaning as a kind of eight-legged arachnid). The extended metaphor is clearly analogical, in that one domain (the spider's world) provides a source that is mapped to a target (the realm of the soul). Focal metaphors are often woven into more extended metaphors. For example, in the second stanza of Whitman's poem, "the ductile anchor" constitutes a focal metaphor. In general, a focal metaphor lies toward one end of what is actually a continuum. But as we will see when we explore the psychology and neuroscience of metaphor, there are reasons to think that focal metaphors differ from more extended ones in how people process them (roughly, focal metaphors invite conceptual combination, whereas extended metaphors invite analogy). In chapter 9 I will draw some related distinctions based on how the source and target are situated within a text.

One might wonder if the basic definition of metaphor I've adopted is too restrictive. Must a metaphor necessarily depend on the affordances of *language*? Analogy, a central mechanism underlying metaphor, is a kind of thinking that can be applied to pictures and other nonverbal media.[27] And it is certainly natural enough to talk about nonverbal metaphors, such as those expressed in art.[28] For example, consider the abstract drawing *Jacob's Ladder*, shown in figure 3.1. The title evokes a famous biblical story from the book of Genesis, in which the patriarch Jacob dreams of a ladder that links earth to heaven. Here the artist Yaron Dotan depicts what can be interpreted as a three-dimensional space within Jacob's head, ascending toward someplace that can never be seen. The image becomes a metaphor for the wellspring of consciousness that guides each of us on our own personal odyssey. Notice how the visual work of art interacts with the linguistic cue provided by the title of the piece.

I don't wish to restrict anyone's use of the term *metaphor*. The basic definition can readily be extended to nonverbal media. For example, a metaphor conveyed as a drawing depends on a comparison guided by the affordances of drawing. But this is a book about poetic metaphor, and poems are written in language. So I will use the term *metaphor* in its literal sense that comes down from Aristotle, as a phenomenon that operates in language via the concepts that underlie words and their meanings. Extensions to other media, one might say, involve metaphorical metaphor. The

Figure 3.1
Yaron Doyle, *Jacob's Ladder*, 2016. India ink on painted panel, 24" × 24".

focus in this book is on cases that are *literally* metaphors—cross-domain comparisons expressed in human language. But as we will see, the neurocognitive mechanisms that support the generation and appreciation of poetic metaphor are involved in many forms of creativity—literature more broadly, the sister arts such as painting and music, scientific discovery, and the humble insights that arise in everyday life.[29] Poetry presents itself as a case study for understanding human creativity—in all the realms where the spider launches its threads.

4 The Road from Xanadu

"Kubla Khan, or, a Vision in a Dream: A Fragment" by Samuel Taylor Coleridge

In Xanadu did Kubla Khan
A stately pleasure-dome decree:
Where Alph, the sacred river, ran
Through caverns measureless to man
   Down to a sunless sea.
So twice five miles of fertile ground
With walls and towers were girdled round;
And there were gardens bright with sinuous rills,
Where blossomed many an incense-bearing tree;
And here were forests ancient as the hills,
Enfolding sunny spots of greenery.

But oh! that deep romantic chasm which slanted
Down the green hill athwart a cedarn cover!
A savage place! as holy and enchanted
As e'er beneath a waning moon was haunted
By woman wailing for her demon-lover!
And from this chasm, with ceaseless turmoil seething,
As if this earth in fast thick pants were breathing,
A mighty fountain momently was forced:
Amid whose swift half-intermitted burst
Huge fragments vaulted like rebounding hail,
Or chaffy grain beneath the thresher's flail:
And 'mid these dancing rocks at once and ever
It flung up momently the sacred river.
Five miles meandering with a mazy motion
Through wood and dale the sacred river ran,
Then reached the caverns measureless to man,
And sank in tumult to a lifeless ocean;
And 'mid this tumult Kubla heard from far

Ancestral voices prophesying war!
  The shadow of the dome of pleasure
  Floated midway on the waves;
  Where was heard the mingled measure
  From the fountain and the caves.
It was a miracle of rare device,
A sunny pleasure-dome with caves of ice!

  A damsel with a dulcimer
  In a vision once I saw:
  It was an Abyssinian maid
  And on her dulcimer she played,
  Singing of Mount Abora.
  Could I revive within me
  Her symphony and song,
  To such a deep delight 'twould win me,
That with music loud and long,
I would build that dome in air,
That sunny dome! those caves of ice!
And all who heard should see them there,
And all should cry, Beware! Beware!
His flashing eyes, his floating hair!
Weave a circle round him thrice,
And close your eyes with holy dread
For he on honey-dew hath fed,
And drunk the milk of Paradise.[1]

To make a leap, to launch a rocket, the first step is to find a solid start-ing point—firm ground to press down against so that gravity pushes back and generates lift. So before we launch into recent developments in under-standing metaphorical thinking in terms of computations performed by the human brain, we need to establish a launchpad. This chapter will paint a picture in broad strokes of how ideas about metaphor developed. I survey the past from our current vantage point, aiming to convey what early ideas mean to us now.

The ideas presented in this book owe intellectual debts to many. But three names of the past two centuries loom larger than any others: Samuel Taylor Coleridge, I. A. Richards, and Max Black. Besides shaping modern views of metaphor, these figures weave an intriguing story of how the fields of poetry, literary criticism, and psychology shaped one another, drew apart, and now are coming back together. We can think of our triumvirate as the explorer, the pioneer, and the settler. Coleridge the explorer threw out ideas he sometimes downplayed as "hints and first thoughts." Richards the pioneer worked with Coleridge's hints, added a great deal more, and formulated the first systematic description of metaphor. Finally, Black the settler refined Richards's ideas, added some important nuances, and laid out a concise proposal that became the benchmark to which all subsequent accounts of metaphor must be compared.

The way metaphor as a field developed reflected the intellectual orientations of its originators. Each of these three figures had broad interests, but their primary identities were as poet (Coleridge), literary critic (Richards), and philosopher (Black). Across the two centuries, as the baton was passed from poet to critic to philosopher, and on to more contemporary linguists and psychologists, metaphor and poetry underwent a separation. For Coleridge, poetry was the center of it all, the prime example of human creativity and imagination. Black, by contrast, explicitly set aside poetic symbolism as beyond the scope of what he aimed to explain.[2] In the most recent four decades or so (i.e., post-Black), poetry has been further boiled out of the study of metaphor—largely (though certainly not entirely) ignored.[3] Discussions have emphasized the reading of metaphors, generally neglecting the question of how poets make them. I aim to swim against the current of recent history, bringing poetry and its creation back to the foreground. And so to set the stage our story will begin with the poet Coleridge, and end with him as well.

————

Samuel Taylor Coleridge is primarily remembered today as the cofounder, with William Wordsworth, of the Romantic movement in early nineteenth-century British poetry.[4] Besides "Kubla Khan" he gave us the "The Rime of the Ancient Mariner" (with its memorable image of a sailor whose shipmates hang an albatross around his neck). But he was much more than a poet. A more complete description of the man and his career would include: political commentator, journalist, preacher, critic, philosopher, opium addict, drunkard, trekker, mountaineer, diplomat, hypochondriac, depressive, failed husband, thwarted lover, adoring but largely absent father, translator, scholar of Greek, Latin, and German literature and philosophy.

Coleridge's greatest poems appear timeless, and over the past two centuries his ideas about poetry and the imagination have inspired many. Yet somehow his dominant image remains that of a failed genius—a man

whose life and work both seemed comprised of loosely connected fragments. Though Coleridge's life had many tragic aspects, his misadventures
sometimes veered toward the comic. My personal favorite is an episode
when, having dropped out of Cambridge University, the debt-ridden young
poet impetuously enlisted in the cavalry under the alias Silas Tomkyn
Comberbacke. This magnificent nom de guerre preserved the initials and
syllabic flow of his real name (and resonates with the moniker of an illustrious English actor of our own time—Benedict Cumberbatch). Fortunately
for the future of poetry, after a brief military career that consisted primarily
of writing love letters on behalf of his fellow dragoons and cleaning horse
stables, Coleridge's family was able to buy his release from duty.

His opium addiction (he used laudanum at first to cope with physical ail-
ments, but lost control) has garnered the most attention, in part because of
its alleged link to his creative powers. The earliest surviving copy of "Kubla
Khan," called the Crewe manuscript (now in the British Museum), is in
Coleridge's own handwriting. He included the annotation: "This fragment
with a good deal more, not recoverable, composed, in a sort of Reverie
brought on by two grains of opium taken to check a dysentery, at a Farm
House between Porlock & Linton, a quarter of a mile from Culbone Church,
in the fall of the year, 1797." He later reported losing his train of thought
when he was interrupted by a visitor, known to us only as the "man from
Porlock." "Kubla Khan" exists as a fragment of some greater whole that
never was. So was born the fabled Romantic notion that creative ideas often
bubble up from altered states of consciousness.

To understand Coleridge's ideas about poetry and metaphor, two aspects
of his background and life are critical. One aspect is political. Both Coleridge
and Wordsworth came of intellectual age in their twenties, during the last
decade of the eighteenth century, and were shaped by the impact of the
1789 French Revolution. (Wordsworth was in France that year, where he
fathered an illegitimate child with a Frenchwoman.) The violent overthrow
of an absolute monarchy hastened the end of feudalism in Europe and
elevated the ideals of democracy ("liberté, égalité, fraternité"). The impact
of the revolution was immediately felt in Britain and the rest of Europe.
Among its indirect consequences were the rise of early feminism and the
quest for universal suffrage, the first laws to regulate child labor (in 1803
in Britain), and the movement to abolish the European slave trade (accomplished by 1807). The Romantic movement in poetry, initiated by the two

poets, was very much in keeping with the revolutionary spirit of the day—individual creative liberty linked to an idealized brotherhood of humanity.

The reaction to the French Revolution was almost as immediate. By 1793 the ideals of popular democracy had been twisted into the Reign of Terror. By the decade's end the nation was ruled by the dictator Napoléon Bonaparte, and France was at war with Britain (after Napoléon invaded Egypt). A British supporter of the ideals of the French Revolution might be open to a charge of treason. For many, including Coleridge, unbridled enthusiasm for popular democracy and social transformation was soon tempered by evidence that the "will of the people" could easily become the rule of the mob, or of a tyrant. Two centuries on, the repercussions of the French Revolution continue to unfold. For Coleridge and others who felt its first blasts, the complexities and paradoxes shaped their lives.

A second key aspect of Coleridge's life was his friendship and collaboration with Wordsworth—perhaps the most intense ever between two poets of their stature. The two met briefly in 1775, then in 1777 Coleridge dropped in unannounced on Wordsworth and his sister Dorothy at the country home the siblings shared. He initially stayed two weeks with them; over the next few years they were nearly inseparable. This "they" was not simply a duality but a trinity, with Dorothy integral to the emotion-laden collaboration. As Coleridge famously summarized, "tho' we were three persons, it was but one God."[5]

Coleridge recognized Wordsworth (correctly) as the greatest poet of their era. For his part Wordsworth, like many others, delighted in Coleridge's gift for conversation. He observed that Coleridge's talk was "like a majestic river, the sound or sight of whose course you caught at intervals, which was sometimes concealed by forests, sometimes lost in sand, then came flashing out broad and distinct, then again took a turn which your eye could not follow, yet you knew and felt it was the same river."[6] The critic William Hazlitt would offer a more cynical assessment: "Coleridge was an excellent talker if allowed to start from no premises and come to no conclusion."[7] Probably both observations carry substantial grains of truth.

The fruits of the collaboration came quickly. Working individually, Coleridge wrote "Kubla Khan" and "Ancient Mariner" in 1797 and 1798. Then in 1798 Wordsworth and Coleridge published *Lyrical Ballads*, a joint collection of their poems. The book was anonymous, with no indication that it had two authors. The bulk of the poems were by Wordsworth, but

Coleridge's "Ancient Mariner" was placed first. "Tintern Abbey," an early masterpiece by Wordsworth, became the closing poem. ("Kubla Khan," considered just a "fragment," was omitted; it was finally published in 1816 at the urging of Lord Byron.)

As Coleridge would put it later, the two collaborators aimed to create poetry that channeled emotion at least as much as reason, using direct rather than ornate language. This was their reaction against the previous generation of poets, exemplified by Alexander Pope, who had directed their work to the perceived tastes of the upper class. *Lyrical Ballads* explored two approaches to creating a new kind of poetry. One was to focus on nature and on the everyday lives of common people living in the countryside close to nature—to take the familiar and make it new. This was Wordsworth. The other was to evoke "persons and characters supernatural" and give them a human nature and poetic truth by encouraging a "willing suspension of disbelief" in the reader—to take the unreal and make it real. This was Coleridge, foreshadowed by Aristotle: "The poet should prefer probable impossibilities to improbable possibilities."[8] The overall aim (as literary critics in later centuries would observe) was to elevate beauty to the sublime by adding "strangeness."

And thus was born the Romantic movement. Its reverberations still roll on, like those of the French Revolution, even in the twenty-first century. A core legacy is the idea that the subject of a poem may—perhaps should— be the consciousness of the poet. The two intervening centuries brought increasing democratization to poetry, including a highly personal "confessional" style. Constraints on the content and form of poems were weakened or broken, and the ranks of poets (if not their readers) were expanded. In chapter 10 I will have more to say about the influence of Romanticism on subsequent developments in poetry, particularly in the use of symbols.

But like the revolution, the idealistic collaboration of Wordsworth and Coleridge was to founder on the shoals of human nature. For another two years the emotional trinity continued, and the two poets prepared a second edition of *Lyrical Ballads*. Coleridge did much of the editorial work for the expanded volume and worked intensely on a new contribution of his own, called "Christabel." But just before the volume was to go to the publisher, Wordsworth vetoed Coleridge's anticipated poem (it was incomplete and may have crossed a line by intimating a lesbian encounter). The second edition of *Lyrical Ballads*, which appeared in 1800, was no longer anonymous.

The title page listed a single author—William Wordsworth—though his new preface mentioned that a few of the poems were contributed by "a Friend." "Ancient Mariner" was still there, but shifted from first to last position in the ordering. The greatest poet of the era, William Wordsworth, had asserted his individuality and preeminence.

Coleridge was crushed. The collaboration withered, and the friendship never fully recovered. But neither did it end. A telling scene two decades on: The two famous poets both attended a literary dinner party in London, sitting at opposite ends of a long table. The guests broke into two clusters, each listening to one of the poets. At one end of the table, Coleridge recited from memory poems by Wordsworth. At the other end, as if in competition, Wordsworth held forth—also reciting poems by Wordsworth.[9]

Another historical detail is too rich to pass by without mention. In the 1790s, Coleridge became friends with the political philosopher William Godwin and his wife, the early feminist Mary Wollstonecraft, and met their infant daughter, also named Mary. The girl grew up to become Mary Shelley, wife of one of the stars of the next generation of Romantic poets, Percy Bysshe Shelley.[10] On a stormy midnight in July 1816, Percy, Mary, and friends were gathered in a villa by Lake Geneva, Switzerland, and the companions started reading ghost stories to one another by candlelight. Lord Byron recited the supernatural poem "Christabel"—the one rejected from *Lyrical Ballads*. Byron's hypnotic reading apparently caused Percy Shelley to become hysterical. In the aftermath, Mary Shelley was inspired to write a short book that remains the most famous icon of the Romantic era—*Frankenstein*.

———

Coleridge's ideas about poetry are sprinkled throughout his scattered writings, which span decades, but the single most important source is his "literary (auto)biography," *Biographia Literaria*, published in 1817. I. A. Richards, who a century later mined this sprawling muddle of autobiography, literary criticism, and nascent psychology, characterized it as a "lumber-room of neglected wisdom which contains more hints toward a theory of poetry than all the rest ever written upon the subject."[11] The passing of a second century has not altered that assessment.

Let's review a few key ideas (many elaborated and augmented by Richards and Black) that trace to Coleridge. The poet said next to nothing about metaphor per se because poetry itself was his concern, and (anticipating

Robert Frost) he took it for granted that poetry was "just made of met-aphor." On poetry, his famous definition—"the best words in their best order"—is about as pithy as it gets.[12] The phrase sounds like a flippant joke, but in fact it fits very nicely with my own definition of a poetic metaphor, which emphasizes that it must *cohere* with other constraints honored in a poem, ideally forming a unified whole. Metaphorical meaning, therefore, cannot be divorced entirely from the poetic context, nor can synonyms be freely substituted. "The Child is father of the Man" (Wordsworth, in "My Heart Leaps Up") is a poetic metaphor; "the youngster is the male parent of the male adult" is trash that could not possibly fit into any poetic context.

Coleridge resisted the perennial urge to define what makes a text a poem. His succinct definition was of a poetic *ideal*, not of everything that passes for poetry. Call the immortal calendar rhyme beginning "Thirty days hath September / April, June and November" a poem if you like, but the real issue is what characterizes the *best* poems. Moreover, the ideal for a poem may be realized in many different ways: "Do not let us introduce an act of Uniformity against Poets" was his plea for a "big tent" attitude.[13] Different styles provide different affordances and constraints; whatever constraints are honored by the poet implicitly determine what makes a metaphor part of a harmonious whole.

At the same time, Coleridge was a critic and did not hesitate to pass value judgments on poems (including some measured criticisms of Wordsworth's poetry). A bit harshly perhaps, he charged some of the poetry of Alexander Pope (a *bête noire* of the Romantics) with "claiming to be poetical for no bet-ter reason, than that it would be intolerable in conversation or in prose."[14] It is tempting to speculate how Coleridge would have responded to the free-est of twentieth-century free verse, which dropped all constraints. How then to define "the best words in their best order"? I. A. Richards, who lived in that later era, complained that "we can ... shift the words about very often in Walt Whitman without loss, even when he is almost at his best."[15] Yet more recently, T. S. Eliot acknowledged that "a great deal of bad prose has been written under the name of free verse."[16]

Debates have long raged about whether metaphor is merely "figurative" (a kind of ornamentation for language), and whether it is at root a phenom-enon of language only, or of thinking more broadly. Coleridge gave a clear answer to both questions. He argued that poetic metaphor is an expres-sion of the essence of human creativity—certainly not merely decorative, and certainly not based on language alone. Yet he also viewed language with reverence, seeing poetry as the product of creative intelligence acting through *Logos* (Word), a divine principle of reason and creativity. Fast-forward to I. A. Richards: "*Thought* is metaphoric, and proceeds by comparison, and the metaphors of language derive therefrom."[17] Or as we might now say, poetic metaphor flows from creative thought pressed through the catalytic converter of language.

Of all the titles and epithets that might be applied to Coleridge, one is unexpected, yet especially relevant to us now—he was a psychologist. He mused that "metaphysics and psychology have long been my hobby-horse."[18] The oddity is that modern psychology is generally dated from the waning years of the nineteenth century—more than sixty years after his *Biographia*. Anticipating some of the interests of the illustrious American psychologist William James (one of the acknowledged founders of the field), Coleridge wrote about religious mystics and observed the influence of nitrous oxide ("laughing gas") on his own conscious experience. He was a kind of phenomenologist—following the dictum "Know thyself," he tried to glimpse the operation of his own creative processes by casting an inner eye on the furtive shadows haunting the borders of the conscious mind. He even coined a word that at the close of the nineteenth century was to be reinvented and thrust into the popular culture: *psycho-analytical*.[19]

Most famously, Coleridge sketched a theory of the creative imagination. He considered and rejected associationism, the philosophical antecedent of behaviorist psychology. Rather than serving as a passive receptacle for whatever information the senses convey about the external world, the human mind at its best actively constructs its own reality. For Coleridge, imagination is a creative engine that "dissolves, diffuses, dissipates, in order to recreate: or where this process is rendered impossible, yet still at all events it struggles to idealize and to unify. It is essentially vital, even as all objects (as objects) are essentially fixed and dead."[20] He anticipated the central role of analogy, urging that the creative mind needs to become "accustomed to contemplate not *things* only, but likewise and chiefly the *relations* of things."[21]

Coleridge the psychologist placed *thought* in the position of intermediary between language and the outer world.[22] In what could be taken as a warning to linguists of the centuries to follow, he wrote, "It is a fundamental mistake of grammarians and writers on the philosophy of grammar and language to suppose that words and their syntaxis are the immediate representatives of *things*, or that they correspond to *things*. Words correspond to thoughts, and the legitimate order and connection of words to the *laws* of thinking and to the acts and affections of the thinker's mind."

Coleridge distinguished between a lower form of creative process that he called *fancy* and the higher process of *imagination*. From our vantage point, these might be considered distinctions based on the degree to which inputs are transformed and reorganized in the course of creating new concepts. It is certainly the case that experience provides part of the input to creativity. Consider the wild romantic vision of "Kubla Khan." The poem, taken as a work of art, is extraordinarily original—a paragon of the Romantic movement. Yet many of its elements can be variously traced to old books Coleridge had read about travel and mythology, to his knowledge of Milton's *Paradise Lost*, to his experiences exploring caves in childhood, and to his walks along streams that tumbled down to the English seacoast. But these raw ingredients underwent dramatic changes as they were integrated into a poetic expression of the destruction and creation of a creative paradise. To take one example, the River Alph was probably inspired by tales of a mythical river in ancient Greece, the River Alpheus, which was said to descend below the surface, pass under the sea, and rise again. *Alph* evokes *alpha*, the first letter of the Greek alphabet, which perhaps symbolizes the creative source of literature and art. The poem is the product of imagination, not mere fancy.

Let's take a more mundane example that may help in grasping Coleridge's distinction between fancy and imagination. It's not too hard to create imaginary beasts by rearranging the parts of actual animals. We can visualize a goat with a fox's head, or a dog with wings. It wouldn't be hard (as we'll elaborate in chapter 14) to write a computer program to generate novel animals by simply recombining parts in some quasi-random way. Most of these would simply be monsters, not only impossible but (much worse) incoherent, such as an octopus sporting a lion's tail and panda eyes.

For Coleridge, our program would illustrate the operation of fancy—a mechanical process operating on fixed parts to create novel combinations of them. (Actually, he would consider the really crazy combinations that lack good sense, like our monster octopus, to be products of something even more primitive than fancy.) Still, if we let our program run long enough, it might well spit out a horse with the single spiraled horn of a narwhal—inventing the "unicorn." Here we have a creation that is not real, yet seems coherent and indeed beautiful.

But of course, the idea of a unicorn extends beyond an image of a one-horned horse. In many cultures, a unicorn is a magical creature, the symbol of innocence and enchantment: "Dreams are the playgrounds of unicorns."[23] Our computer program lacks the capacity to create this poetic symbol. *This* unicorn, for Coleridge, is the kind of fluid whole that stems from the true imagination. In an extended analogy (later to have a direct impact on Richards's theory of metaphor), Coleridge compared the active imagination to the organic growth of vegetation—a complex whole emerging from inner forces that generate its parts, and the parts of those parts, where the final form cannot be fully anticipated yet displays an essential unity. In our own time, the idea of "organic" origin and growth is deeply embedded in the everyday notion of creativity, as well as in the related (rather mysterious) concept of *authenticity*. (More on this in chapter 14.)

In addition to reflecting imagination, Coleridge insisted that poetry should exhibit "good sense." This vague concept (along the lines of "good taste") can be roughly interpreted as meaning that a poem should have something worthwhile to say. Of course, different people at different times will have different conceptions of what is worthwhile, and therefore what counts as "good sense." But subjective though it is, the notion of good sense calls attention to the fact that what makes a poem successful is not just the way it was created, not just the presence of engaging images and metaphors, but also the value of the emotions and ideas it transmits.

Though his life was neither as colorful nor as tragicomic as that of Coleridge, Ivor Richards (universally referred to by his initials, I. A.) also embraced intellectual contradictions. Writing primarily in the 1920s and 1930s, he was the hard-nosed founder (with his friend T. S. Eliot) of what became known as the *New Criticism*.[24] The basic idea was that the meaning and value of a text are best assessed by a "close reading" of the text itself, divorced from the intentions of the author and the cultural context of its composition—as if every text arrived as anonymously as a message in a bottle. Our multiple, contextualized readings of "A Noiseless Patient Spider" would earn us a scolding from New Critics (though strict adherents are now an endangered species). Richards firmly believed that poems, like all works of art, can be evaluated by objective criteria (a point emphatically made by the title of one of his book chapters, "Badness in Poetry").[25] Yet he was also interested in how people arrive at divergent readings of poems. He conducted the first empirical study of how students interpret and evaluate anonymous poems—"practical criticism" in action.[26]

Where Coleridge had foreshadowed modern psychology, Richards was steeped in its early manifestations. He was particularly influenced by then-recent work on learning as a form of associative conditioning (a psychological descendant of the philosophical ideas about associationism that Coleridge had rejected). Inspired by early work on the physiology of the nervous system, he described memory in terms of the operation of a neural network.[27] Differences in associations between experiences, he believed, could explain differences among people in their ability to create art: "The greatest difference between the artist or poet and the ordinary person is found ... in the range, delicacy, and freedom of the connections he is able to make between different elements of his experience."[28] Richards proposed a general theory of word meaning, viewing words as symbols that link their referents in the world to ideas in the mind:[29] "Words are the meeting points at which regions of experience which can never combine in sensation or intuition, come together."[30]

It would be a mistake, however, to think of Richards as someone who simply applied associationist ideas to language and literature. His views about metaphor were also shaped by the Gestalt psychologists (a movement that gave rise to the slogan "the whole is different from the sum of its parts").[31] This influence led to what I term the *coherence principle* that governs human thinking (as will be elaborated in chapter 6). It also elevated the constructive approach to thinking that Coleridge had advocated—the notion that the active imagination aims to create a coherent unity. Indeed, Richards was extremely appreciative of Coleridge's ideas. In 1934 he published *Coleridge on Imagination*, a book that offered a critical analysis and expansion of those "hints and first thoughts" he found buried in the *Biographia Literaria*.

Richards laid out the basic analysis of metaphor that has guided all work since.[32] A metaphor depends on a comparison between two parts, corresponding to what we are terming the source and target; whatever relates the two (their differences as well as similarities) provides the *ground* for the metaphor. He described how novel metaphors work their way into literal language and proposed a basic test of whether a metaphor is psychologically active: can we identify two parts that are being compared? "If we cannot distinguish [target] from [source] then we may provisionally take the word to be literal; if we can distinguish at least two co-operating uses, then we have metaphor."[33] Some years later, the philosopher Nelson Goodman summarized the process of literalization:[34] "What was novel becomes commonplace, its past is forgotten, and metaphor fades to mere truth."

―――――――

It was left to Max Black to summarize the essential elements of Richards's analysis of metaphor and to contribute some further key ideas. Black argued for an *interaction* theory of metaphor, based at least in part on analogy: "a conception of metaphors which postulates interactions between two systems, grounded in analogies of structure (partly created, partly discovered)."[35] The "partly discovered" aspect is critical: "It would be more illuminating in some of these cases to say that the metaphor creates the similarity than to say that it formulates some similarity antecedently existing."[36] Though the interaction theory is sometimes contrasted with the traditional view of metaphor as comparison, Black clearly meant that *some* metaphors (not all) create new similarities *in addition to* the preexisting ones that guide the initial comparison.

Richards had spoken of how metaphor involves "the interanimation of words."[37] As Black elaborated, "A memorable metaphor has the power to bring two separate domains into cognitive and emotional relation by using language directly appropriate to one as a lens for seeing the other; the implications, suggestions, and supporting values entwined with the literal use of the metaphorical expression enable us to see a new subject matter in a new way."[38] Black acknowledged explicitly what Coleridge had assumed: to make or grasp a metaphor is a creative act.[39]

Black also emphasized ways metaphorical meaning defies complete paraphrase. The interpretation is not just a simple list of preexisting and inferred similarities, but rather a network of connections between the source and target. Like a neural network (as Richards had also recognized), the pattern is nuanced in that links can be differentially weighted—not just present or absent, but present to some degree: "The implications of a metaphor are like the overtones of a musical chord; to attach too much 'weight' to them is like trying to make the overtones sound as loud as the main notes—and just as pointless."[40]

The idea of metaphor as a network of connections has implications for the perennial question of what the grain size of a metaphor really is. A word? A sentence? An entire poem? It is often useful to identify a particular word or words (what Black called the focus) embedded in a larger context (the *frame*), where the focus undergoes a significant shift from its conventional meaning. (As noted in chapter 3, I have adapted Black's focus to provide a name for what I term *focal* metaphors.) The focus literally refers to the source, but its meaning is altered as it is transferred over to the target. For example, in the well-known saying "the eyes are the windows to the soul," *windows* acts as the focus, or focal word, that undergoes a meaning shift. A *strong* metaphor, in Black's terms, is one rich in implications and for which no other words could substitute for the focus—one that has "the best words in their best order."[41] Or to use the term suggested by Harold Bloom, the expression strikes the reader as *inevitable* (yet not merely predictable).

The examples of metaphor that modern linguists have emphasized tend to be isolated sentences (and the experiments performed by psychologists are even more biased toward metaphorical snippets devoid of context). However, poetic metaphor involves much more than an individual word in a phrase or sentence. Nelson Goodman, inspired by Richards and Black, proposed that metaphor often involves the transfer of a schema—not a single element, but a complex network of inferences among many interrelated elements.[42] As the poems we've already discussed make apparent, metaphors can be found at all levels of a poem (or other text), often hierarchically embedded. T. S. Eliot remarked that Dante's epic *Divine Comedy* is really one extended metaphor (an allegory).[43] And consider this passage from Eliot's own "The Love Song of J. Alfred Prufrock":

> The yellow fog that rubs its back upon the window-panes,
> The yellow smoke that rubs its muzzle on the window-panes,
> Licked its tongue into the corners of the evening,
> Lingered upon the pools that stand in drains,
> Let fall upon its back the soot that falls from chimneys,
> Slipped by the terrace, made a sudden leap,
> And seeing that it was a soft October night,
> Curled once about the house, and fell asleep.[44]

One might, to a first approximation, summarize Eliot's passage in a focal metaphor, "the fog is a cat." But the metaphor expressed by the entire passage is (to use Black's term) far stronger than that.

———

In the chapters that follow, we will often return to ideas that trace back to those "hints and first thoughts" that Coleridge launched like filaments into the air—gossamer threads that Richards, Black, and others caught and wove into the web of metaphor. I close this chapter with an early vision of the spider's thread.

"The Poet and the Spider" by Samuel Taylor Coleridge

On St. Herbert's Island, I saw a spider with most beautiful legs, floating in the air on his back by a single thread which he was spinning out, and still, as he spun, heaving on the air, as if the air beneath was a pavement elastic to his strokes. From the top of a very high tree he had spun his line; at length reached the bottom, tied his thread round a piece of grass, and reascended to spin another—a net to hang, as a fisherman's sea-net hangs, in the sun and wind to dry.[45]

5 Make This River Flow

"Like Water Chasing Water" by Koon Woon

under the bridge,
we are who we are because of the flow,
the limpid, octave gargle
that follows sons and daughters
of liquid empires, forever
subsumed to the undercurrent pull.
Because of this, we repeat generation upon generation
of the chase, the continuous rush
to fill erroneous time.

And if man the fisher
casts forever
lines and lines
    and water falls
        and birds circle freely
           and not a moment
    is without its color
then the days will relax their rigidity
    become supple
        and bless us with the liquidity of beliefs
    at once bearable and expandable
        and assume the proportions
           of lakes.

And so make this river flow into lake

    and take this swelling
and make it an ocean.[1]

A philosopher deeply interested in metaphor once remarked, "There is no shame in being taught by psychology."[2] One aim of this book is to advance the field of literary psychology, focusing on poetry.[3] The idea that psychology can help understand what poetry is about has often been associated with the psychoanalytic tradition, going back to Freud and Jung. I will have more to say about those connections, but in the next few chapters I will look for clues in areas of contemporary psychology and neuroscience. It's time to take a look at what the neurocognitive approach may be able to tell us about poetic metaphor. But first we need to lay some groundwork. "This chapter," to quote William James as he introduced his idea of the *stream of consciousness*, "is like a painter's first charcoal sketch upon his canvas."[4]

Let's first lay out a bird's-eye view of what it takes to compose and respond to poetry. In keeping with the Coleridge tradition, our ultimate concern is with the operation of the mind at its finest—the ideal Poet and Reader, not the hack writer or the bored student in a required English class. To characterize these ideals, we can turn to "The Rime of the Ancient Mariner."[5] In that long ballad, the Mariner relates the tale of his strange and tortured sea voyage, where the pivotal moment is his shooting of the albatross, an act that triggers deep guilt and the need for expiation. The poem is framed as a tale told to a Wedding Guest. It begins when the Guest, on the way to the wedding, is unexpectedly and aggressively interrupted by the Mariner. Toward the end of the poem, as his tale concludes, the Mariner describes his compulsive need to wander and tell his story to strangers.

Let us say, by analogy, that the Mariner is the ideal Poet, and the Wedding Guest the ideal Reader.[6] Here, then, is the Poet:

> I pass, like night, from land to land;
> I have strange power of speech;
> That moment that his face I see,
> I know the man that must hear me:
> To him my tale I teach.

And here is the Reader, stopped by the Poet:

> He holds him with his glittering eye—
> The Wedding-Guest stood still,
> And listens like a three years' child:
> The Mariner hath his will.

The Poet has passed through some transformational event, a psychological journey perhaps painful and dangerous, returning with "strange power of speech," and a compulsion to compose a poem that will have meaning for someone. But not just for anyone: in an earlier line, the Mariner "stoppeth one of three." That special "one" is the Wedding Guest, "the man that must hear me." In our idealization, a poem is meant for a Reader who is somehow prepared for it; and that Reader, held as by the Poet's "glittering eye," is gripped "like a three years' child." The Poet hath his will. Some bond links Poet with Reader, a bond that neither fully understands.

―――――

Let's hold in mind our Poet and Reader as capitalized ideals, but now we must plunge earthward to make contact with the real poet and reader. Real readers sometimes approximate their ideal counterparts—for example, a psychological study has analyzed the ways Coleridge's "Ancient Mariner" often elicits intense emotional engagement in its readers.[7] And a serious poet is moved by some creative impulse that requires expression. "Poetry," according to Sylvia Plath (not perhaps an unbiased observer), "is the most ingrown and intense of the creative arts."[8] A serious reader of poetry is engaged by it and feels an emotional response to it—indeed, may well return to read some particular poem repeatedly over many years. As we will see, these characteristics do not mesh well with the methods used in typical experiments conducted in psychology laboratories. So, a first caution: much of what has been learned from psychological and neural studies of metaphor applies to poetry only obliquely. Nonetheless, psychological evidence supports a close linkage between the states of mind for writers and their readers: if the writer of a poem feels inspired, readers of the poem are more likely to find inspiration in it.[9]

How does human psychology relate to poetry? To begin with what is obvious (and therefore easily overlooked), poetry arises out of the inner experience of the poet, who aims to impact the inner experience of the reader. Or to borrow an analogy from Harold Bloom, "Consciousness is to poetry what marble is to sculpture: the material that is being worked."[10] It might be objected that the analogy is muddled, because where a sculpture is carved from marble, a poem is made out of *words*. However, there's a subtle but important difference: marble is a raw material provided by the earth, whereas words have a very different origin. The words of natural language are themselves the product of consciousness—distributed across the generations of human speakers who molded their meanings. Consciousness impacts all the arts, but its connection to poetry runs deepest.

The stream of consciousness that William James described more than a century ago is a metaphorical echo of Heraclitus, two and a half millennia earlier: You can never step into the same river twice—for on the second occasion it will not be the same river, nor you the same person.[11] Our waking consciousness, the flow of thoughts and feelings, presents itself as a continuous stream—interrupted by intervals of sleep but with a subjective unity (very much like Wordsworth's description of Coleridge's talk: "a majestic river ... sometimes concealed ... yet you knew and felt it was the same river").

One of the most remarkable aspects of consciousness is that it allows us to adopt many different points of view (including Nagel's vision of objectivity, "the view from nowhere").[12] In a poem, as in one's mind, the perspective can move like a movie camera, cutting or zooming from a close-up to a wide shot and back again. And in a poem, as in one's mind, immediate perception can be superimposed or blended with memories and imagined possibilities.

Although consciousness is continuous, nonrecurring, and confined to a single individual, humans proceed to extract from it discrete concepts that recur and can be shared with others via language. Literal language is *compositional*—it involves the application of systematic rules for combining discrete conceptual elements (represented by words) so as to form "complete thoughts," or *propositions*, which can be true or false. I see a cat, and a rug, and the cat asleep on it, and say to you, "The cat is on the rug." You understand what I mean and your inner experience is altered in response—you may visualize the scene, perhaps feel a sense of peaceful domesticity.

But though the stream of consciousness feeds into the discrete elements of language, it is not so easy to revive any close approximation to the continuous stream from a combination of discrete words and propositions. Or to state the crucial point more generally, *it's easier to cut than to join.* If you cut a ribbon into pieces and try gluing them back together, you'll discover how hard it is to make the mended ribbon look altogether new.

Similarly, literal language, composed as it is of discrete words and sentences, can't readily communicate the richness of the continuous stream of consciousness. The gap is particularly apparent when we consider the emotional aspects of inner experience. We feel happy and sad and bemused and astounded and so much more—it's hard to express our nuanced feelings in words.

Although it is conventional to treat thoughts and feelings, reason and emotion, as disjoint types of internal events, that is not the view of contemporary psychology. Rather, the neurocognitive approach suggests that what we think and how we feel are intimately bound together.[13] We would hesitate to say somebody fully grasps the meaning of "Your mother is dying" if that sentence (uttered in a context that leads the person to take it as a true statement) did not evoke some sort of emotional response. That response might be sorrow, pain, or fear, or maybe a kind of numbness, perhaps even relief—or some mix of all of these responses and more. Even a thought that might seem utterly cold and rational, like "I've derived the theorem," is likely to bring with it certain feelings, ranging from cessation of boredom to quiet satisfaction to joyous exultation. And it is the emotional aspects of the stream of consciousness that give personal meaning to it all. As Koon Woon says in his poem, "we are who we are because of the flow." So in this book I conceive of "meaning" in its most general sense—cognitive meaning and emotional impact bound up with one another so as to give a sense of meaning to the life we each are living.

What can be done, then, to communicate the richness of the inner experience that falls between the gaps, so to speak, of literal language? Humans have many options. We communicate not just by words but by gestures, by touch—by a smile, the wink of an eye, a kiss. Given suitable talents, we may turn to art in any of its manifestations. Many art forms afford a kind of continuity that language lacks—a painting with its nuances of form, color, and texture; a symphony with its blend of instrumental timbres, its integration of point and counterpoint; a movie with its visual and auditory depictions of human characters in motion, interacting with one another over time.[14]

But perhaps most audaciously (if not miraculously), we try to overcome the grave limitations of language by using—language! Language has one great advantage as a communication system—every typically developing person has considerable expertise in it. Many of us are lousy painters and musicians, but at least we can talk to one another.

To understand how language can in some sense transcend language, we need to look a bit more closely at the ingredients that go into a human language, as these determine its affordances—what we can do with it.

Language can be characterized by four basic components: *phonology, syntax, semantics,* and *pragmatics.* Phonology is the system of sounds—both the sounds of individual phonemes (the difference between *cat* and *bat*) and the larger-scale properties extending across syllables, words, and sentences, which yield differences in stress and intonation. Syntax refers to the rules for forming grammatical sentences, which in turn constrain meaning—"The cat is on the rug" means something quite different from "The rug is on the cat." Lexical semantics focuses on the meanings of individual words (a *cat* and a *dog* are similar but different types of animals).[15] Finally, pragmatics focuses on the way language is used in context.

As we will see, all four aspects of language bear on meaning in the broadest sense of that term, and all impact poetry. In particular, the larger-scale properties of the sounds of speech, collectively referred to as *prosody*, provide the basis for poetic rhythm and meter. Prosody in turn is closely linked to pragmatics, which has the greatest potential to expand the power of language to convey nuances of inner experience. So far we've pretended that a literal sentence has a fixed meaning independent of how it is said, where it is said, why it is said, or who says it. But a much more subtle picture of the affordances of language has been sketched by modern philosophers of language, such as John Austin, Paul Grice, and John Searle.[16] An utterance in context becomes a *speech act*—it *does* something, such as asserting a belief, making a promise, or hurling an insult. In chapter 11 we will consider what kinds of speech acts can be accomplished by a poem.

A key insight about pragmatics is that communication by language depends on a tacit contract between the speaker and listener (or author and reader): the speaker will say something that the listener can be expected to understand, and the listener will do their best to recover the meaning the speaker intended. This is Grice's *cooperative principle*: participants in a conversation normally aim to be informative, truthful, relevant, and clear.[17] Critically, in many situations what will be understood will be more than (or different from) the literal meaning of a sentence. Suppose a couple is sitting in the kitchen of their house with a window open, and the wife says to her husband, "It's chilly in here." The husband may be expected to grasp that he should close the window, even though that is not what was (literally) said. If the communication is successful, the listener will have made an inference by integrating what was explicitly said with the relevant contextual cues. Suppose instead it is the husband who speaks first, saying, "Sure is warm in here." This utterance can be understood as *irony*—what is meant, and what the shivering listener is likely to grasp, is that the literal meaning is decidedly *false* (and also that it might be a good idea to close that window). Thus meaning (again in its broadest sense) involves one person intending to produce a response from another by causing that person to recognize the intention.[18]

One useful way to think of metaphor, then, is as a pragmatic, contextually guided extension of literal language. The affordances of language are exploited by mental operations that are not specific to language—particular ways of *thinking*, such as analogical reasoning. By integrating two mental objects (the source and target, each as complex as we like) in relation to one another, where one or both objects can be at least partially described in literal language, we can create a metaphor. And metaphor generates meaning that goes beyond what literal language can say.[19] Pieces cut from inner experience are joined so as to revive it.

"There is a mystery at the heart of metaphor," said the philosopher Ted Cohen.[20] Recognizing the deep value of the emotional aspect of inner experience, Cohen emphasized the close linkage between the use of metaphor and the capacity for *empathy*—the ability to understand and feel what it is like to be some other sentient being. At a basic level, the human capacities for thinking and for feeling are intertwined. The mystery at the heart of poetic metaphor is the heart itself. So it has always been. This is how the preface to the Chinese *Book of Odes*, three millennia old, describes the impetus to poetry:

Poetry is where the heart's wishes go. What lies in the heart is "wish," when expressed in words, it is "poetry." When an emotion stirs within one, one expresses it in words; finding this inadequate one sighs over it; not content with this one sings it in poetry; still not satisfied, one dances unconsciously with one's hands and feet.[21]

6   The Mind Is Like This

"Mind" by Jay Parini

The wind knows nothing,
tossing every leaf and light blue hat
that it surrounds,
invisible but violent of purpose,
single-minded in its sweep
and unselective grasp of everything before.

The mind is like this,
moving forward, sideways, backwards
through the object-world,
undoing what was given, smothering,
unmaking in its wake, then making light
of its destruction, moving on.[1]

T. S. Eliot famously remarked, "The poem which is absolutely original is absolutely bad."[2] Human creativity, which poetry exemplifies, almost inevitably depends on the reuse of old ideas in new ways. The psychologists John Kounios and Mark Beeman, writing on the neuroscience of creativity, define creativity as "the ability to reinterpret something by breaking it down into its elements and recombining these elements in a surprising way to achieve some goal."[3] The mind, as Parini's poem intimates, is a force of creative destruction, of "undoing" and "unmaking."

Notice the intriguing ambiguity of the description of what the mind does in the aftermath: "making light / of its destruction." Perhaps the mind is simply unconcerned, like a playful and irresponsible child who carelessly broke a vase. Or perhaps, out of its own destructive activity, the mind "makes light"—creates new insight or knowledge. Or maybe (for poetry is peculiarly comfortable with superimposed meanings) the mind is all of these things—destructive, playful, creative.

This is the expressive capacity that allows metaphor to recreate a sense of the continuous flow of inner experience—the metaphor creates a plurisign. As another example, the poet and songwriter Leonard Cohen entitled a volume of his collected poems *Stranger Music*.[4] The title is a kind of metaphorical pun—the poetry (music) is said to be "more strange" and "that of a stranger." Rather than setting up a contradiction, the two senses harmonize into a unified meaning, yet with an aura of vagueness that invites its own questions. Stranger than what? Stranger to whom? Music composed by a stranger? For a stranger? Both? One piece in the collection, a song written a quarter century before the book was published, is called "The Stranger Song." Does it offer clues to help interpret Cohen's larger body of work? The plurisign acts as an invitation to consider new combinations of possibilities.

Literary works and everyday conversation exhibit many varieties of *blended* concepts—a cartoon duck wearing clothes and speaking English with a quacky accent, or Sylvia Plath's "melon strolling on two tendrils."[5] In recent decades, cognitive scientists have learned a great deal about how people recombine elements of what they know to generate new concepts or ideas. In this chapter I'll introduce two mechanisms that appear to be especially important in metaphor: analogical reasoning and conceptual combination. Although it's very likely that other mechanisms are also involved in metaphor processing, I'll focus on these two for several reasons. First, there is good evidence that each has broad psychological functions that extend beyond metaphor—metaphor is simply an important special case. Second, models of each process have been implemented as computer programs (which provide greater precision than purely verbal descriptions). Third, we know something about how these processes are realized in the brain. After the two mechanisms are introduced here, chapter 7 will give an overview of how the brain operates when a person is thinking or finding new ideas. Chapter 8 will then go into greater detail about how analogical reasoning and conceptual combination make it possible to grasp metaphors.

———

A core mechanism for idea generation is reasoning by analogy. As we intimated near the end of chapter 3, metaphors are often based on analogies that cross the conventional boundaries between concepts. The poet and critic Wallace Stevens emphasized the centrality of analogy, which links not only metaphor but also such related concepts as model, myth, allegory, and archetype: "Poetry is almost incredibly one of the effects of analogy. ... To identify poetry and metaphor or metamorphosis is merely to abbreviate the last remark."[6] Where Frost claimed that poetry is simply made of metaphor, there is reason to argue it must be made at least partly of analogy.

The notion that analogy is central to metaphor boasts a venerable history tracing back to Aristotle. The poet Allen Tate suggested that "the reach of our imaginative enlargement is perhaps no longer than the ladder of analogy."[7] Still, as Max Black complained, "it is easy enough to mutter analogy"—as usual, the devil is in the details.[8] Here we delve into the story of what cognitive psychologists and cognitive neuroscientists have learned about how people reason by analogy, and how analogy relates to metaphor.

To introduce psychological work on analogy, I'll start with an example that is not at all poetic, but nonetheless forms a kind of extended, cross-domain metaphor. Along the way I'll point out both how this example is similar to poetic metaphor and how it differs (the differences being at least as instructive as the similarities).

Our example is one in which a source analog serves the specific purpose of solving a novel target problem. This use differs from that of a poetic metaphor, which typically has the more diffuse aim of eliciting an emotional response and deeper understanding of the target. Though analogies can be nonverbal (analogy being a kind of thinking rather than a strictly linguistic process), I have chosen as our example one that is verbal and semantically rich, as metaphors are. Its origin traces to the Gestalt tradition in early twentieth-century psychology (which, as we saw in chapter 4, influenced the thinking of I. A. Richards). This tradition gave rise to what I term the coherence principle, which characterizes human thinking: whenever people try to understand a situation, their relevant attitudes, beliefs, and emotions tend to shift so as to form a coherent pattern.[9] The coherence principle, to which we will return shortly, applies to analogy and metaphor, but its full scope is much broader. Finally, this example has the virtue that I know it inside out (that is, from the inside as well as the outside view): the analogy was created for use in psychological experiments I conducted decades ago in collaboration with Mary Gick.

Gick and I asked college students at the University of Michigan to role-play solving a medical problem.[10] A doctor is faced with a patient suffering from a malignant stomach tumor. The tumor is inoperable, and the patient will die unless it is destroyed. There is a kind of ray that will destroy the tumor if the rays reach it at a high intensity. But unfortunately, such high-intensity rays will also destroy the healthy tissue they pass through on the way to the tumor. At lower intensities the rays will not damage the healthy tissue, but neither will they remove the tumor. How can the doctor use rays to destroy the tumor, while at the same time sparing the healthy tissue?

The tumor problem had been introduced decades earlier by the Gestalt psychologist Karl Duncker, who recorded peoples' solutions and analyzed the ideas underlying them.[11] For example, people sometimes suggest applying a chemical treatment that would protect the healthy tissue from the rays. This idea aims to solve the doctor's problem by removing a problematic equivalence: the doctor wants the rays to damage the tumor but *not* damage the healthy tissue.

The novel twist that Gick and I added was to provide some of the participants with a story in advance of the tumor problem. The story was introduced in the context of what was ostensibly a different task—people were asked to memorize it or write a brief summary. One version of the story, called "The General," went along these lines: An evil dictator controlled a fortress situated in the center of a small country. Many roads radiated out from the fortress "like spokes on a wheel" (a simile embedded in the story). A general raised an army at the border, vowing to capture the fortress and overthrow the dictator. The general was about to send his entire army down one road to capture the fortress, when he learned that the dictator had mined each road so that although small groups could still pass, a large army would set off an explosion. The general then had a clever idea: he divided his army into small groups and dispatched each group to the head of a different road. On his signal, each group charged down a different road. All the groups passed safely to the fortress, where the entire army attacked the fortress in full strength. In this way the general captured the fortress and overthrew the dictator.

You may want to stop and think for a moment about how *you* would solve the tumor problem.

Did it occur to you that the story about the general might suggest a solution to the doctor's problem? If so, you may have come up with a solution proposed by some of the participants in our experiments. If you develop the mapping between the source and target, a number of systematic correspondences can be identified. The general becomes the doctor, the fortress the tumor, and the army the rays. So, just as the general employed small converging groups of soldiers to cross safely to the fortress and capture it, the doctor could use several ray machines positioned around the patient to direct multiple low-intensity rays at the tumor simultaneously. The key idea is that each beam will pass harmlessly through healthy tissue, but the converging weak rays will summate at the focal point of the tumor, destroying it.

It's not easy to come up with this "convergence" solution (which is actually quite similar to standard medical practice for radiation therapy) without the aid of an analogy. As shown in figure 6.1, only about 10 percent of the students generated this solution in the absence of the General story (dotted horizontal line). (This estimate turns out to be quite stable— Duncker found the same level of performance decades earlier in experiments he conducted in Germany.) When the students read the story just prior to working on the tumor problem, roughly 30 percent *more* of them generated the convergence problem spontaneously. That is, these students

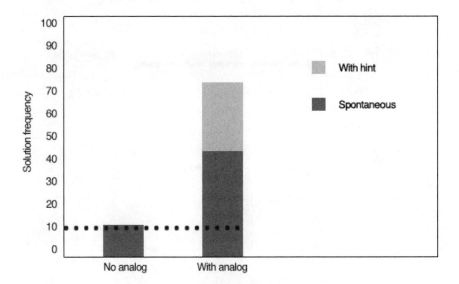

Figure 6.1
Frequency of producing the convergence solution to the tumor problem, either without any analog or after reading the General story (a potential source analog), in a study by Gick and Holyoak (1980).

noticed that the General story was relevant and used it to solve the problem. When the experimenters followed up with a simple cue that "the story you read earlier might give some hints," another 30 percent succeeded in finding the convergence solution. The overall picture we get from these experiments is of a glass half full or half empty—a substantial proportion of people spontaneously used the source analog to solve the problem, though about as many initially failed to notice its relevance (yet often succeeded later when given a hint).

Let's pause to consider how this analogy relates to metaphor (referring to figure 6.2). The General story is the source and the tumor problem is the target. The two analogs come from very different areas of knowledge (military and medical), making it a cross-domain comparison. Just as a reader needs to recognize the presence of a metaphor, the problem solver needs to *access* the source when the target is encountered. The grounds for the analogy/metaphor take the form of a coherent *mapping* between the elements of

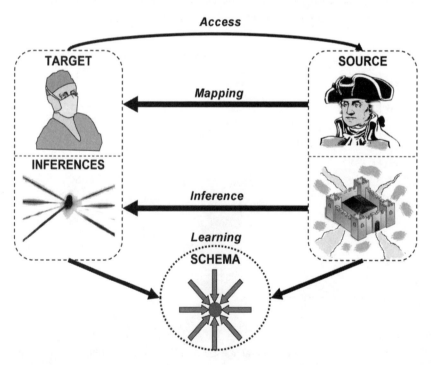

Figure 6.2
The analogy between the General story and the tumor problem.

each analog. It's not enough to simply compare the two situations and observe that they are similar in some loose sense. Rather, a full understanding depends on discovering that the doctor corresponds to the general, the tumor to the fortress, and the rays to the army. In keeping with Black's interaction view of metaphor (see chapter 4), the analogy goes beyond a comparison of preexisting similarities. Using the mapping of elements, the problem solver can *infer* a novel solution to the target problem by creating a new idea ("apply converging weak rays") based on information initially provided by the source alone ("send small groups down many roads").

Finally, in the aftermath of exploring the analogy it is possible to *learn* something new, by forming a more abstract schema that captures the commonalities between the source and target: roughly, when a large force can't be safely applied to a centrally located object, apply multiple converging small forces instead. Just as a metaphor, if encountered in multiple contexts, may eventually foster a new literal meaning, so repeated examples that fit a common analogical schema will set up a positive feedback loop— people find it easier and easier to spontaneously apply the schema to additional examples.[12]

It is instructive to step back a moment and consider how the convergence analogy came to be. For the students in our experiments, the target (tumor problem) was supposed to serve as a retrieval cue to gain access to a source (General story) that was already in their memory. But before there can be readers, there must be writers. Where did the General story come from in the first place? Well—Gick and I just made it up. We were trying to study problem solving by analogy, and we were drawn to the tumor problem because Duncker had shown that people come up with a variety of solutions to it. It therefore seemed plausible that providing a source analog could push around the probability of arriving at the convergence solution, which was relatively rare but potentially practical. So, we deliberately created a story that would show a parallel solution in a different domain of knowledge.

Notice that Gick and I couldn't simply retrieve the General story from memory, in the way students in our experiments sometimes did, because for us—its authors—the story didn't already exist. The story was not based on a "real" event. Though it hardly counts as a piece of literature, it was a product of imagination (however limited). We aimed to make the story somewhat plausible, though it has elements of fantasy—a vaguely medieval setting, with the landmines adding an anachronistic touch (and whoever heard of landmines calibrated to let small groups pass over them safely?). The key to the story's value as a source analog is that it explicitly sets up a landscape in which multiple routes converge at the fortress. This detail is what provides the key insight for the tumor problem—a hint toward the possibility of using rays targeted on the tumor from multiple directions. What makes the General story a potent source is not that it is true, or more familiar, or more concrete, but simply that it is *more informative* than the statement of the tumor problem. If the General story is presented without its solution (and without an analogy), people usually solve it (because its statement mentions multiple routes).

Poets and other creators of metaphor similarly have the freedom to construct their sources from whatever mix of reality and imagination works for them. I don't know how Whitman came up with the idea of comparing a spider to the soul in "A Noiseless Patient Spider," but his thinking might have followed either of two possible directions. The first possibility is that Whitman (like a student in our experiments) was confronted with a target problem—for the poet, the problem of expressing his heartfelt loneliness—and that something about this target—perhaps an emotional response, perhaps the idea of trying to connect, or some mix—reminded him of a solitary spider tossing out its filaments. If this is how Whitman first thought of the spider as source analog, he operated something like a student who encountered the radiation problem, was spontaneously reminded of the General story, and put the latter to work to solve the former.

But it's also possible that the direction of reminding was quite the opposite. A poet or other creator is likely to be on the lookout for anything that might spark an idea for a new work. Perhaps Whitman happened to think about or observe a spider spinning its thread (much as Coleridge did on St. Herbert's Island; see the end of chapter 4), and something about this potential source—perhaps an emotional reaction, perhaps a sense that the spider was trying to make a connection, or some mix—reminded the poet of his own loneliness. In other words, rather than starting with a poetic target problem—"describe the state of my soul"—the poet may have first seen the opportunity to make something interesting out of a spider as source analog, and only then realized that his own longing made a compelling target analog. This hypothetical example also illustrates how a negative emotion such as loneliness can become the positive impetus for poetic creation. In chapter 13 we'll look more closely at cases in which poets turn their sorrows into art.

There is thus no fixed order of which is chosen first, target or source, and no single recipe for finding or creating a source. But however Whitman hit on the spider-soul analogy, he had more work to do to fashion the source analog in his poem. In the first stanza Whitman sketches a gentle spider launching its filaments, one that is devoid of those "creepy" aspects that cause many people to fear actual spiders. Similarly, in the first stanza of his poem "Mind," to set up the key analogy between the wind and the mind, Parini describes a wind that is neither a hurricane nor an ocean breeze. The wind he presents us with is strong enough to be mildly destructive, yet still playful. In both of these examples, the poet exploits the freedom to create a specific source that illuminates the target.

Analogies are often used to make inferences in order to solve a specific problem, whereas metaphors typically aim to trigger emotional responses. But nonmetaphorical analogies can also appeal to the emotions.[13] Indeed, politicians and others routinely use analogies to sway people's emotions. For example, in an effort to drum up popular support for a military response to an Iraqi incursion into Kuwait, President George H. W. Bush of the United States likened Saddam Hussein of Iraq to Adolf Hitler—not exactly poetry, but an effective rhetorical device.

Because metaphor is inherently linguistic (whereas analogy is not), a metaphor can exploit the affordances of language to guide the reader to its interpretation. In studies of the use of analogy in solving a problem, experimenters often try to hide the fact that the source might be useful in solving the target problem by presenting each in a somewhat different context. And indeed, Gick and I found that many people failed to notice the relevance of the source (General story) to the target (tumor problem) until a hint was belatedly given. But in metaphor (as we will describe more fully in chapter 9), the author can exploit various affordances of language to make it easier for the reader to grasp what is intended. For example, both the Whitman and Parini poems illustrate the simple device of juxtaposing the source and target in successive stanzas. And in the latter poem, the second stanza starts with an explicit comparison, "The mind is like this." By the cooperative principle, information that is juxtaposed in a discourse or text is expected to be relatable in some sensible way. The pragmatic aspects of language pave the way for recognizing an intended metaphor, and they sometimes guide the mapping so as to reduce the cognitive work required of the reader.

The affordances of language are even more apparent when we consider the kinds of condensed metaphors that often appear in single sentences. Language offers a variety of ways to say, in a manner that can be less or more direct, that two things are related to one another. Though they do not make great metaphors, it is easy to make sense of metaphor-like sentences that could arise in the context of the convergence analogy. "The rays are like the army" is a simile, calling attention to some unstated resemblance. "The rays *are* the army" (a nominal metaphor, where the target is said to "be" the source) implies something a bit stronger. It suggests that (in the problem context) the rays can be identified with the army, or belong to a more abstract category (perhaps "physical force") that the army exemplifies especially well.

We might also say "The rays are the army of the doctor." Here the same basic thought is elaborated as a proportional metaphor of the sort Aristotle described. Notice that by simply stating the implied fourth term ("general"), this metaphor can be translated into an explicit proportional analogy, "The rays relate to the doctor as the army relates to the general" (or more succinctly, *rays* : *doctor* :: *army* : *general*). One might even say, "The rays *marched on* the tumor from different directions," where a focal word (in this case a verb) from the source domain has been displaced to create a description of the target. Now the standard meaning of the focus shifts to accommodate the requirements of its new context (this kind of marching does not demand legs). At the same time, the concepts denoted in the frame are also subtly altered (the rays seem a bit more human than before). In all such cases, the cooperative principle licenses a search for a sensible meaning, and the syntactic form of the sentence provides guidance as to how that meaning may be found. I'll say more about how language can be used to express metaphors in chapter 9.

In this quest for meaning, the cooperative principle that governs normal discourse works hand in glove with the coherence principle that governs attitudes and beliefs. The various metaphor-like expressions that relate the rays to the army all ultimately depend on the overall mapping between the situations described in the source and target. Outside of their situational contexts, rays have little if any connection to armies. So, why is it that when we encounter them *in* their contexts we feel confident that the rays map to the army, the doctor to the general, and the tumor to the fortress? Why are we unlikely to seriously entertain the various bizarre but hypothetically possible alternatives (the rays are the fortress, or the like)? The basic answer is that when we reason by analogy we seek mappings that *cohere* with one another. The solution emerges from a system of checks and balances that hones in on those mappings that get along well with one another. The forces that determine coherence act as constraints that hold between possible correspondences.

As sketched above, we can diagram the constraints that support the favored mappings between elements of the tumor problem and the General story, creating a constraint network. Psychological research has established that analogy is governed by three basic types of constraints, termed *pragmatic*, *semantic*, and *syntactic*.[14] The pragmatic constraint focuses attention on those parts of the analog that most clearly matter given the reasoner's goals, while backgrounding or suppressing those parts that don't seem so important. Since the reasoner is role-playing the doctor, the information shown in figure 6.3 conveys what is important for achieving the doctor's goal. Like the pragmatic aspects of language, the pragmatic constraint on analogy is highly sensitive to the context of use.

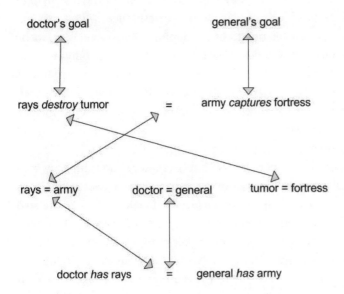

Figure 6.3
The constraint network that supports the "winning" mappings between elements of the tumor problem and the General story.

The semantic constraint favors mapping concepts that are similar to one another even outside of the analogy context. The objects in the two analogs are generally dissimilar, but the doctor and the general are somewhat alike (both human), so these objects are likely to be mapped. The actions of "destroying" and "capturing" are also similar, supporting a mapping between the propositions "rays destroy tumor" and "army captures fortress." This mapping in turn allows the syntactic constraint to come into play: elements that play parallel roles in corresponding propositions should map to one another. So, the mapping between the two propositions supports the mapping of rays to army and tumor to fortress. Similarly, semantic similarity of the shared relation "has" connects "doctor has rays" to "general has army," supporting the mapping of doctor to general and rays to army.

The constraint network as shown in our diagram is oversimplified, in that it includes only the family of constraints that supports the winning set of mappings. In a more complete representation, some additional elements of lesser pragmatic importance would be included. Also, the network as shown includes only *excitatory* links: constraints of the sort "if mapping A holds, then mapping B also holds, and vice versa." A more complete representation would include *inhibitory* links. For example, if the rays map to the army, they probably do *not* map to the fortress. Such inhibitory links encourage a preference for one-to-one mappings. As we will see, poetic metaphors often relax this preference, allowing multiple mappings to combine rather than interfere with one another. But in general, inhibition is essential in order to focus attention on what is important and to weed out incompatible mappings. Finally, a more complete network would include continuously varying weights on all connections, capturing the fact that all the constraints are inherently graded rather than all-or-none.

This kind of constraint network, with its excitatory and inhibitory connections, reflects general properties of the actual neural networks that operate in the human brain.[15] It's no coincidence that I. A. Richards related metaphor comprehension to neural networks, and that Max Black emphasized how the nuances of metaphorical meaning are more like graded weights than discrete propositions. We will have more to say about how constraint networks govern analogical reasoning after we take a look (in the next chapter) at what is known about how the brain supports thinking and language.

Analogy is a powerful engine driving the creative power of metaphor, a tool for breaking ideas into elements and rearranging them into new configurations. The kind of analogical reasoning we've considered so far—what has been termed *explicit* use of analogy—is cognitively demanding.[16] People are typically very much aware that they are using a source analog to think about the target, and (as will see in chapter 7) complex analogies activate specialized brain circuits. However, Chris Schunn and Kevin Dunbar have shown that a source analog can sometimes influence processing of the target in an *implicit* fashion—without requiring an elaborate mapping process, or even awareness that a source is being used.[17] This kind of implicit analogical transfer is based on a very general cognitive mechanism called *priming*—processing something makes it easier to process something else that is similar.[18] Reading the word *doctor* will make it easier to read the word *nurse* immediately afterward. Implicit analogy involves priming of relational concepts. For example, people are able to read *bear—cave* more quickly when preceded by *bird—nest* (same relation) as opposed to *bird—desert* (unrelated).[19] Note that although the pairs *bird—nest* and *bear—cave* share the same relation ("lives in"), the objects themselves are not especially similar. Apparently, reading and understanding the first pair puts the relation into a state of readiness, which makes it easier to process another pair of words that exhibit the same relation. This kind of relational priming very likely plays a role in understanding metaphors.

The coherence principle is by no means limited to analogy (although the specific constraints that govern analogical reasoning differ from those that impact other cognitive processes). For example, a story can be more or less coherent depending on whether the causal connections between events described in it make sense.[20] Constraint networks are used to make decisions in the face of complex, ambiguous, and contradictory information. In a legal setting, jurors are more likely to find a defendant not guilty if all the parts of their alibi are consistent with the facts established by trial evidence, as well as with general expectations about human behavior.[21]

A key aspect of constraint networks is that the connections are generally bidirectional, so that entering beliefs and attitudes actually change to some degree as a decision emerges.[22] If for whatever reason you decide to buy a house that is farther from your workplace but costs less, rather than a more expensive house in a more convenient location, it's likely you'll end up feeling that commuting distance doesn't matter as much as you previously had thought it did. Even moral judgments exhibit these kinds of coherence shifts.[23] If you decide that the actions of a business executive caused harm to the environment, you are likely to view those actions as more intentional, and the harm more severe, than you did at first. In other words, a decision is often more than an isolated conclusion—it's really an entire family of microdecisions about all the relevant factors that constrain one another. As we will see, poetic metaphor depends on coherence of the metaphor with a variety of other factors that contribute to the overall coherence of a poem, collectively determining what counts as "the best words in their best order." Indeed, the coherence principle underlies aesthetic judgments across the entire range of literature and the arts.[24]

Of course, we know that people are quite capable of holding contradictory and incoherent beliefs and attitudes. Yet although *global* coherence may be lacking, people are likely to achieve a kind of local (though often transient) coherence in the course of reasoning and decision making. The coherence principle tends to *create* coherence on the fly, rather than solely depending on preexisting coherence among beliefs and attitudes. This is why the coherence principle fits so well with the cooperative principle that governs communication. A reader who encounters nonliteral language will be inclined to assume that a sensible meaning was intended. A tentative interpretation that makes sense in the context will be favored *because* it creates the expected and sought-after coherence. Coherence is likely to be only partial—analogies and metaphors are inevitably imperfect (varying in what is termed their *aptness*). However, because information that does not fit the emerging interpretation can be actively suppressed by inhibitory links, coherence shares the virtues and pitfalls of a self-fulfilling prophecy. Whatever doesn't make sense in the context is likely to be ignored, so that whatever remains is coherent. Of course, understanding is not completely elastic—sometimes comprehension fails. But the cooperative quest for coherence often takes us a long way.

In addition to explicit and implicit analogy, other cognitive processes also likely contribute to metaphor, and the coherence principle operates in them as well. Analogy is especially prominent in extended metaphors. In contrast, focal metaphors—those involving focal words encapsulated in a sentence or a phrase—often involve a very general affordance of language and thought called conceptual combination.[25] Whereas analogy involves a mapping between multiple elements of the source and target domains, conceptual combination typically involves a comparison of individual concepts considered holistically, making it less demanding of cognitive resources.

Indeed, even the most literal of sentences will typically be understood as a systematic combination of the meanings of the words in it. Suppose we read "While living in London, Sylvia Plath wrote her best poetry despite, or perhaps because of, her struggle with depression." The syntax of this sentence helps to generate its overall meaning from its systematically arranged parts. We understand that Plath wrote poetry—poetry that was better than any other poetry she wrote—while she engaged in a struggle. This struggle was with depression. The struggle may have impeded her in writing her best poetry, or it may have spurred it. This all happened while she was living in London. The rules of language provide a recipe for combining individual concepts into meaningful units, which can be related to one another in a hierarchical fashion.

The simplest example of conceptual combination integrates an adjective with a noun. Suppose I refer to a "green dog." The obvious interpretation is that this is a dog, the color of which is green. We know, of course, that dogs are typically brown, black, or white, and not green. But this one is said to be a green dog, so green it is. Our concept of a dog consists of various typical properties, such as a general shape, tendency to bark, being a pet, and having a color in the brown/black/white range. The force of the conceptual combination is to add a property conveyed by the adjective *green*. To maintain coherence, we cancel the conflicting expectation about color that had been conveyed by the noun. A bit more formally, we start by taking the union of the properties of the adjective and noun, and then to maintain coherence, we inhibit any typical properties of the noun that conflict with those of the adjective. A new concept, our fanciful green dog, has been created by conceptual combination (without using analogy).

Psychologists have discovered that conceptual combination can involve multiple processes and that the meanings of the words being combined often interact in complex ways. As a simple precursor to Black's interaction view of metaphor, even literal conceptual combination of an adjective with a noun depends on the overall interpretation triggered by the conjunction taken as a whole. For example, Douglas Medin and Edward Shoben found that combinations involving a color adjective are interpreted slightly differently depending on the noun to which the adjective is applied.[26] People think that gray clouds are more similar to black than to white clouds, whereas gray hair is more similar to white than to black hair. The reason, of course, is that we know gray and black clouds are signs of stormy weather, whereas gray and white hair are signs of aging. So, even for simple adjective-noun combinations, the derived meaning is based on more than just a combination of properties drawn from the individual words—in this case, knowledge about causal connections also matters. More generally, everything we know about how the world works can potentially impact conceptual combination.

This holistic quality becomes yet more apparent when we move from adjective-noun to noun-noun combinations, where one noun serves as a modifier of the other (the head noun). Many adjectives are essentially one-dimensional (green and gray each convey a value on a color dimension), but nouns are typically much richer in meaning. We know from the work of psychologist Edward Wisniewski and many others that when trying to make sense of a novel noun-noun combination, like *robin hawk*, people follow one of two main strategies.[27] One strategy, *property transfer*, is to interpret the modifier much like an adjective, extracting some salient property from it, which is then applied to the head noun. So, a robin hawk might be a kind of hawk with a red breast similar to that of a robin. A second strategy, *relation formation*, is to find a plausible relation in which each noun plays a role. A robin hawk might then be understood as a kind of hawk that preys on robins.

But how do we predict the interpretation that people will favor for a new combination? People's preferred interpretations vary greatly—some people generally prefer property-based inferences whereas others favor relation-based inferences.[28] But when given a series of novel noun-noun pairs, most people will generate some interpretations of each type. It turns out that prosody matters—if the two nouns receive strong and equal stresses, property-based meanings are found more quickly than relation-based meanings.[29] Putting an equal stress on the modifier seems to encourage searching for a property it exhibits that can be applied to the head noun.

Just as analogical reasoning can be understood in terms of the cooperative and coherence principles, the cooperative principle coupled with coherence constraints seems to guide conceptual combination. Fintan Costello and Mark Keane have shown that people prefer interpretations in which the information used is uniquely salient in at least one of the nouns and the overall meaning is plausible yet informative (i.e., conveys something new).[30] For example, a *cactus fish* might plausibly be a fish that has sharp spines like those of a cactus. "Has spines" is uniquely salient to cactus, and plausible (but not so expected as to be uninformative) as a property of a species of fish. This interpretation is preferable to the alternative possibility that a cactus fish is a green fish—though a cactus is likely to be green, "green" is not very specific, as it is the color of many other types of plants besides cacti. Both property-based and relation-based interpretations obey these pragmatic constraints. The general principle is simple: people expect to find an interpretation that is sensible and informative and are willing to work to find one.

Like analogy, conceptual combination very likely plays a role in forming and grasping metaphors, especially focal metaphors. For example, a kind of metaphorical noun-noun combination, called a *kenning*, was a prominent feature of Old Norse and Old English poetry. In the epic poem *Beowulf* we hear that "in the end each clan on the outlying coasts / beyond the *whale-road* had to yield to him" (italics added), where the kenning is a conventional metaphor for the sea ("the road of whales").[31] In Parini's modern poem "Mind" we find the abstract noun-noun combination *object-world*— the external world of objects that exists outside of the human mind and its perception.

Psychologists have debated whether conceptual combination is somehow dependent on analogy, or whether it is distinct (and probably simpler).[32] I suspect the latter view is correct (although implicit analogy, based on relational priming, is likely to play a role in conceptual combination). But before taking up such questions, we have to first lay some more groundwork. It's time to venture into the labyrinth of the human brain.

7   The Brain Is Wider Than the Sky

"The Brain Is Wider Than the Sky" by Emily Dickinson

The Brain—is wider than the Sky—
For—put them side by side—
The one the other will contain
With ease—and You—beside—

The Brain is deeper than the sea—
For—hold them—Blue to Blue—
The one the other will absorb—
As Sponges—Buckets—do—

The Brain is just the weight of God—
For—Heft them—Pound for Pound—
And they will differ—if they do—
As Syllable from Sound—[1]

Three pounds. If you ever have a chance to heft a human brain, you will not find it a heavy lift. It's a rather small organ, this Johnny-come-lately product of billions of years of Darwinian evolution. Yet it may be said to contain, or support, or generate, or realize (it seems impossible to call up a precise, literal verb) the human mind. And the mind contains humanity's knowledge of the universe, and the sense each of us has of one's self as a thinking, feeling person. And also of course, whatever capacity anyone has to create or appreciate poetic metaphor—we need Dickinson's "Brain" to grasp Parini's "Mind." Three pounds—"just the weight of God," says the poet.

It should go without saying that Dickinson is not speaking literally. I say "should" because it is not unknown for neuroscientists (among those who are also poetry aficionados) to mistake her poem for some sort of ode to materialism (the doctrine that the mental can be reduced to the physical).

But Dickinson's "Brain" is simply an example of *metonymy*—the linguistic device of calling a thing by the name of something closely associated with it, rather than its own name. Unlike metaphor, which is based on resemblance, metonymy only requires some preexisting association.[2] But despite their important differences, metonymy and metaphor often work together in poetry. Here, the down-to-earth "Brain" stands in for the more ethereal mind (and by the final stanza, the yet more ethereal soul). A dissection of a physical brain will not reveal the sky, the self, or the sea—just neurons, blood vessels, and assorted other tissue. But metaphorically (with a boost from metonymy), all that we know, all that we are, is "contained" in the brain. Human cognition is ultimately neurocognition.[3]

How, then, does the brain support the creation and interpretation of poetic metaphor? A couple of unpromising possibilities are best set aside at the outset. Some years ago the popular press touted the discovery of what was dubbed the "God spot"—a single brain area responsible for human spirituality. It did not take long for this simplistic notion to fall into disrepute—in fact, many parts of the brain contribute to a sense of spiritual connection.[4] Similarly, it is not realistic to expect to find a "poetry spot" or a "metaphor spot" in the brain. The general rule is that complex cognitive and emotional processing depends on large neural networks working in coordination.

Another approach best avoided is to simply assert, "It takes the whole brain." This may be roughly true—a complex task like reading a poem will engage many brain areas—but it isn't very helpful. The same description could be applied to such complex but unpoetic tasks as reading a software manual or solving a calculus problem. It's no surprise, for example, that listening to a poem will engage brain areas that support hearing, whereas reading the same poem will engage areas that support vision. But what we really want to know is how neural networks involving multiple brain regions are coordinated to accomplish the core processing required to create or grasp poems.

———

As a start, we will look at what has been learned about the neural basis for several processes, previewed in chapter 6, that likely contribute to the ability to use poetic metaphors. We know something about how the brain supports language, emotion, analogical reasoning, conceptual combination, and creative thinking in general. Individual brain areas and networks will be used in both poetic and nonpoetic tasks, but some particular combination of them may operate together in processing poetry. Our tack is to explore two paths at once—what the brain does and what poetry requires—in hopes of discovering their intersection. This chapter aims to lay out a very rough sketch of the neural basis for cognition in general and poetic creativity in particular. Chapters 12 and 13 will delve deeper into how poetry is produced by the human brain.

At the most global level, thinking and feeling reflect networks of neural activity distributed across much of the brain. The human brain contains roughly 86 billion neurons (nerve cells), of which about 16 billion are found in the cerebral cortex (the outermost layer of brain tissue, which is critical for cognitive functioning).[5] Thinking about a simple concept, like the idea of a cat, involves the activation of vast numbers of neurons connected by synapses (the junctions between neurons). Electrochemical activity serves to transmit a signal from one neuron across a synapse to another, thereby changing the probability that the neuron on the receiving end will *fire*—sending out its own signal. The precise pattern of activity corresponding to "cat" will vary depending on the overall context. The black cat that is being chased by a dog is a bit different than the white one sitting on a child's lap, because the activity of neurons (their *firing rate*) will vary depending on what other neurons are currently active. This basic property of the nervous system supports the contextual shading of word meanings, in literal language and even more so in metaphors.

Also, synapses can be stronger or weaker, and learning can change their effective *connection weights*. "Neurons that fire together wire together"—they have their connecting synapses strengthened, so that in the future whenever one of the neurons fires the other is more likely to also fire.[6] Due to this fundamental type of learning, metaphors that are encountered repeatedly—becoming more familiar or conventional—will be processed with increasing ease and efficiency.

———

The transmission of a neural signal from one neuron to another depends on chemical messengers called *neurotransmitters*. Many different types of neurotransmitters operate in the human brain, of which dopamine, serotonin, and norepinephrine have received the most attention. Global aspects of cognition and emotion (for example, a person's mood) are influenced by the prevalence of each type and the balance between them. We will have more to say in chapter 13 about the role of dopamine in particular. Its wide-ranging functions include modulating the pleasure triggered by various sorts of rewards. Of particular relevance to the neuroscience of metaphor, the regions of the brain in which dopamine serves as a neurotransmitter are deeply involved in tasks that require finding novel connections between word meanings.[7] Some evidence (although controversy remains) suggests that the mental disorder of schizophrenia is associated with a hyperactive dopamine system, which contributes to a tendency toward loose associative thinking. This type of thinking can lead to delusions and hallucinations, but also (in less extreme manifestations) to the discovery of creative connections between concepts that most people would not consider together.

To get a sense of the layout of some of the major brain landmarks that relate to metaphor and to thinking in general, let's walk through a schematic of the surface of the brain. The schematic diagram in figure 7.1 gives a view of the human cortex, showing the left side. The brain is divided into two hemispheres, which to a first approximation are mirror images of one another. (As we will see shortly, the hemispheres differ in ways that are important for understanding creative thinking.) Very crudely, processing

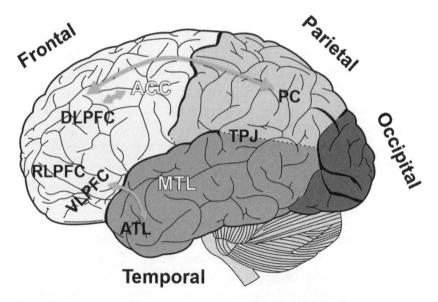

Figure 7.1
A schematic of the surface of the human brain (side view of left hemisphere). See text for details.

moves from low-level sensory processing at the back of the brain to high-level thinking and decision making at the front—perception leading to action.

As shown in the figure, the cortex is divided into four major lobes. (The figure also shows important lower brain areas, the cerebellum and brain stem, which lie beneath the cortex.) Starting from the back of the brain, we see the occipital lobe, which is the center of the earliest visual processing (yes, your eyes are connected most directly to the back of your head!). The other three lobes play much more prominent roles in thinking and language. Parts of the parietal cortex are involved in spatial perception, quantitative calculations, and (especially on the right side) a sense of the self. The figure shows one important parietal landmark, the precuneus (PC). This subregion is involved in mental imagery, thinking about the self, and conscious experience.

The temporal lobe, which provides the neural basis for our sense of hearing, is heavily involved in language. At its border with the parietal cortex we find the temporoparietal junction (TPJ). This area seems to support what has been called *theory of mind*—our ability to *mentalize*, to grasp what others think and know. The left temporoparietal junction is important in judging whether someone is telling the truth. Especially in the right hemisphere, this region appears to support social understanding and empathy—the ability to take the point of view of someone else. Autism, a brain disorder that impairs social understanding, has been linked to atypical activity in the temporoparietal junction.[8]

Two regions within the temporal cortex proper are especially important for human cognition. The medial temporal lobe (MTL) includes the hippocampus and surrounding structures, which are critical for forming new autobiographical memories and being able to retrieve them later. This kind of memory is called *episodic*—memory for episodes, those events of our lives that happened in a certain time and place. As you may imagine, writing poetry is usually guided by memories of personal experiences. Wordsworth famously argued that poetry "takes its origin from emotion *recollected* in tranquillity" (I have added the emphasis on "recollected")—it's as if immediate experience and its attendant emotions need to be transmuted in some fashion by being fed through episodic memory.[9] As we will see, memory and imagination are not really alternative sources of ideas, but partners in the creative process.

The anterior temporal lobe (ATL) is a core region that supports language. It is particularly involved in accessing the meanings of words and combinations of words. This function is often called *semantic memory*, in contrast to the episodic memory based on the medial temporal lobe. In general, the meanings of concrete words like *cat* or *toaster* are encoded by neurons distributed across many areas of the brain, particularly the posterior regions involved in sensory processing.[10] But the anterior temporal lobe operates as a kind of hub for integrating word meanings, and it can add more abstract properties (e.g., a toaster is something "used in the kitchen").[11] Recall the remark by I. A. Richards quoted earlier: "Words are the meeting points [for] regions of experience which can never combine in sensation or intuition." The anterior temporal lobe has the best claim to be the central brain region supporting these "meeting points" in word meanings.

Up above we see the anterior cingulate cortex (ACC), which has strong connections to areas that control cognitive processes (on its dorsal or upper side) and to areas associated with emotion (on its ventral or lower side). The anterior cingulate cortex tends to be active in effortful tasks, and in the early phases of learning a new skill. One of its general functions is to trigger an alert to cognitive conflict—situations that give rise to opposing tendencies that need to be resolved. Conflict is likely to arise, for example, when it is necessary to decide whether to accept competing literal versus metaphorical interpretations of words in a sentence.

Finally, we come to the frontal cortex. Its more posterior subareas provide close connections between sensory information and motor control (i.e., generating instructions to move a part of the body). The large region nearest the forehead is the prefrontal cortex (PFC). This region is critical in cognitive tasks that require holding information in mind, manipulating it, and forming new plans or drawing conclusions. The figure distinguishes three geographic subregions on the surface of the prefrontal cortex. The ventrolateral area (VLPFC) includes Broca's area, which (in the left hemisphere especially) is extremely important for speech production. As indicated by the arrow in the figure, the ventrolateral PFC has strong reciprocal connections to the anterior temporal lobe, the hub for word meanings. More generally, the ventrolateral PFC is involved in inhibitory control— weeding out salient information irrelevant to the current task, and enabling selection between close alternatives (where the loser has to be suppressed). This kind of control is likely to be necessary in understanding metaphors, and more generally in establishing coherence in the face of semantic conflict.

Higher up, we encounter the dorsolateral PFC (DLPFC), which plays a primary role in what is called *working memory*. The dorsolateral PFC holds information in an active state so it can be manipulated, as when we make a mental list of chores and then order them to generate a plan for our day. Notice that the dorsolateral PFC has major reciprocal connections with the precuneus in the parietal cortex (thus relating the current contents of working memory to the self and its needs), and also with the anterior cingulate cortex (reacting to perceived conflict).

Finally, around the front of the brain behind the forehead we find the rostrolateral PFC (RLPFC).[12]This area, which was greatly enlarged over the course of recent hominid evolution, is particularly important in tasks that concern abstract or interconnected relations between concepts, particularly when these relations relate to timing or planning.[13] For example, the rostrolateral PFC is involved in performing tasks that depend on *prospective memory*—making hypothetical plans oriented to the future, along the lines of "Next time I go camping I'll remember to take along a flashlight." The rostrolateral PFC helps to direct attention selectively either to the outer environment or to one's inner thoughts. It can be engaged in processing information that enters from any sense modality, that was retrieved from memory, or that was produced by an act of imagination.

One function is particularly relevant to understanding the processes that may underlie metaphor—the rostrolateral PFC becomes active when a person performs complex analogical reasoning.[14] There is some evidence that the rostrolateral PFC works together with the semantic hub (anterior temporal cortex) in solving analogy problems.[15]

As we mentioned earlier, the two hemispheres of the cerebral cortex are generally symmetrical. A bit of neural folklore is that people are either "left-brained" or "right-brained," but this idea is wildly simplistic. If modern neuroscience has taught us anything, it's that if you want to be a fully functional human being it's best to· keep *both* hemispheres running. Still, the functions of the two hemispheres are by no means identical. For most people (almost all those who are right-handed, and some who are left-handed), language depends primarily on the left hemisphere. Similarly, when engaged in complex reasoning about relations, the left rostrolateral PFC is generally more active than the right.

However, the right hemisphere is also important to many cognitive functions, including language.[16] In broad terms, the right side plays a major role in the pragmatic aspects of language and thought, which I sketched in chapters 5 and 6.[17] As previewed, these aspects are very important to poetic metaphor. If the right hemisphere is somehow impaired, adherence to both the cooperative and the coherence principle is reduced. Damage to language-related areas in the right hemisphere leads to deficits in sensitivity to context, including constraints based on politeness (for example, knowing how to avoid saying something that would be interpreted as a gratuitous insult). In chapter 11 we will consider how politeness is linked to poetry.

Right-hemisphere damage makes it hard to draw the inferences required to establish coherence in conversations or texts. Intriguingly, the right hemisphere is especially important for prosody, which underlies the rhythm and meter of poetry. The nuances of how a poem sounds, especially when read with expression, have much to do with its emotional impact. And as we mentioned, the capacity for empathy with others is primarily linked to the right side of the parietal cortex. Finally, and most directly, right-hemisphere damage impairs the ability to comprehend metaphors, as well as other types of nonliteral language.[18]

Mark Beeman introduced an important idea about how the representation of word meanings may differ between the left and right hemisphere.[19] He suggested that whereas the left hemisphere codes a small number of strong semantic associations for each word we know (e.g., *cut* might be linked to *knife* and *wound*), the right hemisphere codes a larger number of weak associations (e.g., *cut* might have connections to *foot, glass, join, bandage*, and many other words). This type of *coarse coding* in the right hemisphere makes it easier for multiple weak associations to sum up, activating a word that is especially appropriate in a particular context. The sparse representations of strong associations provided by the left hemisphere will be efficient for understanding literal language. However, the broad but weak associations coded by the right hemisphere will be especially helpful in creative thinking, including understanding novel metaphors.[20] In addition, the brain area that selects among competing interpretations (located in the ventrolateral PFC) will have more work to do when processing novel metaphors.

So far we have focused on the mental functions performed by specific brain regions. However, more global properties of neural activity are also critical in understanding how the brain functions. The electrical activity of the brain tends to become synchronized, with billions of synaptic connections firing together in a rhythmic pattern. These patterns of brain waves can be recorded on the surface of the scalp. Patterns at different frequencies are associated with global states of consciousness, such as deep sleep, REM (rapid eye movement) sleep, relaxation, and focused attention. Different mood states are also associated with particular wave frequencies. As we will see in chapter 12, a frequency band called *alpha* (8–12 hertz, the number of cycles per second) seems to have a particularly important connection to creative thinking.[21]

The cortical landmarks sketched above, along with other allied subareas of the brain, typically work together as networks to accomplish complex tasks. In addition to language-related areas, two general-purpose networks are very likely to be involved in the generation and understanding of poetic metaphors. The frontoparietal network consists of subregions within the prefrontal and parietal cortices, which operate together to direct attention and accomplish tasks that need to be broken down into sequential steps.[22] Because these functions provide cognitive control of thought processes— keeping the mind on task—the frontoparietal network is also called the cognitive control network, or to keep it short, simply *control network*.[23] The major components of the lateral surface of the PFC (ventrolateral, dorsolateral, rostrolateral) all contribute to this network, which roughly can be said to come into play when we are thinking hard. Individual differences in the control network—how densely interconnected its major hubs are—have been linked to variations in measured intelligence.[24] Measures of intelligence in turn predict (imperfectly) how successful people are in producing creative metaphors.[25]

A second major network goes by the odd name of *default network*, so called because it seems to be engaged by default when a person is not working on any specific, attention-demanding task.[26] The default network includes the medial prefrontal cortex (medial PFC), which is deeper in the PFC than the areas shown in our figure.[27] This area is activated when engaged in thinking about the self or other people. The medial PFC is also important for maintaining motivation, initiating self-guided action, and integrating information from different pathways—basic processes required to write poetry.[28] Other important hubs in the default network include the posterior cingulate cortex (posterior to the anterior cingulate cortex), which supports conscious awareness, and the precuneus, which seems related to a sense of selfhood. The medial temporal region also operates as a hub within the default network. As we saw, this region is involved in episodic memory and thinking about the future.

Neuroscientists used to think that the default network was basically the mind in idle, but now it's viewed as something much more interesting. For example, the medial PFC—a region within the default network involved in processing information connected to one's self—is active when a person views a piece of visual art that strikes them as highly moving.[29] If you followed our tour of the hubs of the default network and their functions, this network seems to be busily engaged in thinking about one's self and its emotional reactions, one's relationships with other people, and things that have happened or might happen in one's own life—in other words, the things we usually care about. This is the mind turned inward, *not* attending to the immediate surroundings, to the here and now.[30] Instead, the default network often appears to engage in *mind wandering*.

The default network likely plays an important role in composing poetry (a possibility we will explore more fully in chapter 12). From what poets have told us about how they create poems (indeed, from what creative people in many fields have said), a kind of sophisticated mind wandering may often spur the development of new ideas. The novelist Victor Hugo described *reverie* as "one of these ineffable moments when one feels something in himself which is going to sleep and something which is awakening."[31] Edgar Alan Poe claimed that "those who dream by day are cognizant of many things which escape those who dream only by night."[32] The image of the poet wandering about lost in thought, often outdoors in the midst of nature, is a familiar one. We have Coleridge and the Wordsworths of course, but also countless other examples, from Chinese poets centuries ago to the contemporary American poet Mary Oliver.[33] In fact, experiments have shown that walking outdoors stimulates creativity.[34] This simple rhythmic activity can help the mind to wander in creative directions.

The control and default networks might seem to act in opposite ways—thinking hard versus letting the mind wander. But in fact, there is reason to believe that the two networks sometimes work in concert—creative mind wandering can be hard work.[35] Recall that the control network directs attention, and in particular adjudicates between attending to the immediate environment that is impinging on the senses, versus attending to the inner world of the mind. That means that the control network can help to protect the default network from unwanted intrusions by current reality. This is particularly likely to occur when mind wandering is initiated deliberately, as often happens.[36] A poet at work may need to be able to ponder how a remembered dream fragment relates to a childhood fishing trip, the sadness of saying goodbye to a loved one, a glimpse last summer of a heron over a lake, and how the universe might end. Difficult work. Fortunately, the brain is wider than the sky.

8 Breaking It Down

"Breakage" by Mary Oliver

I go down to the edge of the sea.
How everything shines in the morning light!
The cusp of the whelk,
the broken cupboard of the clam,
the opened, blue mussels,
moon snails, pale pink and barnacle scarred—
and nothing at all whole or shut, but tattered, split,
dropped by the gulls onto the gray rocks and all the moisture gone.
It's like a schoolhouse
of little words,
thousands of words.
First you figure out what each one means by itself,
the jingle, the periwinkle, the scallop
    full of moonlight.

Then you begin, slowly, to read the whole story.[1]

In the previous chapters I have tried to break open the many pieces required
to tackle the puzzle of poetic metaphor. Like the shellfish on a New England
shoreline, those pieces are many and varied—language with all its affordances, the cooperative and coherence principles, the capacities to combine concepts and to think analogically, the neural networks that support
thinking and feeling. How everything shines in the morning light! Now we
begin, slowly, to read the whole story—though the story of the neurocognitive basis for metaphor is just beginning.

The central question considered in this chapter has two parts: What
have psychologists learned about how people understand metaphor, and
what do their findings tell us about metaphor in poetry?[2] To start with
the second part of the question, a hard-headed cynic might with some

justification answer, "Precious little." As we intimated earlier, psychologists studying metaphor have overwhelmingly focused on simple focal metaphors, expressed in single sentences, usually accompanied by little or no context. Many pages in journals of cognitive psychology and psycholinguistics have been devoted to discussions of metaphors with minimal poetic appeal, exemplified by "My lawyer is a shark."

Psychologists, we hasten to add, have good reasons for their choice of materials[3]—poetry has seldom been their central interest, and the requirements of psychological experiments impose their own constraints (or as witty psychologists have put it, "Stimulus design is an obstacle course").[4] Each person in an experiment has to be exposed to many examples in a similar syntactic form (so that responses can be averaged to separate real effects from statistical noise), usually with matched nonmetaphorical sentences included for comparison. Of course, reading a long list of unrelated metaphors interleaved with literal sentences, perhaps pressing a button as soon as each has been "understood" by some vague criterion, is hardly the same activity as reading an engaging poem. The emotional impact of metaphor—arguably the most essential component of the response to poetry—has been a focus of psychological studies of literary reading, but virtually ignored in studies of decontextualized metaphors.[5]

But it would be unwise to dismiss the relevance of psychological research to poetic metaphor. When we sift through the available studies carefully, we find some that use poetic metaphors, and some that set metaphors in context. More importantly, it strains credulity to imagine that the processes driving comprehension of simple focal metaphors are unrelated to those involved in grasping metaphors in poetry. "I'm … an elephant," wrote Sylvia Plath—a simple focal metaphor if ever there was one. Psychological experiments on single-sentence metaphors will not complete the story of poetic metaphor, but their findings can help get the story started. As we suggested in chapter 6, focal metaphors lend themselves to conceptual combination. It therefore is not surprising that evidence points to use of conceptual combination as the primary mechanism for comprehending the kinds of metaphors psychologists have tended to study.

———

Let's start by considering some basic questions that have been answered quite clearly. Do people search for a metaphorical meaning only if the literal meaning proves to be absurd? No. Indeed, without performing any experiments at all, we can simply point to the most famous metaphor in twentieth-century American poetry:

Two roads diverged in a wood, and I—
I took the one less traveled by,
And that has made all the difference.

The "I" in Robert Frost's poem may well have been traveling on a road through a wood, but this perfectly sensible and literal interpretation does not deter us from grasping a metaphor for life's choices.[6] This is not a focal metaphor (no single word is the focus that gives up its conventional meaning), but psychologists have found evidence that even for focal metaphors that *are* accompanied by literal incongruity, metaphorical processing is evoked without waiting for literal comprehension to fail.[7] For example, Sam Glucksberg and colleagues asked college students to judge whether sentences were *literally* true or false.[8] They found that people were slower to respond "false" to sentences that were literally incongruous but had a possible metaphorical interpretation (e.g., "Some surgeons are butchers") than to false sentences that lacked a metaphorical interpretation (e.g., "Some apples are oranges"). For simple metaphors, people appear to automatically detect a glimmer of metaphorical truth even when it interferes with their assigned task of judging literal falsity. A metaphorical meaning is hard to ignore.

Though metaphor processing starts early, it will often be harder than literal processing. Metaphors can be grasped more easily when preceded by two or three sentences of meaningful context.[9] With a prior context, metaphors may be processed about as fast as literal meanings, but without a context, metaphors can take much more time than literal processing. In general, metaphorical meanings become active relatively quickly (even without a prior context) when the metaphor is highly familiar or especially apt.[10] People start to become sensitive to metaphorical interpretations before literal processing is completed, but metaphorical meanings often require more time to fully grasp than do literal meanings—early to start, slow to finish. The cooperative principle motivates a search for the intended meaning, which typically continues until a satisfactory interpretation has been achieved.

What seems likely, then, is that metaphors are processed using augmented versions of the same processes used to comprehend literal language[11]— metaphor is part of normal language understanding. Almost universally, psychologists and cognitive linguists have accepted the "Coleridge view" of metaphor we sketched in chapter 4—we moderns are Romantics.[12] Metaphor is not simply a decorative veneer affixed to the surface of literal language, but a creative act involving what I. A. Richards called "the inter-animation of words." In one way or another, modern work has pursued Max Black's interaction theory, emphasizing how metaphorical meaning emerges from the interplay of the source and target, going beyond whatever prior similarities might link the two domains.

Roger Tourangeau and Lance Rips investigated the emergence of metaphorical meaning. Their study exhibits the rare virtue of including poetic metaphors. Given a metaphor such as this one, from a poem by Dylan Thomas,[13]

> Now as I was young and easy under the apple boughs
> About the lilting house and happy as the grass was green,

college students were asked to pick which of two interpretations seemed preferable. One choice specified a property shared by the source (vegetative life) and target (a child), such as "The happiness of the child is dependent on nourishing substance." The other described a property that seems to emerge from the interaction of source and target but is not salient a priori in either, such as "The happiness of a child is essential and intrinsic." People overwhelming preferred the emergent interpretation. Metaphorical meaning is not simply the activation of prior knowledge—it's the creation of something new.

If I've inadvertently conveyed the impression that the psychology of metaphor has given rise to a scientific consensus, we had best correct that happy illusion. Despite the broad agreement about general issues, the devilish details have fueled decades of controversy. How is it that the human mind is able to grasp metaphor? A dozen or more serious theories merit consideration, but the disparate views can be boiled down to two major alternatives, which I foreshadowed in chapter 6. Conceptual combination is generally easier and faster than analogical reasoning. Analogy (at least the explicit variety) is slower and more difficult but can lead to deeper understanding. As I will argue later, the two processes need not be separate alternatives—for metaphors of some complexity, they may work together.

Within modern cognitive science, the hypothesis that analogy underlies metaphor comprehension was first advanced by Roger Tourangeau and Robert Sternberg, and later elaborated by Dedre Gentner and her col-leagues.[14] The most prominent variant of what I term conceptual combi-nation is the *categorization* theory proposed by Sam Glucksberg and Boaz Keysar, later refined as a computational model by Walter Kintsch.[15] A pos-sible compromise called the *career-of-metaphor* hypothesis, put forward by Brian Bowdle and Gentner, argues that novel metaphors are understood using analogy, whereas more familiar ones can be handled by categoriza-tion.[16] Let's take a look at the evidence for and against the various views.

Most of the debate has centered on focal metaphors in the syntactic form *X is Y*, as in the example "My lawyer is a shark." This form, called a nominal metaphor (because it links two nouns), has been viewed as capturing the essence of a metaphorical comparison between a source and target. Accord-ing to the analogy account, such metaphors are understood by first think-ing about the source and target in terms of their constituent elements and relations. A mapping between the two domains is then identified. Alterna-tively, the categorization theory claims that the source (here *shark*) is rein-terpreted as a more abstract category (rather than being a vicious fish, *shark* is construed as the category of vicious things, of which a literal shark is an especially prominent example). This abstract category is then understood as a predicate to be applied to the target, resulting in a representation much like the conceptual combination "vicious lawyer." This type of conceptual combination may sound complicated (and it is certainly nontrivial), but as we will see, the process can be accomplished by relatively simple computa-tions based on the semantic features associated with individual words.

Analogy and conceptual combination clearly share some core proper-ties. In essence, both rely on breakage—breaking the source and target into elements, which are then compared and somehow integrated so as to cre-ate coherence. But the question of how the two processes may be related has been clouded by conflicting interpretations of what "comparison"—that venerable idea about metaphorical processing passed down from Aristotle—really means. Max Black, as we saw in chapter 4, was careful to acknowledge that his interaction theory did not eliminate an important role for comparison of properties of the source and target—emergent prop-erties do not emerge from nothing. But in psychology, some researchers have conflated comparison with analogical reasoning itself.[17] This confla-tion has led to arguments about whether metaphorical thinking evokes comparison (because it's based on analogy) or not (because it's based on conceptual combination). But as I have emphasized, analogy is just one variety of comparison. As we will see, when conceptual combination is considered carefully as a kind of mental computation, it also requires some sort of comparison (between associations of the source and target).

The tendency to identify comparison with analogy (and vice versa) leads to conceptual confusion. Much as some enthusiasts for metaphor have seen it everywhere in language, to the point of abolishing the literal, some enthusiasts for analogy see it in every comparison. A honeybee is capable of some sort of comparison between the color of a new flower and that of one encountered earlier (being more likely to alight on the new blossom if a previous one of the same color had yielded nectar).[18] But is the honeybee thinking by analogy? One can use the word *analogy* this loosely if one wishes, but venturing a scientific leap from foraging by insects to human metaphor invites a nasty fall. Human analogical reasoning—the ability to identify systematic correspondences between superficially dissimilar situations based on shared patterns of relations, and to use the discovered mappings to make inferences about new cases—provides a basis for creative insights. But this ability appears to be the product of a late development in hominid evolution, which (like language) distinguishes humans from all other species with whom we presently share the earth.[19]

We know that analogical reasoning (of the explicit sort required to solve the tumor problem by analogy to the story about the fortress) is often hard—it taxes working memory and inhibitory control and reflects individual differences in intelligence. It takes more time to find mappings based on shared relational correspondences as compared to direct similarity of objects.[20] At the neural level, analogical reasoning pushes the cognitive control network into high gear.[21] (The honeybee, by the way, lacks a prefrontal cortex altogether.) As we noted in chapter 7, numerous studies have shown that complex analogical reasoning is almost invariably accompanied by activation of the left rostrolateral PFC.[22] Let's take a careful look at this neural evidence, because it will help us evaluate the various proposals about metaphor processing.

Many of the neuroimaging studies of analogy have tested analogies presented as pictures or diagrams, but the major conclusions can be illustrated using an experiment that posed verbal analogy problems. As shown in figure 8.1, Adam Green and his colleagues asked students and others from a college community to generate completions to verbal analogies in the form $A{:}B :: C{:}?$[23] On each trial, the problem was first posed, and then the student

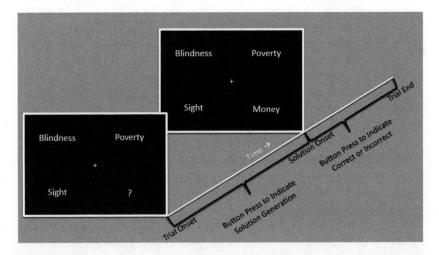

Figure 8.1
Generating solutions to verbal analogies: the events on each trial in a neuroimaging experiment.
Copyright © 2012 by the American Psychological Association. Reproduced with permission from Green et al. (2012, figure 1, p. 266).

pushed a button after thinking of a good completion for the missing *D* term. At this point the answer appeared and the participant pushed a button again to indicate whether their generated answer was correct.

During the interval when the student was trying to find the solution, the neural activity in their brain was being measured using a technique called *functional magnetic resonance imaging* (fMRI). As shown in figure 8.2, Green and colleagues found that a region in the left rostrolateral PFC (panel A) was active during the solution period. Moreover, as shown in panel B, this rostrolateral PFC activation increased with the semantic distance between the source (*A:B*) and target (*C:D*). For example, a problem (with its solution) like *blindness* : *sight* :: *deafness* : *hearing* involves a source and target that are semantically close to one another (i.e., highly similar) and that would not activate the rostrolateral PFC very much. By contrast, in the earlier example (shown in figure 8.1), *blindness* : *sight* :: *poverty* : *money*, the source and target are much more distant, crossing conceptual boundaries (sensory perception and economic status). Solving a semantically dissimilar problem of this sort produced a much larger neural response in the rostrolateral PFC.

To sum up, the evidence is compelling that solving complex analogy problems, including verbal ones in which the source and target are

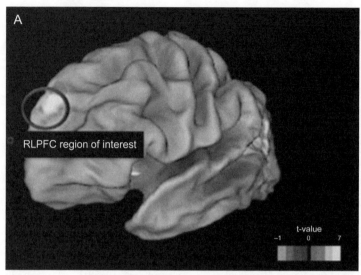

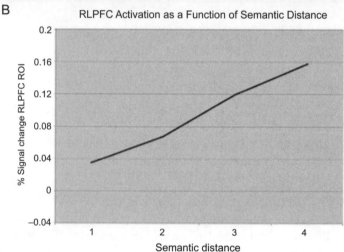

Figure 8.2
Neural response to semantic distance when generating solutions to analogy problems. A: A region of the rostrolateral PFC (circled) is sensitive to semantic distance. B: Activity in this region increases as a function of increasing semantic distance.
Copyright © 2012 by the American Psychological Association. Adapted with permission from Green et al. (2012, figure 2, p. 267).

semantically distant (as they are in metaphors), reliably activates the left rostrolateral PFC. Moreover, a further study by Green and his colleagues has shown that a type of electrical stimulation applied to this brain area helps people generate more creative solutions to verbal analogy problems. Let's make the leap (one I find reasonable given the neural evidence, though open to challenge) that explicit analogical reasoning between a dissimilar source and target inevitably activates the rostrolateral PFC (in one or both hemispheres) as its neural signature. To be clear, I'm not saying that analogy *only* involves the rostrolateral PFC (it generally activates the entire control network), nor am I saying that the rostrolateral PFC *only* becomes active during analogical reasoning (it supports other high-level cognitive functions). What neuroimaging studies indicate is simply that when complex analogical reasoning is evoked, the rostrolateral PFC becomes active.

The next step is to see whether neural studies of conceptual combination and metaphor understanding also reveal reliable neural activity in this region. In the case of conceptual combination—at least for simple, literal compounds like *young man*—the answer appears to be "no." The main region that becomes active is the semantic hub—the anterior temporal cortex.[24]

In the case of metaphor, findings from over 60 studies have been summarized in recent reviews.[25] In interpreting these results, we need to keep in mind that all of these studies used simple focal metaphors—usually in the nominal form, sometimes in a predicate form (e.g., "The flowers purred in the sunlight," where the focal word is the verb). Surveying the available studies, a number of brain areas tend to be activated when processing metaphors as compared to literal language. Notable areas that support metaphor include broad regions of the temporal cortex and several subareas of the frontal cortex. Frontal areas linked to metaphor processing include the ventrolateral PFC (probably because of the need for semantic selection), sometimes the dorsolateral PFC (when working memory is necessary), and sometimes the medial PFC (perhaps because interpreting metaphors often involves thinking about people, including oneself). Activation is bilateral, but sometimes more pronounced in the right hemisphere for relatively novel metaphors.

And what of the rostrolateral PFC, our alleged neural signature of complex analogy? So far, it seems that neural studies of metaphor processing have not found any evidence that the rostrolateral PFC becomes active when processing focal metaphors. To draw an analogy from Sherlock Holmes, we seem to have a "curious case of the dog in the night-time."[26] The rostrolateral PFC, like the dog that did not bark, remains conspicuously silent when people are processing focal metaphors.

The neural evidence, then, undermines the view that analogy (at least the explicit variety) is the dominant process involved in comprehending (or producing) simple metaphors.[27] What about the career-of-metaphor hypothesis, according to which explicit analogy is used to process novel metaphors, then is gradually replaced by categorization as the metaphor becomes more conventional?[28] A neuroimaging study tested this hypothesis by using metaphors that were initially novel, and having people read them repeatedly so that the expressions became increasingly familiar.[29] This study found that the rostrolateral PFC was not selectively engaged by metaphor processing at *any* stage in the process of conventionalization. Interestingly, broad areas of the right hemisphere were somewhat more active when the metaphors were novel.[30] In general, overall neural load decreased with repeated exposure to the metaphors, but there was no compelling evidence of a qualitative shift in processing strategy. Apparently, the career of a simple metaphor can proceed quite well without requiring complex analogical reasoning, even to get it launched.

———

Based on the available neural evidence it seems that simple focal metaphors are generally *not* understood using explicit analogical reasoning. But we need to be careful not to overstate this conclusion. Neural studies of analogical reasoning have found that the rostrolateral PFC becomes active when the task is made hard in some way. Sometimes, as in Green's experiments, the source and target domain are semantically distant and no linguistic or pragmatic cues are provided to help relate the two. In other studies that used nonverbal analogies, multiple relations needed to be considered together to identify correspondences.[31] In contrast (as we will explore in chapters 9 and 10), a poetic metaphor is often based on familiar symbols embedded in a linguistic context that provides strong cues to help find an interpretation. In such situations, the poet may have made it relatively easy for the reader to interpret an analogy.

In any case, given that we lack evidence for the use of analogy to interpret simple focal metaphors, it's worth considering how conceptual combination might manage to create metaphorical meaning. Over the past two decades, a powerful approach to word meaning has been developed in the field of cognitive science (the interface of cognitive psychology, artificial intelligence, and psycholinguistics). The basic idea is that as a person (or computer) acquires experience with language (spoken or written), the meanings of words modulate one another—the meaning learned for any individual word depends on the meanings of the other words in its semantic neighborhood. It's possible to represent the meaning of a word, as stored in semantic memory, by an ordered list or *vector* of feature values (roughly 300 is a standard number). These vectors, which we can think of as relatively stable word meanings, would be realized in the brain by neural networks. The vectors can be estimated from the frequencies with which words co-occur in passages taken from texts.[32]

A second major idea is that a word's stable vector can be modified by the context in which the word appears. That is, each word's meaning-in-use is a combination of its stable meaning and the meanings of the other words with which it *now* co-occurs. This mechanism begins to capture the exquisite context sensitivity of word meanings. For example, the word *runs* is used quite literally in both "The horse runs" and "The river runs." However, we readily imagine the action of the horse, but probably not the river, to be *galloping*. The meaning of *horse* operates to shade the meaning of *runs* in the direction of equine movement. (But notice a possible metaphor for a stretch of rapids: "The river gallops.")

Using this general framework, the psychologist Walter Kintsch developed a computational model of how the meaning of simple focal metaphors can be constructed by a form of conceptual combination.[33] He applied his model to nominal metaphors, such as "My lawyer is a shark." These are the kinds of metaphors that Glucksberg viewed as categorizations, and indeed, Kintsch's model is very much in the same spirit. The general approach has three steps. (1) Starting with the stable vectors for the target (*lawyer*) and source (*shark*), activate those words that are most closely associated with the source (perhaps the top 500). (2) Identify those associates of the source that are also associated (above some criterion value) with the target. (3) Merge the stable vectors for the target and source with those for the words in the set of shared associates to create a new vector, which represents the meaning of the metaphor as a whole.

Applied to "My lawyer is a shark," Kintsch's model alters the stable meaning vector for *lawyer* so that the metaphorical conceptual combination becomes more similar to "vicious" (and even a bit "fishlike")—properties transferred from *shark*. But other salient properties of sharks, like "swims," are *not* transferred because they do not have associative links to *lawyer*. The model creates *coherent* conceptual combinations, enhancing those properties that link source to target and suppressing those that do not. Because only some of the properties of the source are transferred to the target, the source itself (here *shark*) acts like an abstract category, meaning something like "vicious creature."

Kintsch's model captures a number of important phenomena about metaphor comprehension that psychologists have observed. First, they are generally not reversible.[34] "My shark is a lawyer" doesn't make much sense, metaphorically or literally. "The surgeon is a butcher" and "The butcher is a surgeon" both are metaphors, but with very different meanings—the former is a terrible surgeon, the latter an exceptionally skilled butcher. These differences in meaning are explained by Kintsch's model because it transfers meaning asymmetrically—the strong associates of the source have a greater impact on the constructed interpretation than do the strong associates of the target.

Also, people have more trouble finding a metaphorical interpretation if the metaphor is preceded by a literal sentence that primes features of the source that prove irrelevant to the metaphor.[35] For example, reading "Sharks can swim" interferes with understanding "My lawyer is a shark." This is because the literal sentence causes *swim* to become highly active, which interferes with access to other associates of *shark* (some of which connect to *lawyer*). Conversely, if the metaphor "My lawyer is a shark" precedes the literal statement "Sharks can swim," reading the metaphor makes people slower to agree that the literal statement is true.[36]

Kintsch's model explains all of these phenomena, which follow from the coherence principle we have encountered repeatedly. Conceptual combination activates those properties that make sense together in context, while deactivating properties that don't fit the context-driven interpretation. In keeping with Black's interaction view, the metaphorical combination of concepts can create similarities that did not preexist. Kintsch discusses the example "That girl is a lollipop"—a metaphor that arguably can be interpreted as meaning something like "That girl is frivolous."[37] In this case, not only are the stable meanings of *girl* and *lollipop* dissimilar, but the source (*lollipop*) is not associated with the property *frivolous*. Nonetheless, a few associates of the source, like *friendly*, *smiled*, and *carnival*, intersect with those of girl, and these cause the derived feature vector for the compound to move in the direction of *frivolous*. In other words, multiple weak and indirect associations that cohere with one another can create an emergent meaning.

The resulting meaning is a coherent blend of the stable word meanings (of the source, the target, and their shared associates) that contribute to it. Conceptual combination thus captures the elusive power of metaphor to fill the gaps between preexisting word meanings. When used well, metaphor provides a way to express precisely that for which there are no words.

Although less cognitively demanding than complex analogical reasoning, conceptual combination poses its own cognitive challenges. As we noted, neuroimaging studies of metaphor typically show activation not only in language areas of the temporal cortex, but also in regions of the frontal cortex. In particular, processing focal metaphors tends to place a neural burden on the ventrolateral PFC (which supports the enhancement and suppression of semantic information) and the dorsolateral PFC (which supports working memory). People with greater working-memory capacity are able to generate more apt interpretations of metaphors, more quickly, than those with less working-memory capacity.[38]

Recall that as a rule of thumb, Kintsch's model of metaphor comprehension depends on the activation of about 500 associates of the source. By comparison, a literal conceptual combination requires activation of far fewer (and stronger) associates (perhaps 20). Based on Beeman's coarse-coding theory (chapter 7), it seems likely that the right hemisphere plays a special role in activating the many weak associates that impact metaphor comprehension. Of course, people are not conscious of all these associates, but they do need to expend mental effort to perform the search required to activate them. Although the route of conceptual combination processes metaphors by extending a process used in literal comprehension, the metaphorical extension takes extra mental and neural work.

It might seem we have abandoned analogy altogether, given the evidence that simple focal metaphors can be understood using the nonanalogical process of conceptual combination. But here we return to the point at which we started this chapter. The metaphors so far studied by psychologists almost always can be analyzed as the integration of one focal word into its local sentence context—typically either a noun with a noun ("My lawyer is a shark") or a verb with a noun ("The river galloped"). For such metaphors, conceptual combination is enough to generate an interpretation.

But something else is required to deal with more extended metaphors.[39] It would hardly do to take "A Noiseless Patient Spider" and reduce it to one conceptual combination, "The soul is a spider." A richer interpretation requires grasping the interconnections among a system of interrelated elements—the spider, alone on its promontory, launching its filament into a void, hoping it will take hold somewhere; the soul alone in the immensity of the universe, yearning to connect with someone or something. From a cognitive perspective, the essential difference is that understanding an extended metaphor requires keeping in mind *several* elements of both the source and the target. Moreover, it's also essential to keep track of the *relations* among those elements. Technically, this relational information poses the *binding problem*—the need to track not only the individual elements, but also "who is doing what to whom."[40]

I conjecture that the apparent absence of evidence for activation of the rostrolateral PFC in neural studies of metaphor reflects the paucity of studies using more complex metaphors. Future work in literary neuroscience needs to close that gap. Even slightly more complex focal metaphors, such as the proportional metaphors that Aristotle linked to analogy, introduce significant additional complexity.[41] For example, Karl Marx claimed that "religion is the opium of the people." The intended meaning is not just a conceptual combination of *religion* and *opium* (though that may be part of it), but an invitation to explore cause-effect relations—Marx was asserting that religion, like an addictive drug, causes psychic numbness and is hard to overcome.

Cognitive scientists have constructed computational models of this sort of complex analogical thinking.[42] Some of these models operate within humanlike working-memory limits.[43] In addition, some are capable of processing an extended analogy in sequential pieces and are sensitive to the coherence of texts (as are people, who find coherent texts easier to read and understand).[44] Semantic and pragmatic cues can make the mapping process much easier, so that grasping a metaphor is more like getting an insight than working out an intellectual puzzle.

Is it possible that analogical reasoning and conceptual combination actually complement one another? As we saw in chapter 6, analogical reasoning provides a set of correspondences between the source and target. Pairs of mapped elements then become candidates for conceptual combination, which can shade the meaning of the target element in the direction of its corresponding source element. For example, by the end of Oliver's poem "Breakage," a correspondence has been created between words and shellfish on a shore. And the meaning of *words* has been shaded to become more like a protective cover of something growing—more alive.

This kind of neurocognitive process (foreshadowed in chapter 3), and the meanings that emerge from it, create analogical resonance. As I will elaborate in chapter 9, the basic idea is that analogy, augmented by linguistic cues, creates correspondences or *couplings* between words and their associated concepts.[45] These couplings invite comparisons, which cause meanings to resonate and modify each other (as exemplified by Kintsch's model of conceptual combination). Because each individual will have unique memories and associations between concepts, the products of resonance will differ to some degree across individuals. In general, resonance may highlight both similarities and differences between concepts, and create new, context-dependent meanings that coexist with the more literal word meanings used in the interpretive process.

I'll close this chapter with an example of analogical resonance—a famous "meditation" by the seventeenth-century English poet John Donne. This excerpt was written as a prose paragraph with no line breaks, but it exhibits the compression and symbolism characteristic of poetry. It has often been called a *prose poem*. Returning to Howard Nemerov's poem that provides the epigraph for this book, one might say Donne's passage represents "a moment that you couldn't tell" prose from poetry. In the version below, line breaks have been imposed to highlight its poetic character.

The "Meditation" is rich in examples of all the major forms of figurative language. It begins with a striking negative metaphor, "No man is an island," which serves as a compelling counterexample to the notion that a metaphorical meaning is sought only if literal meaning fails. Truly indeed, no man is (literally) an island—which is entirely beside the point! After the negative metaphor, a positive one: "every man is a piece of the continent." The striking phrase destined to provide the title for a novel by Ernest Hemingway, "for whom the bell tolls," is a metonymy—by association, the tolling bell symbolizes death. And the entire piece forms a *synecdoche*, a special type of metonymy in which a part refers to the whole (or vice versa). Here, the fate of an individual stands for that of all humanity. These devices work together to evoke mappings between the small and the great, between people and geological formations, between the reader and a suffering stranger. This network of conceptual and emotional connections triggers analogical resonance and yields poetic coherence.

From "Meditation XVII: Devotions upon Emergent Occasions" by John Donne

No man is an island,
entire of itself,
every man is a piece of the continent,
a part of the main.
If a clod be washed away by the sea,
Europe is the less,
as well as if a promontory were,
as well as if a manor of thy friend's
or of thine own were:
Any man's death diminishes me,
because I am involved in mankind.
And therefore never send to know for whom the bell tolls;
it tolls for thee.[46]

9 Spinning the Web

"旅夜書懷" by Du Fu

細草微風岸
危檣獨夜舟
星垂平野闊
月涌大江流
名豈文章著
官應老病休
飄飄何所似
天地一沙鷗[1]

"Thoughts Written While Traveling by Night" by Du Fu

The fine grass
by the riverbank stirs in the breeze;
    the tall mast
in the night is a lonely sliver.

Stars hang
all across the vast plain;
    the moon bobs
in the flow of the great river.

My poetry
has not made a name for me;
    now age and sickness
have cost me the post I was given.

Drifting, drifting,
what do I resemble?
    A lone gull
lost between earth and heaven.

Recall how the ancient Chinese *Book of Odes* linked poetry to dancing. In modern times the poet Paul Valéry turned the link into an analogy: Where prose is like walking, poetry is like dancing.[2] We walk, in general, to get somewhere—to reach a chair, to cross the street. Exactly how we move our legs is seldom the main concern (generally, the way of least effort is best) as long as we reach our destination. But in dance, the movement is everything. Rather than holding to a straight line, the dancer may swirl in circles, bend, and weave—it's not the destination that matters, but the dance itself. The dancer has no aim except to dance—in the limit, "How can we know the dancer from the dance?"[3]

When a person hears or reads ordinary prose, what is remembered after a few minutes is the meaning, not the exact words.[4] As the psychologist Michael Apter observed, it's as if the words are transparent—we see their meaning, but the words themselves are scarcely noticed.[5] The same information can usually be paraphrased in different ways. The goal in comprehending prose is to extract the information being conveyed. Once that's accomplished the words, like emptied shells, can be let fall.

But the words of a poem are more likely to be appreciated and remembered than those of a prose passage.[6] The words are more than a means to the end of conveying information:

> Do not go gentle into that good night,
> Old age should burn and rave at close of day;
> Rage, rage against the dying of the light.[7]

Continuing Apter's distinction between poetic metaphors and ordinary prose, the words in poetic metaphors seem to become "visible." Just as we see a painting as both an object in itself and as a representation of what it depicts, the words in poetry are important both as words and as cues to multiple levels of meaning. What Dylan Thomas means, we might say, is that we ought to live life to the fullest, even (perhaps especially) at its end. But the paraphrase rings hollow. We prefer to go back to *his* words—the best words in their best order.

In chapter 8 we considered what psychologists have learned about how people think about short metaphors presented with little if any context. Now it's time to put metaphor back into poetry. In chapter 4 we defined a poetic metaphor as one that honors the constraints of a poem. The coherence principle still applies, but now we have to consider not simply how the source coheres with the target *within* a metaphor, but how the metaphor coheres with the poem that incorporates it.

We immediately face the question: What *are* the constraints of a poem?[8] They prominently involve the *sounds* of the language in which the poem is written—what T. S. Eliot and many others have called "the music of poetry." The sounds of language have the power to convey and arouse emotions, especially in individuals with heightened sensitivity. One person with a high degree of sensitivity was Yeats: "All sounds, all colours, all forms, either because of their pre-ordained energies or because of long association, evoke indefinable and yet precise emotions."[9]

More generally, sounds have affinities for specific meanings—not just in the crude examples termed *onomatopoeia* (pots that *clang*, frogs that *croak*), but in far more subtle manifestations. A *rock* is not a *stone*, observed Mary Oliver—*rock* ends abruptly with its mute consonant *k*; *stone* begins with the soft sibilant *s* and ends with the lingering *-one*.[10] The sounds of the words prepare us to imagine a jagged rock, a smooth stone.

The legacy of poetry, accumulated over the centuries from many different languages and cultures, is enormously varied. Nonetheless, the basic nature of poetry appears to be near universal across societies as diverse as those that have flourished across Europe, Africa, the Middle East, China, India, and New Guinea.[11] Most poetry has followed constraints based on repeating sound patterns, particularly meter and rhyme, taking the form of regular verse. Both meter and rhyme enhance the emotional impact of poetry.[12] Meter, defined by repeating patterns of major beats, is a stylized extension of the rhythms of speech. As we mentioned earlier, rhythm is a key aspect of prosody—the global "sound shape" of speech patterns. It conveys emotion and links speech with music and dance. You've doubtless noticed how the hypnotic rhythm of ocean waves can have a powerful emotional impact. That impact can be turned into poetry, as illustrated by this passage from Matthew Arnold's "Dover Beach":

> Listen! you hear the grating roar
> Of pebbles which the waves draw back, and fling,
> At their return, up the high strand,
> Begin, and cease, and then again begin,
> With tremulous cadence slow, and bring
> The eternal note of sadness in.[13]

Rhythm is basic to life. Infants as young as seven months are sensitive to it.[14] Rhythm focuses attention on expected beats.[15] It finds expression in activities of the body, ranging from breathing to sex. Rhythmic brain activity creates neural codes for visual and semantic patterns.[16] Listening to metrical music helps older dementia patients recall memories from decades past.[17]

More than any other constraint, poetic rhythm fuses the meanings of words with the sound patterns they create. Poetry arose thousands of years ago in many cultures as an oral tradition. Shamanism and magical incantations were among its earliest uses. A century ago, Yeats emphasized the role of rhythm in preparing the mind to grasp symbolic meaning. "The purpose of rhythm … is to prolong the moment of contemplation, the moment when we are both asleep and awake, which is the one moment of creation … to keep us in that state of perhaps real trance, in which the mind liberated from the pressure of the will is unfolded in symbols."[18] Rhythm creates and maintains the state of "reverie" described by Victor Hugo—something within is falling asleep, and something awakening.

Of course, not all poetry honors the sound constraints of regular verse. Free verse (negatively defined as the rejection of regular meter and rhyme) became dominant, though many notable poets continued to work in verse forms. The young T. S. Eliot warned, "No verse is free for the man who wants to do a good job."[19] A quarter century later, reflecting on the contemporary style he had done so much to mold, he wrote, "Only a bad poet could welcome free verse as a liberation from form.[20] It was a revolt against dead form, and a preparation for new form or for the renewal of the old; it has an insistence upon the inner unity which is unique to every poem, against the outer unity which is typical."[21]

As Mary Oliver reminds us, "Time—a few centuries here or there—means very little in the world of poems."[22] Fashions in poetry change, and they sometimes recur (with variations). For present purposes, we can take our cue from Eliot—a poet should insist on the "inner unity" of an individual poem, whether that unity arises directly from the forms of earlier poetry or more indirectly from the poet's choices among the constraints available.

Some of the core constraints that contribute to poetic unity are so general—so deeply rooted in human psychology—that they appear to govern almost all verse, regular or free.[23] Poems are divided into lines, which may or may not correspond to syntactic units. The poetic line is the primary device for creating structure in a poem in a way that transcends the ordinary syntax of language. The resonance of a poem involves connections between words and units that are sufficiently close together to share space in the limited working memory of a human being. Poetry therefore tends toward semantic density—much is conveyed in small, compressed units.

The natural rhythms of poetry tend to create groupings based on two to four stressed syllables (usually with one or two slack syllables intervening between successive stresses).[24] These numbers are small because human working memory is only able to hold about four "chunks" of information at once.[25] A line in the familiar meter of iambic pentameter, with its five beats per line (see the lines from Dylan Thomas quoted above), usually can be decomposed into smaller groups of stresses (2 + 3, or 3 + 2, or occasionally 1 + 4). Indeed, it's these sorts of variations in groupings that allow a poem to be written in a regular meter without becoming monotonous. Very long lines (the style of poetic passages in the Bible, or many poems by Walt Whitman) tend to be heard as a sequence of smaller units, or of hierarchical groups themselves composed of smaller units.

The excerpt quoted from Dylan Thomas—an example of poetic constraints in action—exhibits regular meter, as well as rhyme at line endings (*night* and *light*). End rhyme is salient even when a poem is read silently, and makes a simple aphorism more convincing.[26] For example, people judge "What sobriety conceals, alcohol reveals" to be more accurate as a description of human behavior than "What sobriety conceals, alcohol unmasks" (which substitutes a close synonym that doesn't rhyme). The rhyming version gives the aphorism a sense of inevitability and closure, which people tend to translate into a judgment that it's likely to be true. And as you would expect, rhyme and meter help to make poetry memorable, which was immensely important for oral traditions in which poems had to be committed to memory in order to be preserved.[27]

Other sound-based constraints in poetry include *alliteration* (repetition of initial consonant sounds), as in "Do not *g*o gentle into that *g*ood night," and *assonance* (repetition of vowel sounds), as in "Old *a*ge should burn and r*a*ve at close of d*a*y; / R*a*ge, r*a*ge. ..." The sounds of words matter in poetry and merge with meaning. The words are not simply meant to be understood and then discarded.

Given the centrality of sound in poetry, it seems natural that a key insight into the nature of poetic constraints can be traced to one of the founders of the modern field of phonology, Roman Jakobson.[28] The basic idea (as elaborated by Samuel Levin and others) is that poetry provides *extrasyntactic* cues to compare and contrast words and concepts. To understand what counts as an extrasyntactic cue, let's start by recalling the basics of conceptual combination at its most literal. If you hear "The brown dog barked," the syntax of English indicates that the meaning of the adjective *brown* should be combined with that of the noun *dog* to form the concept of a certain individual dog (marked by the definite article *the*) of a specific color. The meaning of this integrated noun phrase is to be combined with the meaning of the predicate conveyed by the verb *bark*. The syntax in essence provides a set of instructions—syntactic cues—for taking a string of words and building the meaning of a proposition.

Jakobson and others have argued that poetry makes extensive use of additional, nonsyntactic cues that create couplings (to use the term introduced by Levin) between words (and the concepts that words evoke). Many of these cues are based on sound, including those types we just surveyed— rhythm, meter, rhyme, alliteration, and assonance. In "Do not *go* gentle into that *good* night," the alliteration couples *go* with *good* (and hence with the phrase *good night*). These sound connections convey a sense of soft movement by choice or acceptance (*go gentle*) into something apparently inviting (*good*) but actually threatening (*night*, a symbol of death)—a possibility against which the voice of the poet issues a warning (*do not*). Meanwhile, the fact that *night* and *light* rhyme and occur in salient parallel positions (line endings) encourages a coupling between these two words. And this coupling focuses attention on the familiar contrast between *night* (death) and *light* (a symbol of the day, and hence of consciousness and life).

Because poetry is organized hierarchically, couplings can connect units of meaning at any level, not simply individual words. The first and third lines are linked not just by the coupling between *night* and *light*, but also by parallel meter and syntactic parallelism—the negative imperative "Do not go" is answered by the positive imperative "Rage, rage." If we return to Whitman's "A Noiseless Patient Spider," the stanza structure creates long-distance couplings. Most notably, the first line of each of the two stanzas stands out because it is shorter than the others. Just as the first line of stanza 1 introduces the spider, so the matching line in stanza 2 introduces the soul, encouraging a coupling between the metaphorical source and target.

We see, then, that the kinds of correspondences created by metaphor are of a piece with other couplings—those created by phonological similarities in coordination with parallelism of poetic form. It's this entire network of couplings—the web of connections between words and their associated concepts, based on both sound and meaning—that drives the "interanimation of words" within a poem. Couplings trigger a network of comparisons, drawing attention to similarities and contrasts at multiple levels of meaning.

Now let's return specifically to the role of metaphor in poetry. How exactly do metaphors get introduced into the nexus of couplings within a poem, creating analogical resonance? The possibilities are virtually endless, but it's helpful to sort them into three basic types. These form an ordering from most indirect to most direct, and also from simplest to most complex (where simplicity is defined by the linguistic form, not the meaning—a simple form can convey a complex meaning). At the indirect and simple end, the metaphor can be stated as the *source only*. The poet simply starts talking about the source and lets the cooperative principle do its work, encouraging the reader to figure out what the poem is *really* about. This is what Frost did in "The Road Not Taken"—it's up to the reader to decide what that road refers to—what it is a symbol of.

Poetic symbols (which we will look at more carefully in chapter 10) often function as a source that needs no direct explication. Take the word *night* in Dylan Thomas's poem—we're prepared to interpret "that good night" as death, or something like it. From the title of Langston Hughes's poem "Night Funeral in Harlem," we learn not only that the poem is about a death, not only that it's the death of an African American (a strong associate of Harlem)—we learn it's a death half-hidden, unacknowledged by the world.[29] The same word, *night*, can shift its symbolic meaning in different contexts, though death often lurks in its neighborhood. When in another poem Frost wrote, "I am one acquainted with the night," we sense he's referring to a side of life that's mysterious and ominous.[30] The poet does not need to spell it out. Metaphors presented in source-only form are inherently analogical. They tell a story using symbols or allusions that refer to something beyond themselves.[31]

The next type of metaphor presentation can be called *juxtaposition*—the source and target are each stated, often using some form of verbal parallelism, but without explicit mention that they are related to one another. Instead, the cooperative principle encourages the reader to consider why two disparate things happen to be laid out side by side in the poem. A simple but striking example (from Theodore Roethke) is "my memory, my prison."[32] We encountered juxtaposition in Whitman's "A Noiseless Patient Spider": the first stanza describes a spider at work, the second the struggles of the soul. We are invited to consider the former as the source for understanding the latter as target. Juxtaposition was a favored device in classical Chinese poetry.[33] In the Tang dynasty (eighth century CE), the fabled poet Li Bai composed the twinned lines

> Floating cloud, wanderer's mind.
> Setting sun, old friend's feeling.

The floating cloud and the setting sun are both conventional symbols in Chinese poetry. Here they are coupled with one another by their parallel positions in adjacent lines. Within each line, a symbol based on the heavens is coupled with the human world. The result is a metaphor between metaphors, told by juxtaposition.

Finally, the most direct, most complex, and most varied type of metaphor presentation can be called *merged*—all the myriad ways syntax can stitch together a source and target using the syntactic devices of natural language to invite comparisons.[34] We have *simile*—"O my Luve is like a red, red rose," sang Robert Burns, drawing an explicit comparison between the rose—symbol of love—and his own muse. In "Mind," Parini introduces a deft simile—"The mind is like this"—to open the second stanza, prompting an explicit comparison between the mind as target and the wind (already introduced in the first stanza) as source.

Then we have the many varieties of what are conventionally counted as metaphors, where the target and source are merged in some way without using the language of explicit comparison. "Juliet is the sun" (Shakespeare) exemplifies the kind of *X is Y* expressions on which psychologists have focused (see chapter 8).[35] Such examples abound in poetry, as simple as "I / am a horizon" (Donald Justice). An adjective may be added to qualify the source, as in "Folly is an endless maze" (William Blake), or "deepest shades / Were deepest dungeons" (John Keats). The source may instead be elaborated by a prepositional phrase, as in "wisdom is the property of the dead" (Yeats). More complex proportional metaphors can be expressed in many ways. Examples include "Time, the subtle thief of youth" (John Milton), and the Old English kenning "sea-stallion" (i.e., "a ship is the stallion of the sea"). The metaphorical complexity deepens in an example from the modern Swedish poet Tomas Tranströmer, who talks about

Battlegrounds within us
where we Bones of the Dead
fight to come alive.

Poetic metaphors also flourish in verbs, as in "He glides unfelt into their secret hearts" (John Dryden), as well as in adjective-noun combinations, such as "I indulge myself / in rich refusals" (Donald Justice).[36] A verb may interact metaphorically with an adverb, as in "Music had driven their wits astray" (Yeats), where *driven* creates the sense of a physical force operating to change the location of *wits*, with *astray* describing their destination. There are even examples where an adverb metaphorically subverts a noun, as in "a grief ago" (Dylan Thomas), where the adverb *ago* turns *grief* into a unit of time.

Metaphors—whether their form is source-only, juxtaposed, or merged—interact with poetic constraints to create analogical resonance. Let's consider a more extended example of how metaphor, sound, and poetic form operate together in a short poem.

Every poem provides its own set of constraints, but particular forms that recur (such as the English sonnet or the French villanelle) offer a set shared by all poems written in that form. For our example, we'll look at a poem from Tang-dynasty China—"Thoughts Written While Traveling by Night" by the great master Du Fu. This poem, presented to open this chapter, is shown both in its original classical Chinese characters and in an English translation (by me). Our example will serve to illustrate the problems that arise in translating poetry across languages—especially those as different as Chinese and English.[37] If a poem is written as Coleridge advocated—in the best words in their best order—then pity the poor translator who aims to recreate the poem in a new language! Some words may lack an exact translation. The syntax will have to change, as will the sounds of individual words and the more global prosody—so meter and rhyme may not be translatable. Not surprisingly, different translators are likely to produce very different translations. In essence, each translator has to decide which constraints of the original to keep and which to give up.

For a century now, translations of classical Chinese poetry have had a strong impact on the development of western poetry, particularly in English. As we'll discuss in chapter 14, new writers learn from their predecessors, yet also struggle to transcend them. Translation is a special case in which the influence necessarily crosses the boundaries of language and culture. Ezra Pound, one of the earliest and still most influential translators of classical Chinese poetry, in 1917 claimed that "a great age of literature is perhaps always a great age of translations; or follows it."[38] He referred in particular to the impact that translations of classical Greek and Roman plays had on the creative work of Shakespeare and other playwrights during the Elizabethan era.

Pound's translations often traded accuracy for poetic impact. Inspired by the strong sensory imagery in the Chinese poems, he created a style of free verse in English known as *Imagism*. Ironically, as I'll describe below, poems written by Du Fu and other poets of the High Tang era were not "free" at all—they followed a strict form. But in the world of literature, original work may depend on a kind of creative misunderstanding of predecessors, which Harold Bloom termed *misprision*.[39] One kind of misprision is to generate inaccurate translations that inspire successful new poetry in the target language. Regardless of my degree of success in capturing the originals, my own primary aim in working on translations from Du Fu was to try to get a sense of his spirit or poetic essence (in Chinese, *yijing*). Later, I tried my hand at writing original poems in English guided by the style of my Chinese translations.[40]

I'll assume you are a reader of English who does not know Chinese. (If you happen to be bilingual in Chinese and English, congratulations! You can fairly judge for yourself the aptness of the translation.) Without understanding Chinese at all, we can still describe the general constraints honored in the Chinese original. The poem is written in what is called *Regulated Verse* or *New Style*, which Du Fu perfected. (The latter label is a bit incongruous, of course, given that the poem is more than 1,200 years old!) Look first at the Chinese version. Each line has exactly five characters. Since in Chinese each character corresponds to a single syllable, we can also say that each line is five syllables long. There is usually a slight pause between the second and third syllable in each line, creating two groupings (in accord with the near-universal principle that sound groups may not exceed size four). Each line expresses a complete thought (basically, a sentence—though classical Chinese writing lacks punctuation).

A New Style poem is exactly eight lines long. The lines are organized into couplets; the poem consists of four couplets. A general formal constraint is that the paired lines in particular couplets exhibit a kind of parallelism, both in sound and meaning. The sound parallelism is based on correspondences between the *tones* (systematic pitch variations) of corresponding vowels. Since the phonology of English lacks tones altogether, this Chinese sound constraint defies translation.

The parallelism of meaning is best described after we turn to the English version. But first, notice how some of the formal constraints in the original have been modified to fit the very different affordances of English. Each line of the original is translated as two semilines—two beats followed by three beats. That is, Chinese syllables (five per line) have become five metric beats, broken into two followed by three (to correspond to the pause in Chinese between the second and third syllable). English words are generally longer than Chinese words, and English demands prepositions and other function words that classical Chinese omits (letting the context disambiguate the meaning). The English version is therefore more expansive and less ambiguous than the dense Chinese original. Such changes may result in an aesthetic loss—metaphors that in Chinese create Wheelwright's plurisigns may seem less resonant when rendered into English.

The four Chinese couplets have become four English stanzas, separated by blank space on the page. The Chinese version has a single rhyme that falls on the even-numbered lines (i.e., the final syllable of each couplet). The English version makes a weak rhyming gesture, with similar-sounding two-syllable words at the end of each stanza (*sliver* and *river*, *given* and *heaven*).

Now, on to the meaning. It may be helpful to know that Du Fu's life was marred by poverty and ill health. He lived through a ferocious civil war that brought China to the brink of ruin. In general, his poetry is marked by his compassion for the poor and for the victims of war. These "night thoughts" were composed toward the end of his life during a journey down the immense Yangzi River.

Each of the first two stanzas illustrates verbal parallelism. The fine grass is coupled with the tall mast, the riverbank with the boat. Together, the first couplet links the movement of the grass (nature) with the movement of the human speaker down the river. In the second stanza, the parallel lines couple stars with the moon, which together symbolize the heavens, while also linking heaven with earth (the river).

Then in the third stanza, the perspective shifts dramatically. This is an example of the way a poem, like consciousness itself, can suddenly alter the psychological distance between the observer and what is being observed. Here the shift is from the remote and impersonal to the immediate and highly personal. No longer calmly contemplating the heavens and the natural world, Du Fu plunges down to take stock of his own individual human life. What he finds is disappointment—a sense of futility as his life's ambitions wind down in old age, unfulfilled. In the final stanza, Du Fu sees his life adrift, moving with the wind, with the river—forces beyond human control. The poem ends with a magnificent simile: What am I like, what do I resemble? The poet becomes a gull—symbol of the soul—flying alone somewhere between the bitterness of life on earth and a transcendent vision symbolized by the sky.

The poem ends, the poet falls into silence. But analogical resonance, generated by the web of poetic couplings, continues to reverberate.

10   What Rough Beast?

"The Second Coming" by William Butler Yeats

Turning and turning in the widening gyre
The falcon cannot hear the falconer;
Things fall apart; the centre cannot hold;
Mere anarchy is loosed upon the world,
The blood-dimmed tide is loosed, and everywhere
The ceremony of innocence is drowned;
The best lack all conviction, while the worst
Are full of passionate intensity.

Surely some revelation is at hand;
Surely the Second Coming is at hand.
The Second Coming! Hardly are those words out
When a vast image out of *Spiritus Mundi*
Troubles my sight: somewhere in sands of the desert
A shape with lion body and the head of a man,
A gaze blank and pitiless as the sun,
Is moving its slow thighs, while all about it
Reel shadows of the indignant desert birds.
The darkness drops again; but now I know
That twenty centuries of stony sleep
Were vexed to nightmare by a rocking cradle,
And what rough beast, its hour come round at last,
Slouches towards Bethlehem to be born?[1]

Yeats's poem has been called "the most thoroughly pillaged piece of literature in English."[2] Pieces of it have been plucked out and repurposed as titles
and catchphrases for books, essays, newspaper articles, and heavy-metal
albums. Line by line, we hit upon phrases that sound vaguely familiar, and
yet strangely remote and ominous: "the widening gyre," "the falcon cannot

hear the falconer," "things fall apart," "the center cannot hold," "the blood-dimmed tide," "the ceremony of innocence," "the best lack all conviction," "the worst are full of passionate intensity," "blank and pitiless as the sun," "vexed to nightmare," "slouching towards Bethlehem." This chapter adds to the legion of admiring plunderers—"what rough beast" is this?

It is, above all else, an example—a quintessential one—of the use of poetic symbols, introduced briefly in chapter 3. A symbol is something that stands for, or represents, something else. Words, used literally, are symbols. For example, the four-letter English word *rose* is the symbol of a familiar kind of flower, the rose. Other languages use different words as symbols for a rose (for example, *roos* in Dutch, 玫瑰 in Chinese). But a poetic symbol is something more. Now the *thing*—that which corresponds to the concept named by the word—represents something beyond itself. The rose, in Robert Burns's poem (see the preface) and many others, is a symbol of love and all that is associated with it, such as the fragility and transience of beauty. With this step, the English word *rose* (or its equivalent in another language) becomes a second-order symbol—the linguistic symbol of a thing that in turn represents something else. When coordinated with the other constraints that govern a poem, a second-order symbol is poetic.

Yeats's poem is basically written in poetic symbols. Take the word *gyre* in the first line. For Yeats, the gyre (a spiral or vortex, such as a circular pattern of ocean currents) symbolized his grand vision of the mind and of human civilization. Each of these, he thought, moves in a circular path from an initial point through an expanding series of cycles, and then reverses direction to trace a contracting series of spirals back toward the point of origin.[3] Yeats turned the gyre into a poetic symbol.

As linguistic devices, poetic symbols occupy the borderland between metaphor and metonymy—in varying degrees, resemblance and prior association are both at work. The key psychological question is: where do poetic symbols come from? The cooperative principle implies that the poet will use symbols that the reader can grasp (perhaps after some effort that itself contributes to the reader's appreciation). The poet may provide clues by establishing a suitable context, in the poem or perhaps in their larger body of work. Sometimes a poet makes an allusion to the writings of others—anyone who now uses the symbol of the gyre is almost certainly making an allusion to Yeats. But some poetic symbols with deep roots in cultural history (in western poetry, the apple from the Garden of Eden; in Chinese

poetry, the moon illuminating the roofless court of vanished kings) transcend any individual writer.[4] It's best to think of symbols as falling along
a continuum of generality across history and cultures. The most general
symbols, which can be termed *archetypal*, appear in the poetry of many
cultures (the cave as a store of secret knowledge, sexual union as a mystical
connection between the human and divine). When archetypal symbols are
combined to form patterns (often as a narrative, such as a hero's descent
into an underworld and eventual return with new knowledge or power),
the result is an *archetype* (a term made famous by Carl Jung).[5]

Before we consider the possible origins of symbols and archetypes,
let's use Yeats's "Second Coming" as an example of how symbols relate to
metaphor in poetry. About two decades before he wrote this poem, Yeats
affirmed that "symbolism said things which could not be said so perfectly
in any other way, and *needed but a right instinct for its understanding*" (italics
added).[6] In the language of current psychology, his idea was that symbols
(of the right sort—those for which the reader is properly prepared) evoke
their intended meanings with little cognitive effort. Arguably, "The Second
Coming" is an example par excellence of what Yeats meant by a poem that
unfolds in symbols. You very likely have encountered this poem before, but
let's approach it as if for the first time, and see what comes to mind.

The first thing to notice is that the poem as a whole is a source-only metaphor. It describes a situation that is clearly intended to have some deeper
meaning, without explicitly mentioning what the target domain might be.
This poetic structure is very different from an analogy in which a known
source is explicitly mapped to a stated target. Instead, the poem itself acts
as a source analog composed of concrete symbols carefully melded with
abstract descriptions. The poet's creative mission is to produce the source;
the reader's creative mission is to grasp its target.

There is another key difference between the way symbolic poetry operates and the way analogies are used to solve problems (chapter 6). Rather
than comparing a concrete source and target to generate an explicit and
separate schema, poetic symbols often create concrete universals (introduced in chapter 3), which act as a kind of plurisign. "The Second Coming" intimates something universal yet intimately bound to the symbols
that give rise to it. The poem has two stanzas. The first conveys a very
general picture of a world in turmoil. The symbolic gyre in the first line
becomes a concrete image in the second: a falcon is turning in rising and

widening circles until it's eventually disconnected from its controller, the falconer. I'm reminded of Major Tom, the lost astronaut in David Bowie's song "Space Oddity": "Ground Control to Major Tom / Your circuit's dead, there's something wrong."[7] The next two lines, abstract yet chilling, state the predicament: "Things fall apart; the centre cannot hold; / Mere anarchy is loosed upon the world." This abstract summary is followed immediately by key symbols: "the blood-dimmed tide" drowns "the ceremony of innocence." This can't be good! Then the state of humanity is laid bare: "The best lack all conviction, while the worst / Are full of passionate intensity."

Whereas the first stanza is generally a description, the longer second stanza sets this disturbed and threatened world into narrative motion. We have a "Second Coming," which of course evokes the Christian belief in the expected Second Coming of Christ. But this is no Redeemer who's returning, but rather "a vast image out of *Spiritus Mundi*" (a key concept for Yeats—more on it below). The image is that of a sphinx come to life and on the move, its "gaze blank and pitiless as the sun." More Christian symbols follow, their emotional impact inverted—"a rocking cradle" that has created a nightmare, culminating in the "rough beast" that now "Slouches towards Bethlehem to be born." The verb *slouches* is especially ominous. The word usually characterizes a weak and careless posture, but here we imagine the immense shoulders of the awakened sphinx propelling it forward with a kind of mindless strength.

One other element of the second stanza is especially notable. Whereas the first stanza is a third-person description, the second stanza introduces a first-person narrator who puts "those words out," and for whom the terrifying image "troubles my sight." The persona who speaks seems to assume the voice of a prophet, watching extraordinary events unfold from some privileged position. A first-person pronoun occurs just once more, in the line "The darkness drops again; but now I know...." What does the prophet know? The final four lines begin to lay out a vision and prediction. But something curious happens. The initial "now I know" is an exclamation in the voice of the authoritative prophet. Yet in the final two lines, the prophecy devolves into a question: "what rough beast ...?" It's as if even the prophet uttering the poem "lacks all conviction."

So, what is the target analog elicited by this vision of an ominous sphinx come to life? Though often interpreted as foreshadowing the catastrophic events of the 1930s that ravaged Europe and then the world, Yeats actually wrote this poem in 1919, in the aftermath of World War I and at the beginning of the Irish War of Independence. But whatever the impact of those then-current events on the poem's origin, the greater influence was Yeats's complex symbolic interpretation of cycles of civilization. What the poem means for our own times, I leave you to ponder. As I. A. Richards remarked about poetry in general, "The poem is a quest"—one that can continue indefinitely.[8]

Yeats himself had an answer to the question of where poetic symbols (especially those that are archetypal) come from. He spoke of their source often, including in "The Second Coming," where the "vast image" is said to emerge from *Spiritus Mundi*. The term is Latin for "world spirit"; sometimes Yeats called it *Anima Mundi*, "world soul." He first laid out his basic ideas in an essay called (appropriately enough) "Magic," asserting that "many minds can flow into one another," "our memories are a part of one great memory," and "this great mind and great memory can be evoked by symbols."[9] Yeats's concept of a "great memory" was echoed by the *collective unconscious*, a core component of the psychological theory developed by Carl Jung. Indeed, the fact that such similar ideas were proposed by two contemporaries, one a poet and the other a psychologist, gives rise to an intriguing intellectual puzzle. Did (at least) two minds flow into one another?[10]

Jung drew a direct connection between his psychological theory and literature: "It is obvious enough that psychology, being the study of psychic processes, can be brought to bear upon the study of literature."[11] The Jungian version of the theory of symbols and archetypes became a driving force motivating the earliest work in literary psychology by scholars such as Maud Bodkin.[12] It also had a major impact on literary criticism, reaching its zenith with Northrup Frye in the mid-twentieth century. Around the same time, the mythologist Joseph Campbell discussed archetypes and *monomyths* that recur across different cultures and times. The "hero's quest," for example, can be found both in the legends of the Holy Grail and the plot of the earliest *Star Wars* movies. Arguably, Jungian theory has found its deepest applications not in the psychology of individuals, but rather in analyses of literature and myths.

In more recent decades, literary theorists have for various reasons turned away from the Yeats/Jung view of symbols and archetypes.[13] Scientific psychology, meanwhile, has largely ignored Jung's theory because it seems impossible to test. For example, both Yeats and Jung claimed that archetypal symbols sometimes occur as elements of dreams, but it's unclear how this proposal can be evaluated in an objective way.[14] (In chapter 12 I will have more to say about dreams as possible sources of poetic symbols.) Nonetheless, the idea that stories can be based on archetypes retains a hold on the popular imagination. This very fact can perhaps be taken as suggestive evidence that the concept has some kind of psychological reality.

Jung conjectured that archetypes have a genetic basis, but this idea strains credibility. In fact, it's not too hard to imagine how some very general symbols and patterns could arise from the normal experiences of people living on planet earth, and then be transmitted by language and culture. Consider some very basic aspects of the human condition. Sometime in middle childhood, children almost inevitably ask questions like "Why am I here? Where was I before I was born? What happens to people after they die?" These questions feel extremely important, yet lack obvious answers. The powers that we assume to govern human existence are largely hidden from us. Mythologies and religions arise to provide answers.

Everywhere people see cycles of change and renewal. The day-night cycle, the phases of the moon, the cyclic seasons—nature moves in systematic recurrences. Human intelligence makes it possible to think about relations such as cycles in a general way, abstracted from specific manifestations. We can draw analogies. At temperate latitudes the vegetative world seems to die each winter and come back to life in the spring, so perhaps the death of an individual human is a phase change, not an end.

The lifespan of a human follows a natural course from the helplessness of infancy through the dependency of childhood to the strength of maturity and on to the decline of old age. The continuation of society depends on successful transitions from one generation to the next. Yet the relations across generations create natural sources of conflict, both between individuals and internal to each. It seems natural that children will be grateful to the parents and other elders who raised them, but eventually the grown children must replace these same elders. The father figure—particularly one who has achieved great power, such as a king—may be reluctant to relinquish his position to the natural heir, blocking the essential renewal that depends on new blood. Siblings may grow up as friends, yet compete for power as adults. Then throw in all the complexities of sex and love. The tensions inherent in human relationships provide a fertile field for tragedy—and for the great archetypes embodied in *Oedipus Rex*, *King Lear*, and *Romeo and Juliet*.

Normal human experience, from the earliest times into our indefinite future, exposes us to things that naturally symbolize elements of the complex patterns arising from our deepest concerns. In the words of Northrup Frye, "Some symbols are images of things common to all men, and therefore have a communicative power which is potentially unlimited. Such symbols include those of food and drink, of the quest or journey, of light and darkness, and of sexual fulfillment."[15] These are the symbols that "need but a right instinct" to be understood. The vocabulary of poetic symbols is not simply a list of words that take on odd nonliteral meanings, but a source of nuanced conceptual combinations and novel analogies. The "blood-dimmed tide" has the symbolic power of a rising sea merged with the added power and violence symbolized by blood, and the "rough beast" seen slouching toward Bethlehem is a demon that couples overwhelming strength with an utter lack of humanity. Symbols of this sort provide a language to express mysteries and emotions—"things which could not be said so perfectly in any other way." When a symbol triggers its own interpretation, an analogical mapping may emerge without the cognitive and neural burden imposed by the need to process multiple relations at once. Individual elements will find their place in a coherent and emotion-laden whole.

But Yeats's notion that "a right instinct" suffices to grasp symbolic poetry has its limits. A psychological account will eventually have to grapple with the interpretation of what might be called "extreme metaphor"—poems where words are used in ways that make it difficult to understand the source, or even to distinguish source and target. Let's consider a few examples, extending from the eighteenth to the twentieth centuries, which highlight the uncertain boundary between insightful plurisigns and obscurity.

A major influence on Yeats was the English poet William Blake. Fifteen years older than Coleridge, he was largely ignored (or written off as insane) in his lifetime, but eventually was recognized as a brilliant and exceptionally innovative poet. Shortly after his death, Wordsworth reportedly gave this memorable assessment: "There was no doubt that this poor man was mad, but there is something in the madness of this man which interests me more than the sanity of Lord Byron and Walter Scott." (We'll consider the possible impact of mental illness on creativity in chapter 13.) Blake's work anticipated and influenced poets, artists, and thinkers of later centuries, including not only Yeats but also Jung, the surrealists (see below), the Beats of the mid-twentieth century (see chapter 11), and popular American songwriters such as Jim Morrison and Bob Dylan.

Here is one of Blake's most striking poems, which remains famous more than two centuries on. This short poem is written in clear, simple language, using established symbols. Most readers find it compelling and evocative—and extremely enigmatic.

"The Sick Rose" by William Blake

O Rose thou art sick.
The invisible worm,
That flies in the night
In the howling storm:

Has found out thy bed
Of crimson joy:
And his dark secret love
Does thy life destroy.[16]

Interpretation of the poem hinges on two key symbols. The rose usually represents love, fragile beauty, purity, and innocence. It's under attack by the worm—strongly associated with disease and death, and perhaps phallic (especially in the context of *bed* and *crimson*). But this worm is invisible, and instead of living on or under the ground it "flies in the night / In the howling storm." A mythical dragon? A vision of a "Dementor" (to be realized centuries later in the *Harry Potter* novels)? Moreover, this worm harbors a "dark secret love" for the rose whose life it destroys. Is the poem saying something about the way experience preys on innocence and inevitably corrupts it? That innocence demands experience? I'm reminded that Yeats would later write, "For nothing can be sole or whole / That has not been rent."[17] And in the same poem, "Fair and foul are near of kin, / And fair needs foul."

The aura of ideas, emotions, and reminders can go on indefinitely. As Richards said, "The poem is a quest."

———

Modern poetry brought further developments in the use of symbols to construct what I am terming extreme metaphors. Twentieth-century modernism highlighted free verse, which is most obviously marked by the absence of regular form based on meter and rhyme. But its development was also deeply associated with experiments in metaphorical language. Of course, not all free verse is symbolic (nor is all symbolic poetry in free verse, as the examples from Blake and Yeats attest). But I will focus on ways free verse introduced language that presses the limits of metaphor.

Several trends fostered these developments. One was an increased emphasis on the role of the unconscious in creativity in general, but particularly in the creation of poetry. The idea that important emotional and cognitive activity takes place out of awareness yet influences the conscious mind goes back to antiquity. Poets and others believed in divine inspiration—the power of a muse or daemon. But the modern conception of the unconscious mind (and its name, the *unconscious*, as a noun) emerged early in the nineteenth century, in the work of the German Romantic philosopher Joseph Schelling. His ideas were quickly passed on to the world of English poetry by Coleridge. The Romantic movement made poets and others keenly conscious of the unconscious, so to speak, leading to poetry that was more explicitly psychological.

Poetic developments flowing from Romanticism have had certain broad characteristics. In this book I have been using the term *meaning* to embrace both thought and emotion, on the grounds they are inherently intertwined. But to be more precise, they are intertwined in yin-yang fashion. Any poem conveys some mix of emotion (yin) and thought (yang). The increased emphasis on the role of the unconscious as a source of inspiration brought with it a shift in balance—toward emotion. In the limit, some of the poetry of twentieth-century modernism aimed to make language express emotion directly—bypassing cognitive meaning. The primary aim of such poems is to make the reader feel, not think. Of course, just like yin-yang, neither emotion nor thought can ever fully overcome the other. Consider this caution from Sylvia Plath, one of the originators of the emotion-driven "confessional" style in mid-twentieth century American poetry: "I believe that one should be able to control and manipulate experiences, even the most terrifying, like madness, being tortured, this sort of experience, and one should be able to manipulate these experiences with an informed and intelligent mind."[18]

Another eternal tension in poetry is between a focus on the real world of people and nature and a focus on the ideal—on visions of perfection (of love, or beauty, or freedom, or even pain) that can never be realized in the world, yet in some sense exist in a human mind. Again, we can consider this opposition in yin-yang terms—the yin of idealism versus the yang of realism. (It's interesting how easy it is to see the direction of polarity.) The thrust of the Romantic movement (chapter 4) was toward the ideal. In short, the forces that took hold in poetry at the dawn of the nineteenth century reverberated throughout that century and on into the twentieth. The result was an increased emphasis on emotion (emanating from the unconscious) and on the expression of visions of some ideal—visions that often tortured the poet. These new emphases fostered many changes in the style of poetry, which collectively became what is known as free verse. Here I will focus on one type of change that fed into modernism—the rise of extreme metaphor. This development brought to the fore another polarity that has always been present in poetry—the power of symbolic compression versus the danger of slipping into solipsism and obscurity.

In the later nineteenth century, a group of French poets made a deliberate effort to press the limits of symbolic poetry. The most prominent of these *French Symbolists* were Charles Baudelaire, Arthur Rimbaud, Stéphane Mallarmé, and Paul Verlaine. Their influences included William Blake and the American writer Edgar Allan Poe (author of the famous poem "The Raven" and many horror stories told in prose). Their avowed aim was to explore symbolic meanings of words guided by dreams, visions, and free imagination—not to describe the real, but to evoke the ideal.

As an example, let's consider a poem by Mallarmé. He is less famous now than Baudelaire or Rimbaud—poets whose lives better exemplified the bohemian decadence that captures the popular imagination. But Mallarmé wrote extremely innovative poetry that had a major influence on later poets in the Dada and surrealist movements, as well as on twentieth-century poets such as Wallace Stevens. It was Mallarmé who translated Poe's "The Raven" into French.[19] His work reflects the complex interactions between poetry and the sister arts of painting and music. With respect to painting, his work was greatly influenced by the artistic style of impressionism. He was a friend of the impressionist painter Édouard Manet. Mallarmé's stated aim was "to paint not the thing itself but the effect it produces." With respect to music, his masterpiece "L'Après-Midi d'un Faune" inspired Debussy's composition "Prélude à L'Après-Midi d'un Faune," which in turn inspired a ballet by the great Russian dancer Nijinsky. This suite of works played a prominent role in the rise of modernism across all art forms.

"La Chevelure Vol d'une Flamme" by Stéphane Mallarmé

La chevelure vol d'une flamme à l'extrême
Occident de désirs pour la tout éployer
Se pose (je dirais mourir un diadème)
Vers le front couronné son ancien foyer

Mais sans or soupirer que cette vie nue
L'ignition du feu toujours intérieur
Originellement la seule continue
Dans le joyau de l'oeil véridique ou rieur

Une nudité de héros tendre diffame
Celle qui ne mouvant astre ni feux au doigt
Rien qu'à simplifier avec gloire la femme
Accomplit par son chef fulgurante l'exploit

De semer de rubis le doute qu'elle écorche
Ainsi qu'une joyeuse et tutélaire torche.

"The Flight of Flaming Hair" by Stéphane Mallarmé

The flight of flaming hair at the extreme
West of desires unfurling it forth
Comes to rest (as if it were a dying diadem)
On the crowned brow its ancient hearth

Then sigh for no gold but this cloud that lives
The kindling of an always interior flame
Originally the only one it gives
To the truthful or laughing eye its gleam

The tender nudity of heroes demeans
The one on whose fingers no stars wave or fires
Whose dazzling head is the only means
By which woman simplified with glory conspires

To sow with rubies the doubt she would scorch
In the manner of a joyous and tutelary torch.[20]

As in the example of the poem by Du Fu (chapter 9), we're again dealing with all the issues of poetry translation. However, English is far more closely related to French than to Chinese, and this English version (by Henry Weinfield) closely tracks the form of the original. Notice the near complete lack of punctuation—just one lonely period signifying that the poem has concluded. Punctuation is one of the constraints of ordinary language often altered or eliminated in free verse. By minimizing punctuation, the syntactic ambiguity of the poem is increased, with an attendant increase in the potential for metaphorical plurisigns.

More surprisingly (from our present vantage point, from which Mallarmé is viewed as a forerunner of free verse), "The Flight of Flaming Hair" is extremely regular in form—it's a sonnet, fourteen lines long, using a Shakespearian rhyme scheme. (If you want to check, compare Shakespeare's Sonnet 18 from chapter 3—the stanza breaks introduced in Mallarmé's poem are just a minor variation.) Although Mallarmé also wrote poems in experimental forms (notably his late poem "Un Coup de Dés"; "A Throw of the Dice"), most of his poems were written in standard forms.

But within the structure of this formal sonnet, Mallarmé has created extreme metaphors. The full effect of his poetry emerges from the interplay of symbols and sound, with a musicality in French that is difficult to translate. He also exploited the French language to create complex plurisigns. For example, the French *vol* in the first line can be translated as *flight*, but also as *theft*. The opening lines can be interpreted as suggesting that the flame of ideal beauty has been stolen to create the natural beauty of a woman, who returns that ideal to the brow of the poet. The complexity of Mallarmé in the French original is formidable. T. S. Eliot called him "one of the most obscure of modern poets … of whom the French sometimes say that his language is so peculiar that it can be understood only by foreigners."[21]

The general sense of "The Flight of Flaming Hair" is a juxtaposition of the real (a woman's head of hair) with the ideal, symbolized by the sky. It helps to know that *chevelure* is a recurring symbol for Mallarmé—a woman's hair stands for erotic beauty and experience. In the opening lines of the poem, an image is created of a woman's golden-red hair being combed out at dusk, mapped onto a diadem of light from a fading sun. There is a sense of a correspondence between earthly and astral beauty, but it's far from clear that source and target are separable, or which is which. The poem as a whole perhaps suggests the hope of beauty or meaning against a background of descending night or meaninglessness. But the emotional impact is not readily expressible in any paraphrase.

At the beginning of the twentieth century, Freudian psychology began to influence the arts, including poetry. Although Freud did not invent the idea of the unconscious, his theory increased its popular appeal. During the 1920s, in France and elsewhere, a movement called *surrealism* (literally, "above or beyond the real") blossomed. Surrealists aimed to mine the unconscious through dreams, hypnosis, automatic writing, and free association. One of their forerunners, Comte de Lautréamont, pressed the idea of comparison to its outer limits in the simile "beautiful as the chance meeting on a dissecting-table of a sewing-machine and an umbrella."[22]

The surrealists invented a group game called *exquisite corpse* in which each player in turn adds a contribution to a poem or a drawing based on only part of what has already been produced. (The name comes from the game's first creation, which translates as "The exquisite corpse shall drink the new wine.") The emphasis was on breaking the chains of reason, morality, and conventional aesthetic judgments. Poetry was meant to be fluid and impulsive, guided by symbolic associations. Revision was frowned on. Though the unconscious may offer up psychological insights, it seldom couches them in sonnets. Surrealism thus led very naturally into free verse.

Among the leaders of the French surrealist poets were André Breton and Paul Éluard. The latter was particularly inspired by the poetry of Walt Whitman (whose influence would eventually be reflected back across the Atlantic to America). Much as the French Symbolists were linked with the art movement of impressionism, surrealism in poetry was bound together with surrealism in art. Éluard was closely associated with painters such as Max Ernst, Man Ray, René Magritte, and Pablo Picasso. These ties led to some productive collaborations between poets and artists. Other interchanges were more problematic—Éluard's first wife Gala left him for the surrealist painter Salvador Dalí.

Here is an example of surrealism—a section from a series of love poems written as Éluard's marriage to Gala was crumbling.

"L'Amour la Poésie: VII" by Paul Éluard

La terre est bleue comme une orange
Jamais une erreur les mots ne mentent pas
Ils ne vous donnent plus à chanter
Au tour des baisers de s'entendre
Les fous et les amours
Elle sa bouche d'alliance
Tous les secrets tous les sourires
Et quels vêtements d'indulgence
À la croire toute nue.

Les guêpes fleurissent vert
L'aube se passe autour du cou
Un collier de fenêtres
Des ailes couvrent les feuilles
Tu as toutes les joies solaires
Tout le soleil sur la terre
Sur les chemins de ta beauté.

"Love-Poetry: VII" by Paul Éluard

The earth is blue like an orange
There's no mistake words don't lie
They don't give you anything to sing about
When it's time to hear kisses
The madmen and our loves
She with her mouth of alliance
All the secrets all the smiles
And such indulgent clothing
Making one think she is naked.

The wasps blossom green
Dawn wraps a necklace
Of windows round its neck
Wings cover leaves
You have all the solar joys
All the sunshine on earth
On the paths of your beauty.[23]

The first line captures the essence of surrealism—an extreme simile. What could be simpler—the earth is blue, just like an orange—except that an orange is typically more orange than blue, *n'est-ce pas*? The reader is invited to find their own associations to create a meaning—"There's no mistake words don't lie." So, maybe the earth surrounded by its azure atmosphere exudes the juicy liveliness of an orange—an orange casting perhaps a bluish shadow, becoming a symbol of the earth. Over the next few lines the earth metamorphoses into a lover, beautiful but possibly unfaithful ("She with her mouth of alliance / All the secrets all the smiles"). Very likely you can discover other possible interpretations. Surrealism creates a kind of metaphor in which comparisons are used to create something new that seems to occupy a space that opens up *between* the many sources and targets.

During World War II, Éluard joined the Resistance to the Nazi occupation of France. Copies of his poem "Liberté" were dropped over France by the British Air Force.[24] One stanza reads,

On the foam of the clouds
On the sweat of the storm
On the thick dull rain
I write your name

That name, we learn in the final line of the poem, is liberty.

Let's consider one more example of extreme metaphor, this time a poem written in English by one of the American modernists of the 1920s. Hart Crane is not as famous as T. S. Eliot, Ezra Pound, and a few others in that set of pioneers, in part because he died young. He was inspired by Baudelaire and Whitman (sharing with the latter the challenges of homosexuality). Crane can be counted among the *poètes maudits* ("cursed poets")—at age 32, he committed suicide by jumping off a ship in the Gulf of Mexico. His admirers have included poetic luminaries such as Sylvia Plath and the literary critic Harold Bloom. Crane's best poems give a sense of the power of extreme metaphor to create haunting effects.

"Voyages: II" by Hart Crane

—And yet this great wink of eternity,
Of rimless floods, unfettered leewardings,
Samite sheeted and processioned where
Her undinal vast belly moonward bends,
Laughing the wrapt inflections of our love;

Take this Sea, whose diapason knells
On scrolls of silver snowy sentences,
The sceptred terror of whose sessions rends
As her demeanors motion well or ill,
All but the pieties of lovers' hands.

And onward, as bells off San Salvador
Salute the crocus lustres of the stars,
In these poinsettia meadows of her tides,—
Adagios of islands, O my Prodigal,
Complete the dark confessions her veins spell.

Mark how her turning shoulders wind the hours,
And hasten while her penniless rich palms
Pass superscription of bent foam and wave,—
Hasten, while they are true,—sleep, death, desire,
Close round one instant in one floating flower.

Bind us in time, O Seasons clear, and awe.
O minstrel galleons of Carib fire,

Bequeath us to no earthly shore until
Is answered in the vortex of our grave
The seal's wide spindrift gaze toward paradise.[25]

The poem is generally interpreted as a love poem directed toward Crane's most significant erotic interest (a Danish sailor). The dash that begins the first line marks it as a continuation from the final line of part I: "The bottom of the sea is cruel." The sea is seen as "this great wink of eternity"—a symbol of eternity and yet limited by earth. Its motion and patterns, pulled and bent toward the moon, become linked to the joined hands of lovers. In what reads as an eerie premonition of the poet's suicide a few years later, this sea becomes specifically the Caribbean. The lovers are joined as "one floating flower," drawn toward "the vortex of our grave" to await the gaze of the seal—that gentle sea mammal—directed toward a paradise of ideal life. Throughout the poem, the sea serves as a symbol that conjoins the mother, the lover, sleep, and death.

Crane was very explicit about his poetic aims and about the ways he used metaphor: "As a poet I may very possibly be more interested in the so-called illogical impingements of the connotations of words on the consciousness (and their combinations and interplay in metaphor on this basis) than I am interested in the preservation of their logically rigid significations at the cost of limiting my subject matter and perceptions involved in the poem."[26] His variety of extreme metaphor defies explication through literal language. Symbolic poetry raises questions that lack ready answers.

11 Poetic Lightness

"I, Too" by Langston Hughes

I, too, sing America.

I am the darker brother.
They send me to eat in the kitchen
When company comes,
But I laugh,
And eat well,
And grow strong.

Tomorrow,
I'll be at the table
When company comes.
Nobody'll dare
Say to me,
"Eat in the kitchen,"
Then.

Besides,
They'll see how beautiful I am
And be ashamed—

I, too, am America.[1]

The ideal Poet and Reader, whom we met briefly in chapter 5, share an intimate bond. That bond is an unusual one, however, for ordinarily the two will never meet in what passes for real life. The Poet is the maker of a message, which the Reader encounters some time later—in rare but very significant cases, perhaps centuries on. The first creates, the other appreciates. Their intimacy is nonetheless genuine, especially if we accept the view that poetry operates on consciousness—the inner life of the Poet guides the creation of the poem, which in turn changes the consciousness of the Reader. And it's the *change* in consciousness that's critical.[2] A poem, whether heard or read, unfolds over time—more than an object, it's an event.[3] Humans naturally attend to changes of all sorts—a static object set into motion, the onset of a sound or light. The flip side is that people pay less and less attention to anything that remains constant. Once something has been processed, it can be mentally set aside even though it remains physically present. A change, on the other hand, alerts the brain to pay attention and react. The first encounter with a poetic metaphor can produce a change in consciousness, as if something were seen in a new way. On a subsequent occasion, if the Reader can regain something of the naive attitude that preceded that initial experience, a rereading may again effect a change of consciousness

The writing and subsequent reading of a poem is both similar to and different from everyday communication. (Though I speak of poetry, much the same could be said about art in general.) In many ways, what makes the case of poetry special is what is *missing* relative to an ordinary conversation.[4] If two people meet by chance on a street corner and stop to talk awhile, several conditions will likely be met. The participants are present together—they can see and hear each other in real time, sending and receiving their communications simultaneously. They will likely take turns in the conversation, which will be oral, spontaneous, unscripted, and (barring the use of recording devices) ephemeral. If we set aside oral poetic contests ("battle rap"), none of the above conditions ordinarily hold for poetry. The Poet and the Reader never meet—there's no back-and-forth between them. The Poet's message may be composed over an indefinite time period and is subject to revision. Once the Poet dubs it "finished," the poem acquires the relative permanence afforded by writing.

To understand how a poem serves to communicate, we can start by returning to the cooperative principle that governs everyday human communication—one person (here the Poet) intends to produce a response from another (the Reader) by causing that person to recognize the intention. This principle implies that even if the Poet is a stranger unknown to the Reader, the latter ought to cooperate with the Poet, striving to recognize the intention that led to the poem's creation. The Reader need not believe what the Poet says, but must (as Coleridge advocated) "willingly suspend disbelief." And the Poet, in some sense anticipating the Reader (who may not yet be born), must use the language of the poem to produce the intended response.

Understanding the bond between poet and reader (I drop the capitals as we descend once again to the world of actual humans) takes us into the realm of pragmatics, which we touched on in chapter 5. We need to consider what a poem *does* and the role metaphor plays in that doing. Then we can return to the question of what a poem *means*, and what kind of truth—poetic truth—it may offer.

————

A poem is a speech act. To a first approximation, a poem may do any of the things that language can accomplish, such as praising, ridiculing, exhorting, comforting, lamenting, or amusing. But if we look more closely, we confront the question of exactly who is doing what to whom. On the side of the poet (or more generally, the writer—point of view is also a critical component of fiction), there is a question as to who is uttering the speech. The poet is of course its creator, but the voice of the poem need not be the poet's own. Most obviously, in a dramatic poem the voice may be that of various fictional characters (perhaps Macbeth, Lady Macbeth, or the Three Witches). But in any poem, the poet is free to assume a *persona*—a character distinct from (though often related to) the author. The voice that speaks "Kubla Khan" might be that of Coleridge, and the voice of "The Second Coming" might be that of Yeats—but not necessarily. Between the poet and the poem, a persona—one might even say a character behind a mask—may act as a conduit. A distance is established.

On the side of the reader we may ask, to whom is the poem addressed? To you and me—to its readers? Not so fast. … Let's take the poem "To Celia" by the Elizabethan poet Ben Jonson, which begins with the famous line, "Drink to me only with thine eyes."[5] If you have read it, you might fairly have thought the poem was addressed to you—if your name happened to be Celia, and you lived in England during the early 1600s. But alas, poor Celia, you were fooled—Jonson's poem is largely a translation of one composed in ancient Greece by a man named Philostratus. If a real Celia ever existed, she was Greek (and not named Celia).

Of course, we modern readers are certainly not Celia. We take the poem to be addressed to some suitable female object of desire, not to any specific individual. But even with this generous enlargement of who the addressee might be, a heterosexual male doesn't really fit the bill. And yet any poetry lover may read and appreciate the poem—there doesn't seem to be any gender requirement for being affected by "To Celia."

The lesson to take away is that in general, a poem is *not* addressed to the reader in any direct way. The philosopher John Stuart Mill had an essential insight: poetry is not heard, but *overheard*.[6] The poet (or persona) may be addressing anyone or anything—perhaps a Grecian urn or a nightingale—and simply allowing the reader to listen in. But critically, this is not a case of mere eavesdropping—the poet *invites* the reader to listen in. The aim of an ode addressed to a Grecian urn is not to move the heart of an old relic, but the heart of the human reader.

But notice how indirect the communication has become—the poet takes on a favored persona, the persona speaks, and the reader is invited to overhear. Jorge Luis Borges observed, "When I write, I do not think of the reader (because the reader is an imaginary character), and I do not think of myself (perhaps *I* am an imaginary character also), but I think of what I am trying to convey and I do my best not to spoil it."[7]

One reason that metaphor is so integral to poetry is that indirect language enhances the indirectness of the poetic speech act. The most basic reason to favor indirectness is that poetry aims to convey ideas or emotions that just can't be expressed adequately in any direct way. For example, symbols that serve as concrete universals attach emotional nuances to abstract ideas, which would seem bloodless if stated literally. Poetic plurisigns make it possible to blend meanings that literal language strives to keep separate. In addition, indirect communication requires effort on the part of the reader. This extra cognitive activity may increase engagement and allow the reader to vicariously (re)experience some aspects of the poet's creative process.

There are other reasons why a poet may choose to be indirect. Should a poet aim to criticize those who wield political power, indirectness may provide a cloak of plausible deniability intended to ward off retaliation. During the Tang dynasty, Du Fu wrote a poem called "Ballad of the Lovely Ladies," which on the surface describes a sumptuous court picnic.[8] But though the poem does not "name names," in fact it's a veiled critique of the family of the emperor's favorite concubine. It includes the lines

> The willow's pollen whitens waterpoppies;
> A bluebird's beak snatches a fine red scarf.

An innocuous description of nature's beauty, one might suppose … but these lines symbolically allude to an incestuous affair between the imperial concubine's sister and a cousin (the latter a high minister favored by the emperor). Du Fu filters his contempt through layers of indirectness, which apparently sufficed to keep him safe from retaliation. But poets are not always spared should they offend the mighty. Poor Ovid, for example, was exiled from Rome by the Emperor Augustus, perhaps because his poetry collection *Ars Amatoria* (*The Art of Love*) was deemed insufficiently discreet.

Indirectness contributes to another very general property of poetry, which may not be immediately obvious—*politeness*. A pleasant conversation is normally one in which neither party threatens the "face" of the other, thus helping to ensure that neither party loses it. To put it in positive terms, each of us aims to maintain a sense of self-worth and autonomy. If these aims are thwarted in the course of a social interaction, we will have lost face. To maintain mutual self-worth in the course of a communication, each party must at least pretend to respect (and better yet, share) the values and goals of the other. And if the speaker wants something from the listener, politeness requires avoiding any suggestion of coercion.[9] Here are a few different ways to make a request:

(1)   Looks like a nice day for a little stroll.
(2)   I wonder if you might like to take a walk with me?
(3)   I'm going for a walk—I don't suppose you'd care to join me?
(4)   How about we take a walk?
(5)   Please join me for a walk.
(6)   Follow me.
(7)   That way—move it!

Sentence (1) conveys a casual suggestion. The listener is free not simply to decline, but to act as if no request was even uttered. The listener's autonomy is not threatened, and if the suggestion is not taken up, no one has lost face—nothing was requested, nothing refused. Sentence (2) frames the request with "I wonder if you might like …"—making it merely an expression of interest in the listener's preference. In sentence (3), "I don't suppose" suggests that the speaker doesn't really expect the listener to accede, thus reducing the speaker's potential loss of face if the request is refused. All of these three framings are quite indirect—and very polite.

Sentence (4) is a tad more direct, though the "How about" makes it overtly an inquiry about the listener's attitude to the proposal, rather than a completely bald request. Sentence (5) is in the more aggressive imperative form, but softened by "please." Sentence (6) is a stronger imperative, and sentence (7) is a flat-out order made yet more emphatic by the exclamation point. The latter phrasing would be appropriate for a request made at gunpoint—the listener is being compelled to obey, and furthermore can't be trusted to comply without being kept under the speaker's watchful eye. The complete lack of politeness implies that the speaker has overwhelming power over the listener, and therefore no need to care about the latter's loss of face.

Even sentence (7), raw though it is, is less coercive in and of itself than is actual physical violence (e.g., a command accompanied by a kick to get the prisoner moving). Written language can certainly be insulting (imagine a nonnegotiable demand for unconditional surrender, delivered with a healthy dose of sarcasm). But in comparison to oral speech, a written communication (usually delivered after a delay, and not in the presence of the writer) at least eliminates loud shouting, fist shaking, and other nonverbal aggressive accompaniments.

The characteristic indirectness of a poem tends to make it a polite communication—even when the poem expresses negative emotions, as in a protest poem. For it may not be the poet who is speaking, but a persona, and the one under attack is not (at least directly) the reader. The poet is simply inviting the reader to listen in on whatever the poem is saying. Indeed, this shared intimacy hints that the poet and the reader are in some sense on the same side, at least provisionally.

———

Long after both slavery and the Civil War had ended, intense racial bias was commonplace in the United States. Against that backdrop, in the aftermath of the First World War and lasting until the onset of the Great Depression, a "Harlem Renaissance" flourished in New York City. Harlem in that era was a magnet for migration of African Americans from the South and other regions of the country. The music, art, and literature of African Americans—an outsider culture in a society dominated by white Americans—became a source of pride within the Harlem community and beyond it. Looking back now after another century has gone by, the racial divide in this nation has stubbornly persisted. But the legacy of the Harlem Renaissance also remains. What is now the broader American culture has been shaped in considerable part by African American contributions.

These influences are particularly evident in oral and musical art forms, including poetry. During the decade of the 1920s, Langston Hughes emerged as one of the leading poets of the Harlem Renaissance. Hughes—the descendant of enslaved black great-grandmothers and slave-owning white great-grandfathers—embodied the contradictions inherent in the movement to forge a strong African American identity. He helped originate a style of free verse called *jazz poetry*, which valued spontaneity, improvisation, and public performance. Stemming from the long oral tradition of African poetry and song, jazz poetry (like jazz music) incorporated syncopated rhythms and repetitive phrases. But the poetry of Langston Hughes also had other roots, notably the poetic voice of Walt Whitman. Like Whitman, Hughes was almost certainly a closeted homosexual. And Hughes, like Whitman, was an outsider who longed to "sing America."

Let's take a look at Hughes's poem "I, Too," focusing on how it works as a speech act. The core of the poem is a simple but powerful metaphor—to be treated as an outsider because of race is likened to being marginalized by one's family. In particular, the gathering of the family to share a meal symbolizes what it means to belong to a social group. The "darker brother" is left to eat in the kitchen instead of at the dining table with the others. In various manifestations, some type of segregated dining arrangement had long been the literal norm for African Americans, making the symbolism transparent.

"I, Too" is certainly a poem of protest against racial injustice and exclusion, but its tone is highly nuanced. The first line—"I, too, sing America"—is a direct response to a poem by Whitman titled "I Hear America Singing." Hughes is not damning America but asserting his own voice of praise. Nor does he say "I *will* sing America" (in some hoped-for future)—he is "singing America" right now, in this poem, without waiting for an invitation from anybody.

To whom is the poem speaking? Hughes does not use the pronoun *we*, which might trace a boundary around an in-group audience, but simply *I*. Though he certainly speaks on behalf of African Americans as a group, he does so as an individual proud to speak to all of America. Those being rebuked are referred to as *they*—"They send me to eat in the kitchen." But *they* are not beyond redemption: "They'll see how beautiful I am / And be

ashamed. ..." And notice that we readers—white Americans among us—
are not pigeonholed into the *they* of the poem. Rather, treated as listeners
invited to overhear, Hughes tacitly draws us into his own circle—he lets
us listen to criticism directed elsewhere, so that we readers may have the
opportunity to learn from it without being the direct target. The closest to
an aggressive tone is struck by the phrase "Nobody'll dare"—the speaker is
coming to the family table and will not be stopped. But overall, the voice
of the poem is that of a proud individual both deserving and desirous of
inclusion—with us, the readers. Viewed as a speech act, the indirectness of
"I, Too" makes it a polite communication.

Describing a protest as "polite" might be mistaken for disparagement,
but this is simply the nature of poetry. A poem may advocate rage—whether
against the dying of the light or against The Man—but it does so in a way
that draws the reader closer. Let's take another example of a protest poem,
this one blatantly inflammatory. Allen Ginsberg's "Howl," written in 1955,
became the anthem of the Beat Generation—a group of writers and other
bohemians who took pride in their status as outsiders mocking the establishment culture of the postwar United States.[10] "Howl" begins with a long
section, written in long, Whitmanesque lines that form a single run-on
sentence, describing the joys and tribulations of these outsiders—a short
history of the Beats in their early years. The famous opening lines set the
scene:

> I saw the best minds of my generation destroyed by madness, starving hysterical
> naked,
> dragging themselves through the negro streets at dawn looking for an angry fix.
> ...

Ginsburg and many of his friends were homosexual or bisexual, and
"Howl" glorifies not only drug use but also casual gay sex, in lines such as

> who let themselves be fucked in the ass by saintly motorcyclists, and screamed
> with joy,
> who blew and were blown by those human seraphim, the sailors, caresses of At-
> lantic and Caribbean love,

—lines that triggered legal charges of obscenity, which in 1957 culminated
in a trial held in San Francisco. The defendants were acquitted and "Howl"
was declared not to be obscene. In the aftermath, censorship in the United
States based on sexual content largely ceased. Ovid would have had little to
fear in late twentieth-century America.

By the way, the last line quoted above provides an opportunity for a poetic reminding. Did you notice the allusion to another poem we've encountered?[11]

Unlike "I, Too," which expresses an outsider's claim to belong, the outsider voice of "Howl" has absolutely no desire to join the establishment, which is held in complete contempt. The Beats are *seraphim* and *angels*, while the world of industrial capitalism is symbolized by *Moloch*—the name that the Bible gives to a Canaanite god linked to child sacrifice. Moloch is denounced as the source of the madness that has destroyed "the best minds of my generation."

A poem that rages against the establishment and praises drugs and casual sex, thereby successfully courting an angry reception from many early readers, hardly seems "polite." And yet the poem exhibits the kind of indirectness that spares the reader from direct attack. The voice in the first section is closely identified with Ginsberg himself, who claims the mantle of a prophet or perhaps shaman, looking out ("I saw ...") over a landscape strewn with Beat angels shattered by the destructive power of Moloch. But based on its very title, the poem is not really cast as a verbal address to anyone in particular, but rather as a prelinguistic howl—of rage against capitalist society's suppression of what is human, of joy flowing from individual freedom and expression. A howl is not even a deliberate speech act—it's an automatic explosion of emotion channeled into a vocalization. The effect of the poem is to create a kind of plurisign. At once it bares the poet's deep emotions and asserts his shamanistic vision. We the readers are once again invited to listen in, permitted to hear the voice howl and to make of it what we will. A howl is disturbing to hear and may create an uncomfortable intimacy, but it does not threaten us with a loss of face. The howl has become poetry.

> When old age shall this generation waste,
>   Thou shalt remain, in midst of other woe
> Than ours, a friend to man, to whom thou say'st,
>   "Beauty is truth, truth beauty,—that is all
>   Ye know on earth, and all ye need to know."

In his "Ode on a Grecian Urn," John Keats addresses an ancient Greek vessel, describing in detail the scenes some unknown artist painted on it, which through Keats's eyes become a vision of eternity.[12] In these closing lines of the poem, the poet lets the urn itself speak to future generations "in midst of other woe" with words of comfort: "Beauty is truth, truth beauty. ..." And ever since the poem first appeared in 1820, people have asked in one way or another, "Is that really true? And how would we ever know?"[13]

In "Thirteen Ways of Looking at a Blackbird," the twentieth-century American poet Wallace Stevens plays with that shadowy symbol.[14] One way of looking at it, he says, is this:

> A man and a woman
> Are one.
> A man and a woman and a blackbird
> Are one.

On the surface, these lines comprise two simple declarative sentences, which convey even simpler arithmetic statements: "$1 + 1 = 1$" says the first; "$1 + 1 + 1 = 1$," says the second. A natural question that arises is, "Is that really true?"

Not literally, of course—but is there such a thing as *poetic truth*, and if so, what is it?[15] Literal truth—the only kind acknowledged by logic or science—requires that a declarative statement can be publicly verified as corresponding to objective reality. In this literal sense of truth, beauty and truth may or may not be the same, depending on whether every beautiful thing is true and vice versa.[16] More definitely, a man, a woman, and a blackbird certainly do *not* add up to 1.

But there is another way something may be true, a way grounded not in objective reality but rather in subjective experience. A poetic truth— more generally, an aesthetic experience—provides a novel integration of concepts and emotions within one's own inner experience (shaded by the accumulated memories derived from a lifetime of experiences). The experiencer perceives some value inherent in the way the poem changes their view of some aspect of the world and in so doing changes their view of themselves. As Gabrielle Starr puts it, "Ultimately, all aesthetic experience is the result not so much of perceiving the outside world as becoming aware of our own judgment of what matters to us."[17] Like analogical resonance (which often accompanies it), poetic truth depends on the particularities of the person who encounters it.

Why is a poetic truth called a "truth" at all, rather than merely (say) a poetic "effect"? In everyday usage, we take something to be a literal truth if we can verify it by observation of the external world. Even if it is not (yet) verified, we understand something can nonetheless be true—back when people thought the earth was flat, it truly was round, regardless. Similarly, a poem may provide a truth that not everyone can grasp—that perhaps no one can grasp at all times. But a successful poem is one that has at least the *potential* to alter some reader's consciousness in a way that changes how they feel about themselves and the world. "Yes," says a reader of "Grecian Urn," "I feel the tension between my own transience and the human longing for timeless beauty. It makes me sad yet somehow hopeful. That feels true." By this subjective test, a poetic truth has been realized.

In science, truth is objective in the sense that it does not depend on anyone's particular viewpoint and may in fact be totally independent of human experience (e.g., water is a compound of hydrogen and oxygen atoms; the universe is expanding). But a poetic truth is always a truth about human experience.[18] It also is bound to the context in which it is encountered. In his poem, Keats invites the reader to share a vision of an eternal becoming—a place where a lover caught pursuing the beloved will never reach her, but neither will time be able to steal her beauty. Inside that poetic world, perhaps beauty and truth form a kind of unity—creating a poetic truth. And if we suspend disbelief and allow ourselves to share Stevens's "way of looking," then a man and a woman can of course be one—joined in sexual and emotional union. This is likely a familiar paradox to most readers, quite easy to apprehend as a poetic truth. But what about a man and a woman and a blackbird? Such a greater union is not so familiar, but if we open ourselves to poetic vision, possibilities arise. There is a oneness of humans with the natural world, perhaps; there is a special bond between human lovers who share a certain mood associated with the symbolic bird, perhaps. These are poetic truths.

Notice how the word *perhaps* crept into my attempts to fix a poetic truth using more or less literal words. Such qualification is not simply an expression of uncertainty, as in "It will probably rain tomorrow." The latter statement may be *literally* true, assuming that today's weather forecast provides an accurate assessment of the imperfect cues to tomorrow's weather. Rather, the qualification reflects a property of poetry that, like politeness, stems from its indirectness—what Philip Wheelwright called *lightness*.

To grasp what poetic lightness means, let's first take another look at the basic types of expressions that comprise literal language. Consider these sentences:

(8)   Is your leg broken?

(9)   Your leg is broken!

(10)   Your leg is broken.

These sentences exemplify standard forms of a question (8), an exclamation (9), and a declaration (10). Sentence (10) is the only one that clearly asserts a proposition that may be evaluated as true or false (depending on the state of your leg).

Notice, however, that the exclamation (9) also implies that your leg is broken, even though the form places the focus on the speaker's emotional reaction to that observation. Though the speaker's surprise and/or dismay will not be invalidated even if the leg turns out to be uninjured, the line between exclamation and assertion is somewhat blurred. In fact, a single utterance may convey aspects of a question, an exclamation, *and* an assertion. Consider:

(11)   Omigawd your leg is broken isn't it?!

This sentence places an emotional ejaculation in front of an assertion, then adds an element of doubt conveyed by the tag question (thereby justifying the doubled final punctuation). The absence of commas emphasizes the hurried fusion—the psychological simultaneity—of the speaker's multiple attitudes toward the allegedly broken leg. We have a plurisign.

Notice that if we compare the force of the assertion "your leg is broken" in the straightforward declarative (10) versus the multifaceted (11), it seems a bit more like a *suggestion* in the latter—a serious possibility to be sure, something that demands immediate attention and investigation, but hope remains that it's not as bad as it looks. What was a "heavy" assertion in (10)—stated as literally true without qualification—is made lighter in (11). But notice that "lighter" does not mean "less serious." In fact, the emotion-laden (11) conveys a greater sense of seriousness about the situation than does the matter-of-fact (10).

Poetic truth can be viewed as the exploration of serious lightness. The indirectness of poetry (to which metaphor strongly contributes), coupled with the mutual politeness of the poet's communication with the reader, allows the poem to suggest some truth-in-context without demanding acceptance of its literal truth. Coleridge's notion of "willing suspension of disbelief" implies (in the words of Wheelwright) "that we should be willing to take up residence lightly in whatever poetic situation is offered—willing to accept the partial truth of the insights which are crystallized by a given poetic mood without insisting that their truth must extend unreservedly into all other moods and contexts."[19] Here is another key advantage of indirectness in poetry: unlike direct arguments for or against some conclusion, hints toward some poetic truth do not provoke the reader to weigh the pros and cons. As Borges put it, "When something is merely said or—better still—hinted at, there is a kind of hospitality in our imagination."[20]

A poem (and any poetic metaphor within it) creates a world in which we are invited to "take up residence lightly" and consider truths (perhaps partial) that reside in that context. Notice how we have arrived back at the yin-yang polarity of subjective experience and objective knowledge. To create objective knowledge, humans analyze experiences to identify examples of abstract concepts, which are then reified as concepts and words. From many examples of black-feathered creatures of a certain size and shape, we form the concept of a "blackbird." This generalization is extremely useful precisely because it has been divorced from any specific context, allowing us to make general statements ("A blackbird can fly") that apply to any example. Context-independent concepts are the building blocks for constructing literal language—and the truths of logic and science.

But poetic truths abide in their experiential contexts. One way of looking at a blackbird is "A man and a woman and a blackbird / Are one." But another of Stevens's "ways" is

I was of three minds,
Like a tree
In which there are three blackbirds.[21]

These new blackbirds seem to convey a different meaning—rather than forming a part of some unity, they suggest psychological division. But this apparently incompatible description has a lightness, a suggestiveness (enhanced by the *like* that makes it a simile rather than a full-force metaphor) that encourages coexistence rather than contradiction. Whatever poetic truth is conveyed by either of these stanzas (or the poem as a whole) is tied to its own context. "In art," said Oscar Wilde, "there is no such thing as a universal truth. A Truth in art is that whose contradictory is also true."[22] Yet as we saw in chapter 10, something universal may be conveyed by a concrete symbol that presents itself as part of a particular context. What is being offered is not literal knowledge, but poetic wisdom.

12   The Hunger of Imagination

"Mysticism for Beginners" by Adam Zagajewski

The day was mild, the light was generous.
The German on the café terrace
held a small book on his lap.
I caught sight of the title:
Mysticism for Beginners.
Suddenly I understood that the swallows
patrolling the streets of Montepulciano
with their shrill whistles,
and the hushed talk of timid travelers
from Eastern, so-called Central Europe,
and the white herons standing—yesterday? the day before?—
like nuns in fields of rice,
and the dusk, slow and systematic,
erasing the outlines of medieval houses,
and olive trees on little hills,
abandoned to the wind and heat,
and the head of the *Unknown Princess*
that I saw and admired in the Louvre,
and stained-glass windows like butterfly wings
sprinkled with pollen,
and the little nightingale practicing
its speech beside the highway,
and any journey, any kind of trip,
are only mysticism for beginners,
the elementary course, prelude
to a test that's been
postponed.[1]

Mysticism can mean many things, from an experience of unity with the divine to a dreamy confusion of thought. Poets and others have often spoken of their creative process in terms that hint of some sort of mystical experience. Poetry traces back to rhythmic chants of tribal shamans uttered in a state of altered consciousness, often induced by fasting, liquor, or hallucinogenic plants. Coleridge was working in this time-honored tradition when his opium-induced reverie gave rise to "Kubla Khan." A common theme in first-person accounts by poets (and other creative artists) is that the creative act is accompanied by a loss of the sense of personal control or even identity. The emerging poem is experienced as being in some sense "received" from a source beyond conscious thought, sometimes lauded as a divine spark emanating from a godlike muse or daemon. In modern times, the American poet Amy Lowell provided an intriguing technological analogy: "Let us admit at once that the poet is something like a radio aërial—he is capable of receiving messages on waves of some sort; but he is more than an aërial, for he possesses the capacity of transmuting these messages into those patterns of words we call poems."[2] This sense that a poem can arise in a part of the mind to which the poet lacks conscious access led Jorge Luis Borges to remark, "Perhaps it is better that a poet should be nameless."[3]

Many people at times have a feeling that their self has multiple aspects and wonder, "Who am I (really)?" Most of us have a strong intuition that we can pay attention to people and events around us, set our own goals and pursue them, make conscious decisions, and initiate actions. This is the intuitive sense of free will, closely linked to what psychologists call cognitive control (which as we saw in chapter 7, is supported at the neural level by the frontotemporal control network). "I" feel like a conscious agent, sitting in the driver's seat of my own life.

And yet a little reflection shows that this intuition, though perhaps comforting, is at best incomplete. My seven-year-old son Dylan once asked me, "How do people talk?" As we walked to school together, he explained that he was obviously talking, but that he had no idea how this was happening. What was going on to make words come out of his mouth in the form of sentences? I replied that this was a good question indeed, adding the half-joking observation, "Your brain is smarter than you are!"

The serious half of my joke is that the brain (and the mind that it supports) are more than the "I" of which we are normally conscious when we reflect on ourselves. My son had the insight that much of our apparent intelligence—our ability to perceive, to think, and to act—depends on processes that operate partially or entirely outside of our conscious awareness or control. None of us really knows from direct experience how we manage to create sentences and carry on ordinary conversations, so it's hardly surprising that poets have only vague ideas about how they compose poems. Sensing that their conscious thought processes don't provide the full story, it's only natural that creators have often credited some additional source for their ideas. As I said earlier, the notion that the mind operates in part at an unconscious level predated Freud by centuries, and it has been supported (after dropping the Freudian baggage about repressed sexuality and the like) by recent research in psychology and neuroscience.

The conscious and unconscious aspects of the mind are not separate, but rather interdependent. The emotional color permeating the stream of consciousness is due in part to associations of which we may not be aware. As Koon Woon said in "Like Water Chasing Water," "we are who we are because of the flow," and that flow is guided in part by mental processes that operate outside of our conscious awareness. The great paradox of human consciousness is that there is more to "I" than what "I" am aware of. As the sense of what "I" am expands, the self (that lesser "I") may seem to dissolve.

The influence of the unconscious can feel like a compulsion. As the British poet Stephen Spender observed, "Poets speak of the necessity of writing poetry rather than of a liking for doing it. It is a spiritual compulsion."[4] In yet another core paradox, this sense of compulsion—the hunger of imagination[5]—simultaneously seems like an expression of profound freedom. Poets, according to Spender, strive to reveal "their inmost experiences, their finest perceptions, their deepest feelings, their uttermost sense of truth, in their poetry. They cannot cheat about these things." The paradox of compulsion-as-freedom dissolves once we grasp that our larger self includes the unconscious aspects of our mind. The compulsion to create is not something imposed on the creator—it *is* the creator.

The motivation to create must be *intrinsic*—arising from within, not imposed from without.[6] Poets may write to attract lovers, to earn the favor of their king, or to win a Pulitzer Prize.[7] But at the moment of creation, external motivations and pressures need to be set aside. What matters is simply responding to an urge to give birth to the emerging poem. To decide whether he still needed to keep writing poetry, one poet posed an exacting test for himself: "I'd ask myself, Bukowski, if you were on a desert island by yourself, never to be found except by the birds and the maggots, would you take a stick and scratch words in the sand?"[8] Only when the answer came back "yes" did he consider it worth his effort to keep writing. (And whenever the answer was "no," Bukowski would drink himself into an alcoholic stupor.)

Creative freedom is the sine qua non for a poet or other artist. Most people over most of human history lacked the basic conditions for creative work. Their lives were governed by the exigencies of physical survival. They lacked opportunities for education; their everyday lives were directed by those with greater power—the chief, the lord, the tyrant. With few (but significant) exceptions, access to creative freedom was denied to women— half the population—by their social roles.[9] Even in the most recent phase of modern civilization, when many in the developed world are blessed with "free time" and the apparent choice of how to use it, impediments to creative freedom abound. People are beset by social pressures and disinformation amplified by the echo box of social media. Like sheep herded by dogs nipping at their heels, citizens are nudged into consumerism by corporations, into conformity and often apathy by their governments. The constant external din can easily drown out the still small voice of a potentially creative mind. The creative person needs to follow their own daydreams, their own dreams.

———

Poets have come up with a number of analogies, such as Amy Lowell's "radio aërial," each of which illuminates some aspect of the creative process. Two of the most intriguing analogies trace back to Coleridge. One of these is the comparison of creative imagination to organic growth. Pursuing this analogy, Spender speaks of the need to focus a kind of mental concentration on all the implications and directions of an emerging idea, which he likens to the growth of a plant in multiple directions at once: "towards the warmth of the light with its leaves, and towards the water with its roots."

Coleridge also suggested another analogy, one intended to capture a yin-yang duality in creative thought—the alternation of passive and active impulses. He was struck by the parallel with the motion of insects like the water strider that propel themselves on the surface of water.[10] More than a century later, this intriguing hint from Coleridge inspired Yeats to compose "Long-legged Fly," one of the most significant poems to address the theme of human creativity.[11] Written near the end of the poet's life, each of its three stanzas sketches a scene with an individual who serves as a concrete universal symbolizing creativity (Julius Caesar, Helen of Troy, Michelangelo), and concludes with the refrain,

Like a long-legged fly upon the stream
His mind moves upon silence.

Yeats's "fly" is a water strider; its motion on the stream provides a metaphor for the subtle sense in which the active mind modulates its own stream of consciousness. Armed with high-resolution slow-motion photography, modern biologists have achieved a better understanding of this small natural miracle—insects walking on water.[12] Actually, it would be more accurate to say that the water strider *swims* on water—or in even finer detail, swims *in and above* water without touching it! The six delicate legs of the insect are covered by thousands of tiny hairs that repel water—not only does the insect not sink, it doesn't even get wet. Though the lightweight strider is supported by the surface tension of the water, the weight of each leg creates a tiny hollow or dimple in the water surface. The insect moves by an active stroke, pressing each of its four larger legs (middle and hind) against the side of a water dimple (without breaking the surface). The stroke launches the insect into the air, returning to passively glide along the water surface.

To recall a line from Jay Parini's poem, the creative mind is like this. At multiple timescales, an active impulse alternates with a passive "glide" along a path that is largely outside of conscious control but can be modulated by the active impulse. Amy Lowell describes how she formed the basic idea for a poem about horses, then "consciously thought no more about the matter. But what I had really done was to drop my subject into the subconscious, much as one drops a letter into the mail box. Six months later, the words of the poem began to come into my head."[13] But the unconscious is seldom so generous as to yield a complete poem. The poet Paul Valéry spoke of "one line given" by some mysterious source, which provides a seed for conscious poetic work. The poet, says Lowell, "must fill in what the subconscious has left, and fill it in as much in the key of the rest as possible."

Yeats says that the mind, like the water insect on a stream, "moves upon silence." His conception is reminiscent of Wordsworth's remark that poetry "takes its origin from emotion recollected in *tranquillity*"—here adding the emphasis on tranquillity, on quietude. Though some water striders practice their delicate strokes on ocean waves, a calm pool is easier to navigate. For many if not most people, much of the time the unconscious mind is buffeted by the storms of everyday life—troubles and stressors in all their mundane varieties, the flood of advertising, propaganda, and popular opinion pouring in from media. The emotions and other reactions triggered by external sources of which we are at most dimly aware—and that therefore evade conscious scrutiny—drive the biases and sheer stupidity that lure humans into their myriad follies.[14] The subtle guidance of the creative impulse is easily swamped if delivered to an unconscious mind in turmoil. The creator requires a special kind of autonomy—the ability to connect with one's own unconscious mind and by participating with it, navigate on the stream.

As Spender and others have emphasized, a major part of creative navigation is the activation and transformation of memories linked by shared emotional nuances and by analogical resonance. By consciously focusing on one remembered experience, the active impulse may initiate a wave of associations that then operates largely outside of conscious awareness. Related memories, accumulated perhaps over decades and in very different domains of experience, may answer the call and be made available for conscious consideration. The creative process requires *divergent* thinking— the activation of diverse pieces of information related to some common element—followed by *convergent* thinking—melding it all together in a creative product, such as a poem with its internal couplings between words. Often these two modes operate in a cyclic fashion throughout an extended process of composition and revision.

I don't know how Zagajewski composed "Mysticism for Beginners," but on the face of it the poem exemplifies the process of creation. The poet sees the German in a café reading the book with its odd title and suddenly understands that something unifies an array of diverse experiences he had lived or imagined: those swallows on patrol, those travelers, the white herons standing "like nuns in fields of rice," dusk falling over ancient villages, a sculptured head, the stained-glass windows, the nightingale, and "any journey, any kind of trip." The network of suddenly visible connections has taught the poet something about life and about himself—and also that much remains to be learned before his death, the final test.

———

A basic sketch of the creative process traces back to Graham Wallas, a British social reformer and cofounder of the London School of Economics. Wallas characterized creativity in terms of four phases that unfold over extended time periods.[15] Though the phases have a natural order, they can cycle and be interleaved in various ways. First, *preparation* involves formulation of the general idea for a project, and deliberately acquiring as much information as possible that might help to accomplish it. This phase is largely under the control of the conscious mind. To apply Lowell's postal analogy, preparation composes a hopeful letter of request to be dropped into the mailbox of the unconscious. Second, *incubation* is the phase in which conscious thinking about the problem is minimal, and unconscious activity, such as a search through a network of associations, predominates. Third, if these unconscious processes prove fruitful, a sudden phase of *illumination* yields an insight—conscious awareness and recognition of one or more key ideas. Fourth, a period of *verification* involves a return of control to the conscious mind. In this culminating phase, ideas are developed and integrated to create an actual product—this is the phase in which, as Lowell observed, the poet needs to fill in the gaps left by the unconscious, aiming to keep composing in the same key. Verification may include extensive evaluation and revision. This cycle may iterate indefinitely until the poet is satisfied or simply "runs out of steam." In the end, the poem (to paraphrase Paul Valéry) may not be so much finished as abandoned.

Different neural networks support the various phases of the creative process. In chapter 7 we sketched two broad networks that appear to play especially important roles. The control network that links major areas within the frontal and parietal cortices underlies the conscious, self-reflective mind as it exerts control over its own cognition. When cognitive control of thought is disengaged (either due to inadvertent distraction by internal thoughts or to conscious choice), the default network supports looser associative thinking that is nonetheless guided by current interests and concerns. It would be oversimplified to identify the unconscious mind with the neural default network. Nonetheless, these brain areas are certainly involved in thinking processes that proceed in the absence of direct conscious control. Critically, these relatively unconscious processes seem more directed than the term *mind wandering* suggests. "Not all those who wander are lost"—the mind may wander as it uses incomplete information to search memory in response to some elusive but important concern.[16] As I. A. Richards put it, "The mind is a connecting organ, it works only by connecting and it can connect any two things in an indefinitely large number of ways. Which of these it chooses is settled by reference to some larger whole or aim, and, though we may not discover its aim, the mind is never aimless."[17]

As we saw earlier, the two networks can operate in concert, with the control network protecting the default network from unwanted intrusions by the immediate environment, thereby allowing the flow of thought to be directed inward. Often the default network is activated in reaction to internal distractions—worries, regrets, and fears, usually transient but in the extreme amounting to obsessions. However, while excessive brooding is a recipe for sadness, self-reflection can contribute to creativity.[18] Moreover, people are also able to deliberately turn their thoughts inward, which in neural terms implies that activity of the control network can initiate the default network.[19] A particularly intriguing finding is that people who agree that "I allow my thoughts to wander on purpose" also tend to agree that "I perceive my feelings and emotions without having to react to them." Such nonreactivity to emotions is an aspect of the mental state often termed *mindfulness*. A poet must be open to the emotional impact of memories activated by loose associative thinking, yet not be overwhelmed by them— strong emotion needs to be "recollected in tranquillity." The melancholy feeling triggered by a sad memory may inspire a poem, but it's hard to compose while sobbing in uncontrolled grief. It appears that the control network, when consciously used to initiate the default network, helps to manage emotions generated by reactivated memories.[20]

As sketched in figure 12.1, the stream of consciousness (mimicking the stroke/glide motion of a water strider) tends to alternate between periods of conscious thinking responsive to the immediate environment (white) and periods of internally directed thinking supported by the default network (black).[21] These phases can occur at different timescales and blur into one another (gray) as the mind turns inward and then eventually returns to the

Figure 12.1
Conscious and unconscious thinking constantly alternate.

here and now.[22] Mind-wandering tends to be oriented to the future—people often remember the past in order to imagine a possible future (or in the case of a poet or other artist, perhaps form a vision of a poetic truth).[23] Because people are often unaware that their mind has turned inward, the default network likely plays an important role in the incubation phase of creative thinking.[24]

Mind wandering, or day dreaming, is not the only state that fosters incubation. There is evidence that solutions to problems on a standard test of verbal creativity are more likely to be found after a delay filled by REM (rapid eye movement) sleep—the phase of sleep in which vivid, potentially memorable dreams are most likely to occur.[25] Dreams construct their own internal reality, while the brain is largely cut off from sensory information being generated by the external world: "Sleep opens within us an inn for phantoms."[26] As mentioned in chapter 10, Freud and Jung emphasized that the content of dreams often seems symbolic, as if the dreamer's current concerns and problems have been recast in some altered form.[27] Freud particularly emphasized processes of *displacement*—transfer of emotion to a different object—and *condensation*—attaching multiple associations and ideas to a single dream element. For Jung, some common dream symbols are viewed as archetypes—dangerous animals, mountains, water, falling from a high place, flying unaided. The psychoanalytic view of "dream work" bears a striking resemblance to the symbolic indirectness and semantic density typical of poetry—words operating as plurisigns.

Dreams can help achieve a quality prized in poetry—strangeness. Sometimes, as the surrealists recognized, dreams may pass clues from the unconscious mind to the conscious control network. And as suggested by Amy Lowell's analogy of the conscious mind writing letters to the unconscious, it may be possible for the concerns of the waking mind to influence the content of dreams. This possibility has been developed into proposals for *lucid dreaming* as a tool for both creative problem solving and psychological therapy.[28]

In some instances, a remembered dream may generate Valéry's "one line given"—the seed of a poem. Poets and songwriters have often credited dreams as a source of inspiration. I'll give an example from my own experience, since I can attest to the details. The occasion was the month-long recount that followed the American presidential election in November 2000, which had produced a near tie between Democratic candidate

Al Gore and Republican candidate George W. Bush. Like millions of others, I followed the continuous news reports in a state of anxiety (and suffered bitter disappointment when the Supreme Court eventually awarded the presidency to Bush). I felt in particular that the fate of the earth was hanging in the balance—Gore was a committed environmentalist, whereas Bush had acquired much of his wealth in the oil business. The dangers of climate change strongly affected me. I thought of the earth as a small and fragile planet, the sole place where life is known to exist in our universe. Everything depended on the thin band of gases that formed its atmosphere.

As I suspect is often the case, the emotional impact of such global and societal problems interacted with more personal and less rational concerns. I had just turned fifty, a milestone I marked by falling into a midlife crisis. My marriage was crumbling, and I was plagued by uncertainty about what I wanted to accomplish in my remaining years. Around this time I started to have intermittent panic attacks, which were to recur over the next few years. When I was traveling and spending the night in some unfamiliar high-rise hotel, I would occasionally wake up feeling I was short of oxygen. I would feel compelled to open a window, or (if the hotel's window turned out to be sealed) get dressed and go outside for air. Rather obviously, my irrational fear of suffocation was linked to my concerns about the accumulation of greenhouse gases in the atmosphere.

This tangled nexus of thoughts and feelings became the "letter" I apparently sent to my unconscious. One morning during that month of electoral limbo, I recalled a fragment of a dream. A hole opened up in the atmosphere, a great wind blew, and all of earth's air was sucked into space. As this happened I heard a voice saying something like "The bubble has burst." I immediately felt that this dream symbolized the fundamental insecurity of life, and my own life in particular. And that it was worth a poem.

This was not a case where a poem emerged full-blown from the unconscious. Actually, not even one solid line was given—what I remembered most clearly was the visual image of a monstrous tornado breaking out of earth's atmosphere. But the dream provided core symbols and the emotional tone. Implicitly following Amy Lowell's advice, I worked very consciously at writing and revising my poem over the next nine months, trying to stay in the "key" of the dream that had seeded it. Here is what I ended up with.

"Bubble's Burst" by Keith Holyoak

At dawn that last of days no trumpets sounded,
Or maybe they were drowned in wicked wind.
Though lookouts stared, they spied no spectral horsemen—
Perhaps some hid, well-cloaked inside infernal
Coiled clouds, but no one came. If we had sinned
We weren't told how. Newspapers all propounded
Their theories: sunspots, global warming, normal
And cyclic ice age, like before the first men.

Plain awful weather. Rain, at first a torrent,
Stopped cold as if the heavens were drained of pity.
And something strange was happening up in space—
Satellite signals died, computer networks
Crashed, and the multitudes who filled my city
Felt very lonely. Through the day the abhorrent
Cyclone toyed with the earth the way a cat works
A mouse—pouncing, clawing, licking its face.

Schools let out early, government buildings closed.
The wind grew steady, spun a tightening noose
Round the Tropic of Cancer west to east—
A fevered dervish dancing on the world,
Genie without its master broken loose,
Freed from its bottle, with blind passions roused.
The sun dimmed in green neon sky to herald
Endless dark, and up from the swirling beast

Tornadoes shot like missiles to the void.
A lone voice cried, "Oh, the bubble's burst!"
And then the great wind sucked earth clean of cattle,
Children, nations, poems, oceans and air,
Lovers and prayers, the creatures of deep forest
And of the sea—sanctuaries destroyed,
Monuments broken, beaten earth stripped bare
Of soft looks and the armaments of battle.

Wandering souls still hear that cruel wind blow,
Wailing from light-years off, eons ago.[29]

Rereading the poem now, two decades later and in the midst of writing about the linkage between consciousness and poetry, I notice perhaps for the first time the way the persona who speaks the poem moves through psychological space (a bit like the way psychological distance shifts in

Du Fu's "Thoughts Written While Traveling by Night"). The anonymous speaker begins to describe something awful that apparently happened in the past. In the first stanza, the "we" in "If we had sinned ..." places the speaker among the inhabitants of some city, psychologically close to anxious neighbors and fellow citizens. A close perspective is maintained up to the opening of the third stanza, "Schools let out early ...," but then the persona moves toward a view of the earth from a high altitude, surveying the ominous storms. The fourth stanza highlights one last connection to a fellow human: "A lone voice cried, 'Oh, the bubble's burst!'" After this, blastoff—the persona draws farther and farther away from earth and its people, a disembodied observer of their destruction. The final couplet, set off in isolation from the rest of the poem, fixes the speaker's lingering view at an unimaginable distance—"light-years off, eons ago." And yet the ending hints that the voice of the poem may still belong to one of those doomed people, those "wandering souls"—all drawn close, and yet so far away.

Research has established some of the neural signatures of the moment of insight—the phase that Wallas called illumination.[30] A burst of brain waves in the relatively slow alpha band—associated with wakeful relaxation, eyes closed—tends to occur over the right visual cortex just before an insight enters consciousness. The brain seems to enter a state of tranquillity by withdrawing from visual input, clearing the mind for a new thought. This alpha wave is quickly followed (about a third of a second prior to the moment of insight) by a burst of much faster gamma waves (with a frequency of about 40 hertz), mainly originating in the right hemisphere. Gamma waves seem to arise when a novel collection of neurons begins firing together for the first time.

Most work on the neurocognitive basis of creative thinking has focused on simple laboratory tasks, but a few studies have examined what happens in people's brains when they aim to produce complex creative products. Of particular relevance here, a team led by Siyuan Liu and senior researcher Allen Braun used neuroimaging to trace the neural networks that are active when poetry is being composed and revised.[31] The participants in their study were asked to perform several tasks, including composing a short poem, revising their new poem, and (as a noncreative control) recalling poems they had memorized—all while lying inside a machine that scanned their brains. Some of the participants were novice poets, and others were relative experts (graduate students in an MFA program who had published in poetry journals). Later, a panel of experienced poets evaluated the poems that had been produced, judging their craftsmanship and linguistic creativity.

The findings from this study support the general conception of creativity as depending on a delicate balance between the activity of different neural networks. The dorsolateral PFC and parietal areas, including the precuneus—major landmarks in the control network—were highly active when poems were being revised, but were relatively *de*activated during the prior phase of initial composition. But notably, the rostrolateral PFC—an area activated in complex analogical reasoning (chapter 7) but not in comprehension of simple metaphors (chapter 8)—was highly active during poetry composition. This area may play an important role in linking the control and default networks, acting to guide divergent thinking and make conscious use of the information it activates. The medial PFC and a broad set of language-related areas were also particularly active during the composition phase. The medial PFC—important for motivation and self-initiated action—was highly active in revision as well as composition. The deactivation of parts of the control network during composition may allow unconscious processes to more freely activate ideas, emotions, and words related to the emerging poem. During the revision process the broad control network comes back online to guide self-evaluation of the poem and to identify lines that need improvement.

As would be expected, the experts wrote higher-quality poems than did the novices. Although the basic networks involved in writing poetry were the same for poets at both skill levels, the experts showed a more pronounced deactivation of the control network during composition. This finding has the encouraging implication that expertise in writing poetry can be achieved by refining the activity of neural networks that are already operating in most normal brains. Relative to novices, the expert poets showed greater activation of lower-level, subcortical brain areas during the composition phase. With increased experience, poets may be able to perform some basic subtasks, such as tracking rhythm and meter in an emerging poem, in a relatively automatic fashion. Cognitive control is no longer needed.

The study also revealed some intriguing hints about the neural correlates of writing superior poems. When experts generated poems that garnered high craft scores, the medial PFC was especially closely coupled with language areas, but less closely coupled with posterior parietal areas—the default network apparently was running with reduced direction from the control network. And when experts generated poems rated high in linguistic creativity, the dorsolateral PFC was less closely coupled with sensorimotor areas. It seems that the control network lessened its normal regulation of these areas, allowing sensory imagery (often involved in creative thinking) to become available more freely, so that it found its way into the emerging poem.[32]

This neuroimaging study—a high-water mark in exploration of the poetic brain—was limited to a single session of just over half an hour, with the composition and revision phases artificially segregated from one another. And the "experts" who participated, while accomplished poets, were not composing at the level of the masters. In actual practice, a poet will often interleave composition and revision over an extended time period. As Spender observes, "The work on a line of poetry may take the form of putting a version aside for a few days, weeks or years, and then taking it up again, when it may be found that the line has, in the interval of time, almost rewritten itself."[33]

Spender kept notebooks for his poems and provided us with a careful analysis of how a particular poem evolved across a series of over twenty revisions. His initial version began with the lines

> There are some days when the sea lies like a harp
> Stretched flat beneath the cliffs. The waves
> Like wires burn with the sun's copper glow. ...

In composing this poem, a very early insight was the poet's recognition of the symbolic value of this core imagery. The waves (wires of a harp) are "like a seen music fusing seascape and landscape. ... The sea represents death and eternity, the land represents the brief life of the summer and of one human generation which passes into the sea of eternity." This seems to be the kind of insight central to the creative use of metaphor and symbolism in general. An image presents itself in the mind, intimating a deeper vision. The poet's job is to take this initial insight and move the poem along so as to complete the vision (without stating it directly, which would break the spell).

Of course, we will never know what was happening in Spender's brain when he arrived at his symbolic interpretation of the image of the sea "stretched flat beneath the cliffs." But recent discoveries about the neural basis of creativity certainly encourage a few conjectures. I imagine the default network at work, freed of immediate cognitive control. Brain areas involved in sensory perception and in language are operating in concert. At some point, alpha waves culminate in a burst of activity in the gamma band. In more poetic language,

Like a long-legged fly upon the stream
His mind moves upon silence.

13 Free in the Tearing Wind

"In a Dark Time" by Theodore Roethke

In a dark time, the eye begins to see,
I meet my shadow in the deepening shade;
I hear my echo in the echoing wood—
A lord of nature weeping to a tree.
I live between the heron and the wren,
Beasts of the hill and serpents of the den.

What's madness but nobility of soul
At odds with circumstance? The day's on fire!
I know the purity of pure despair,
My shadow pinned against a sweating wall.
That place among the rocks—is it a cave,
Or winding path? The edge is what I have.

A steady storm of correspondences!
A night flowing with birds, a ragged moon,
And in broad day the midnight come again!
A man goes far to find out what he is—
Death of the self in a long, tearless night,
All natural shapes blazing unnatural light.

Dark, dark my light, and darker my desire.
My soul, like some heat-maddened summer fly,
Keeps buzzing at the sill. Which I is *I*?
A fallen man, I climb out of my fear.
The mind enters itself, and God the mind,
And one is One, free in the tearing wind.[1]

Asked if writing poetry gave her satisfaction, Sylvia Plath replied, "Oh, satisfaction! I don't think I could live without it. It's like water or bread, or something absolutely essential to me. I find myself absolutely fulfilled when I have written a poem, when I'm writing one. Having written one, then you fall away very rapidly from having been a poet to becoming a sort of poet in rest, which isn't the same thing at all. But I think the actual experience of writing a poem is a magnificent one."[2]

At the time of this interview (October 30, 1962), Plath was living in London in a flat in which Yeats had once lived. The loving mother of two children, she had separated the previous month from her husband, the renowned poet Ted Hughes. She was writing poems that would comprise her greatest single volume, *Ariel*. Less than four months later, early one morning of the coldest British winter in a century, Sylvia Plath placed her head in the oven with the gas turned on. She was just thirty—"... you fall away very rapidly. ..."

To be human is to face inevitable loss, for life is transient. Echoing Shakespeare's "lines to time" (chapter 3), the contemporary poet Thomas Kinsella noted that "one of the main impulses to poetry or, for that matter, to any art, is an attempt more or less to stem the passing of time."[3] The attempt may succeed in producing a creative work, but it must inevitably fail to halt time's flight. To be a poet, or any kind of artist, is to be vulnerable. To feel deeply is to risk being hurt. To turn the mind inward and let it enter itself (as in the poem by Roethke, who suffered from bipolar disorder) is to risk arousing demons. Recall our ideal Poet, the Ancient Mariner, whose terrifying voyage left him with a compulsion to take on a different sort of journey, to never rest:

I pass, like night, from land to land;
I have strange power of speech. ...

"Writing," observed Plath, "is ... a way of ordering and reordering the chaos of experience."[4]

We're shocked when someone who's successful—in an endeavor they surely find meaningful—plunges into depression, perhaps even deliberately ends their own life. How could Plath enjoy writing poetry so much, yet kill herself? A first clue lies in the distinction she draws between the poet actively writing and the poet "in rest." Without doubt, what made her feel "absolutely fulfilled" in the process of writing a poem was the introspective experience that the psychologist Mihaly Csikszentmihalyi has termed *flow*.[5] Flow is a state of complete absorption in an activity—what an elite athlete might call "being in the zone." During a flow experience, the mind or body is voluntarily pressed to its limits to accomplish a difficult task the person has chosen to undertake. The person has an intrinsic motivation to succeed, and a justified expectation of doing so. Poets recognized the state of flow before psychologists began to study it. Stephen Spender emphasized that "writing poetry, when a poem appears to succeed, results in an intense physical excitement, a sense of release and ecstasy."[6]

Importantly, the sense of self is diminished during the flow experience. Neural studies of flow have found that the medial PFC—an important component of the default network involved in thinking about oneself—is *de*activated during the state of flow.[7] By contrast, major depression is associated with *greater* activity of the medial PFC.[8] The flow state counters depression—Plath could be happy when she was actively writing.

But alas, the flow state ends when the challenging activity ceases. Spender also noted how a poet may delight in a poem just completed as "my best ever," yet a few days later downgrade it to just another shot that missed its mark. The burst of writing ended, the poet falls back into their usual mood. If that mood is sadness, the memory of recent joy now lost may aggravate the downswing. Happiness is losing the self; sadness is finding it again. Poetry often springs from pain, which the act of creation can momentarily relieve but not erase. "I can make stories out of my heartbreak, beauty out of sorrow," wrote the teenaged Plath in the journal she kept from adolescence until the end.[9] Though expressive writing is not a cure for depression, it can be a valuable part of therapy—writing provides a readily available means to self-medicate.[10]

The suffering artist is in a peculiar position—psychological pain may seem to be an essential source of the creative impulse, yet the flow state that accompanies the creative act may be experienced as the deepest joy. A question arises: How much pain am I willing to suffer in order to create? Often a further question has to be confronted: How much pain am I willing to inflict on those who love me in order to create?

There's no universal answer. But I'm struck by a remark the poet Elizabeth Bishop directed to her close friend, the poet Robert Lowell.[11] Lowell (descended from the same family as Amy Lowell, a poet we met in chapter 12) suffered from bipolar disorder. He had just published a book of confessional poems based on the details of how he had recently left his wife for another woman. His book, which would win a Pulitzer Prize, incorporated (without her consent) passages from letters his now-former wife had written to him. "But," wrote Bishop in a letter to Lowell, *"art just isn't worth that much"* (emphasis in original).

Mental illness is certainly not a prerequisite for creativity—generally it's a severe impediment. For example, schizophrenia (a disease that involves impairment of the frontal and temporal cortices) impairs the ability to comprehend metaphors or proverbs.[12] In general, severe psychoses impede creative success, not to mention the ability to cope with everyday life. Most poets—like most creative people in all walks of life—do not suffer from mental illness. And most are not *poètes maudits*. But they are, as a class— well, peculiar in certain ways. Let's take a closer look at the attributes of creative people, poets included. Along the way we'll consider more carefully the role that mental illness sometimes plays.

———

Poetry acts as a device by which the consciousness of a poet impacts that of a reader. To attract a reader's interest the poet must offer a novel perspective on some aspect of life (or a new way of expressing that perspective). At the same time, the poet's consciousness must not be so foreign to that of the reader as to be inaccessible. In a delightful essay titled "What Is It Like to Be a Bat?," the philosopher Thomas Nagel pointed out that we feel confident these atypical mammals are conscious, even though the nature of their subjective experience (which derives from their special sense of echolocation) is virtually impossible to intuit.[13] I imagine that if bats wrote poetry, we humans would probably not be moved by it. (Nor would a superintelligent and literate bat be likely to appreciate the outlandish poetry of humans!)

In previous chapters we encountered many of the key building blocks for the writing of poetry—intrinsic motivation to create, intense emotional experiences, excellent memory for emotions and sensory details, a grasp of symbolic connections, and of course high verbal ability. Any kind of creative activity will be aided if a person has a rich associative memory in which very different concepts and experiences are linked, directly or indirectly. As we saw in chapter 7, there is evidence that the right hemisphere provides a denser network of relatively weak semantic links than does the left. There is also evidence that individual differences in associative networks are related to creativity.[14] In one study, people were divided into two groups based on their score on a battery of standardized tests of semantic creativity. The participants in this study provided word associations—given a target word, they had one minute to generate as many associated words as they could think of. Using statistical techniques, the researchers were able to reconstruct associative networks that best predicted the typical responses for the groups that scored low or high in creativity, as shown in figure 13.1. Network A is based on responses from the low-creativity group, and Network B is based on responses from the high-creativity group. The network for the high-creativity group appears to be less spread out, less segregated into distinct clusters, and overall more interconnected. The semantic knowledge of creative people is organized in a way that allows greater flexibility in how that knowledge can be accessed and used. This finding was anticipated by I. A. Richards: "The greatest difference between the artist or poet and the ordinary person is found ... in the range, delicacy, and freedom of the connections he is able to make between different elements of his experience."[15]

Is there something distinctive about the personalities of creative people? Creators vary enormously in their general character—they may be humble or conceited, kind or cruel, foolish or wise, gregarious or painfully shy. Still, some general tendencies are apparent. Using standardized tests, psychologists have identified a set of personality dimensions termed the *Big Five* on which people vary—openness to experience, conscientiousness, extraversion, agreeableness, and neuroticism. The first of these—openness to experience—is consistently linked to creativity.[16] People who score high in openness tend to embrace new experiences of all sorts—they have broad interests, like to travel to new places, and are curious about different cultures. They have an advantage on tests of *implicit* learning—picking up regularities in complex and noisy data without a great deal of conscious effort.[17] Of particular note, such regularities include the intricate associations among words and their meanings that guide comprehension of metaphors (see chapter 8). People who are open to experience have an active imagination and tend to fantasize. They are especially sensitive to beauty. Such people are daydreamers—and also tend to remember their nocturnal dreams on waking.[18]

To be open, of course, is to be vulnerable. Those who score high on this personality trait are often impulsive. Their need for novelty is linked to a propensity to use alcohol and mind-altering drugs, and—in the limit—to cross the line into forms of mental illness. An interesting type of phenomenon linked to openness is *apophenia*—the mental generation of patterns that have little or no objective basis. Not content to simply detect regularities

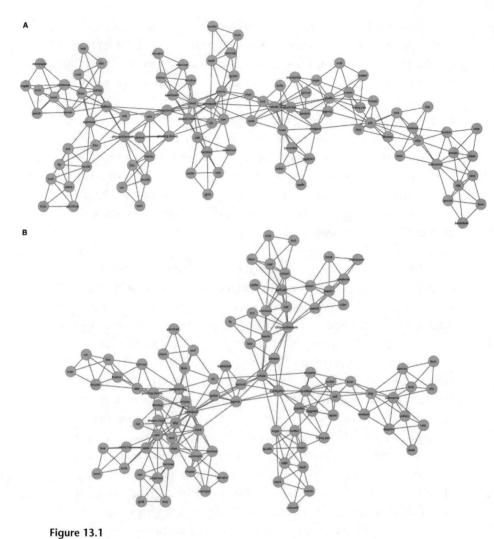

Figure 13.1
The associative network reconstructed for (A) low-creativity group and (B) high-creativity group.
Reprinted with permission from Kennet et al. (2014, figure 1).

in the environment, the open mind may create them. A modest degree of openness leads to a propensity for finding meaningful shapes in clouds by day or the stars by night—and perhaps for creating metaphors.[19] A greater degree of openness leads to magical thinking—the tendency to report paranormal experiences or being abducted by aliens. And schizophrenics—their minds wide open to full-blown apophenia—may respond to commands that seem to emanate from inner voices.[20]

At the neural level, openness in its broad range of manifestations depends on the operation of the neural transmitter dopamine.[21] Higher global levels of dopamine are associated with a preference for novelty, seeking of reward through exploration, and acquiring and using a richer set of semantic associations. These traits are associated with creativity, but also (when taken to extremes) with alcoholism, drug abuse, the manic phase of biopolar disorder, and schizotypy (a less severe version of schizophrenia). As we will see shortly, these behavioral and mental disorders represent the downside risks of creativity, particularly in the verbal realm where poets flourish.

The association between openness and creativity is connected in complex ways to *intellect*.[22] To a first approximation, people high in openness also tend to score relatively high on tests of intelligence—especially when the tests are verbal. A question that has vexed psychologists and others is exactly how creativity and intelligence are related. We use subtly different terms to refer to qualities associated with these interrelated traits. A creative person is likely to be described as *imaginative, original*, or *curious*, perhaps *artistic* or *poetic*. Someone viewed as highly intelligent (but perhaps not especially creative) might be dubbed *intelligent, intellectual*, or *philosophical*.

Highly creative people in all fields tend to be intelligent, but the extent of the connection varies across disciplines.[23] Roughly, scientific creativity depends more on intellect, whereas artistic and literary creativity depends more on openness. In addition, scientists are less susceptible to mental illness than are artists and writers—especially poets![24] Success in science demands a high level of intellectual control, though creative insight is always welcome. In contrast, success in art or poetry first and foremost demands a novel perspective, which is nourished by the spirit of openness—though intellectual control is likely to be helpful, as long as it doesn't get too heavy-handed.[25] The trade-offs, especially as they relate to poetry, can be understood in terms of the intricate dance of the control network and the default network (sketched in chapter 12). In broad strokes, the control network supports intellect, whereas the default network (sometimes) supports openness. If the control network is too domineering, the creative potential of mind wandering will be blocked. But if a balance can be maintained, the control network can guide the operation of the default network, protect it from external distractions, and ultimately transform the partial insights it offers into completed creative works. To borrow the title of a volume of poetry, a successful poem depends on "the ratio of reason to magic."[26]

The idea that the intellect offers protection from the risks associated with openness to experience fits with a general view of the way creativity is related to psychopathology. The psychologist Shelley Carson has proposed a *shared vulnerability* model, depicted in figure 13.2.[27] The overlapping region represents important traits (in part genetic) that creative people share with those who suffer from certain forms of mental illness, notably schizotypy. Both groups show a novelty preference, and both have an especially rich network of associations between concepts (*hyperconnectivity*).

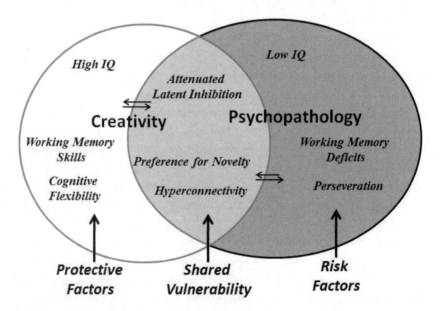

Figure 13.2
The shared vulnerability model: factors common to creativity and mental illness, factors that afford protection from illness, and factors that increase the risks.
Reprinted from Carson (2011) by permission of SAGE Publications, Inc.

Attenuated latent inhibition reflects a departure from a general phenomenon. People usually pay less attention to stimuli that have not proved significant—inputs that have signaled neither reward nor punishment. If such "irrelevant" stimuli recur—but now signal something important—this change is likely to be missed. This pattern—latent inhibition—is reduced for schizotypics and possibly for creative people. Reduced latent inhibition suggests the person may be more prepared to notice when a familiar stimulus takes on a new and significant meaning in a novel context.

These traits shared by creative people and those suffering from mental illness are relatively independent of intellectual capacity or IQ. However, these same traits constitute vulnerabilities. As shown on the right side of the diagram, if a person's cognitive control is relatively weak (manifested in a relatively low IQ score), then the potentially beneficial traits may appear in exaggerated forms associated with psychopathology. If working memory capacity is low, then the cognitive control network is likely to be impaired. The rich network of associations may trigger delusions. Reduced inhibitory control may contribute to *perseveration*—the tendency to become mentally stuck, fixated on particular thoughts or stimuli.

The positive flip side (left part of the figure) is that high cognitive capacity affords protection against the vulnerabilities that accompany creative potential. A well-functioning control network permits flexible thinking, avoiding the dangers of getting stuck in the rut of perseveration. In general, successful creators are people who have some of the vulnerabilities associated with psychopathology, but also protective traits.[28] People who have close relatives suffering from mental illness, but are themselves free of psychopathology, are often especially creative. There may be a germ of truth to the suggestion made long ago by the British historian Thomas Babington Macaulay, "Perhaps no person can be a poet, or can even enjoy poetry, without a certain unsoundness of mind."[29] But I. A. Richards hit the mark more closely in his description of the mind of a poet: "His superficial resemblance to persons who are merely mental chaoses, unorganized, without selective ability and of weak and diffused attention, is likewise clear. Essentially he is the opposite of these."[30]

————

The psychopathologies most closely linked to creativity are schizotypy and bipolar disorder. Schizotypy brings looser associative thinking, but without the more profound thought disturbances of schizophrenia. Bipolar disorder involves periods of depression that sometimes transition into states of excess excitement, or mania. Both diseases are associated with disruptions in the dopamine system. Increases in dopamine (or in sensitivity to it) are linked to increased activation of weak associations between concepts—a symptom of schizotypy that supports creativity. Increased dopamine also contributes to an elevated overall mood, and in bipolar disorder to the transition from depression to mania. In general, creativity is associated with positive mood (or an upswing in mood) for both clinical and nonclinical populations. In the case of bipolar disorder, the depressive phase tends to be incapacitating, with the person stuck in rumination about personal problems.[31] But the transitional upswing may provide an occasion for creative insight, and the manic phase (if not too extreme) can provide the motivation and energy to actually execute a creative work.

Why might psychopathology be more prevalent among poets than in other creative groups? A number of possibilities come to mind. Strong emotions, which are a driving force in the creation of poetry, can reach extremes in mental illness. Roethke feels how "My soul, like some heat-maddened summer fly, / Keeps buzzing at the sill." Is that what bipolar disorder is like? This glimpse of an altered consciousness is part of what makes the poem effective.

In addition, different disciplines impose different constraints on their practitioners. A scientist has to focus on the natural world as it presents itself, because to explain it is the object of science. A poet, by contrast, is free to explore other worlds that exist only in imagination, or perhaps in some ideal world never to be realized. The bounds of poetic truth are more fluid than the bounds of the scientific variety. Moreover, success in some disciplines demands sustained focus over long time periods, which may pose an insurmountable barrier to someone suffering from mental illness (unless they are in remission). Apparent counterexamples usually can be explained when timing of the illness is considered. John Nash, who won the Nobel Prize in Economics even though he suffered from schizophrenia, in fact completed his most important work before the onset of the disease.[32] But writing a poem—especially a short lyric—is advantaged by the fact that the creative product is relatively short and self-contained. A poem might be completed (or at least drafted) during a brief remission from schizophrenia, during the first creative burst of a manic phase, or on an alcoholic's occasional day of sobriety.

Based on historical analyses of eminent creators, it has been suggested that the incidence of psychopathology and suicide has been particularly high for women poets.[33] Tragic cases such as Sylvia Plath and her contemporary Anne Sexton (both winners of the Pulitzer Prize—posthumously for Plath) are certainly suggestive. However, it seems very likely that this sad statistic reflects the sociocultural conditions of the times, rather than any inherent gender difference in suicidality of poets. For most of human history women, with rare exceptions, were excluded from creative professions (indeed, from most professions that conveyed economic or social advantages). In the United States, the first great woman poet was Emily Dickinson, who lived in the nineteenth century. The twentieth century— the primary period surveyed in recent studies of mental illness among creators—brought dramatic changes in the status of women. One of these changes was that women could become practicing poets—publishing their poems in magazines, their collections as books, and in some instances winning major literary awards.

But what is desired, and indeed possible, need not be easy. The women who pioneered their gender's entry into male-dominated professions faced many hurdles. These included their own internal struggles with the conflicts inherent in the juxtaposition of traditional expectations with the newly expanded realm of possibilities. The case of Plath—a brilliant, sensitive, and unstable woman drawn to "the most ingrown and intense of the arts"—is telling. By keeping private journals from adolescence on, writing a novel (*The Bell Jar*) that is barely disguised autobiography, and creating poems in a confessional style, Plath laid her soul bare to posterity to a degree that still feels painfully intimate. A bell jar is a simple inverted bottle, often used to protect and display delicate objects, such as dried flowers. These delicate objects are dead. And so we have Plath's metaphor: "To the person in the bell jar, blank and stopped as a dead baby, the world itself is a bad dream."[34] The poet herself is the delicate, dead object—suffering from clinical depression.

The many manifestations of openness to experience include those related to gender and sexuality. A poet's perspective is likely to embrace aspects of both feminine and masculine experience—the yin and yang of Taoism, the anima and animus of Jung. Openness to the consciousness of both genders is not the same as homosexuality (though many of the renowned poets we've encountered in this book—from Walt Whitman in chapter 2 to

Elizabeth Bishop a few pages back—were indeed homosexual or bisexual). Sylvia Plath was firmly heterosexual but capable of empathy with male as well as female consciousness. At the age of eighteen she recorded in her journal (ellipses included):

I am part man, and I notice women's breasts and thighs with the calculation of a man choosing a mistress ... but that is the artist and the analytical attitude toward the female body ... for I am more a woman; even as I long for full breasts and a beautiful body, so do I abhor the sensuousness that they bring ... I desire the things which will destroy me in the end ... I wonder if art divorced from normal and conventional living is as vital as art combined with living: in a word, would marriage sap my creative energy and annihilate my desire for written and pictorial expression which increases with this depth of unsatisfied emotion ... or would I achieve a fuller expression in art as well as in the creation of children? ... Am I strong enough to do both well? That is the crux of the matter, and I hope to steel myself for the test.[35]

This early passage foreshadows the ambivalence toward conventional gender-based expectations that would find expression in "Metaphors" (see chapter 3). In the end, Sylvia Plath was not strong enough to survive her own contradictions. But she didn't spend her whole life in a bell jar, sheltering against the storm—she lived free in the tearing wind.

14   The Authenticity of Footprints

"Heights of Macchu Picchu: XII" by Pablo Neruda

Arise to birth with me, my brother.
Give me your hand out of the depths
sown by your sorrows.
You will not return from these stone fastnesses.
You will not emerge from subterranean time.
Your rasping voice will not come back,
nor your pierced eyes rise from their sockets.

Look at me from the depths of the earth,
tiller of fields, weaver, reticent shepherd,
groom of totemic guanacos,
mason high on your treacherous scaffolding,
iceman of Andean tears,
jeweler with crushed fingers,
farmer anxious among his seedlings,
potter wasted among his clays—
bring to the cup of this new life
your ancient buried sorrows.
Show me your blood and your furrow;
say to me: here I was scourged
because a gem was dull or because the earth
failed to give up in time its tithe of corn or stone.
Point out to me the rock on which you stumbled,
the wood they used to crucify your body.
Strike the old flints
to kindle ancient lamps, light up the whips
glued to your wounds throughout the centuries
and light the axes gleaming with your blood.

I come to speak for your dead mouths.

Throughout the earth
let dead lips congregate,
out of the depths spin this long night to me
as if I rode at anchor here with you.

And tell me everything, tell chain by chain,
and link by link, and step by step;
sharpen the knives you kept hidden away,
thrust them into my breast, into my hands,
like a torrent of sunbursts,
an Amazon of buried jaguars,
and leave me cry: hours, days and years,
blind ages, stellar centuries.

And give me silence, give me water, hope.

Give me the struggle, the iron, the volcanoes.

Let bodies cling like magnets to my body.

Come quickly to my veins and to my mouth.

Speak through my speech, and through my blood.[1]

What is authentic poetry? What is authentic anything? The term is, to put it kindly, rather subjective. To say a poem (or poet) is *authentic* usually means, "in my opinion, good." Aiming for a bit more precision, one might claim an authentic poem is one that expresses sincere feeling, feeling that comes from the heart, that conveys soul. The work may be a bit rough in its craftsmanship, but the imperfections are forgiven because it's authentic. In our times, authenticity is everywhere a scarce commodity. Which means, it's a commodity—something worth paying a little extra for. As the old saying goes, "The secret of success is sincerity. Once you can fake that you've got it made."[2]

Joking aside, authenticity may be more than (and less than) sincerity. The literary critic Lionel Trilling argued that whereas sincerity strongly implies unalloyed honesty to others, authenticity does not.[3] The word *art* shares its root (from Latin and Old English) with *artifice* and *artificial*. To be true to oneself, perhaps one needs to create a mask or persona (see chapter 11). According to Oscar Wilde, "Man is least himself when he talks in his own person. Give him a mask, and he will tell you the truth."[4] The artistic value of sincerity—authenticity stripped of its masks—is debatable.

Doubtless some good poetry is sincere, but a noted literary critic (echoing another of Wilde's witticisms) claimed "all bad poetry is sincere."[5]

To delve a little deeper into authenticity, let's consider how things are defined. Many concepts—biological kinds such as daisies, raccoons, and humans—refer to things that are born, not made. Let's focus instead on concepts referring to things that *are* made, or are created by the actions of animate beings. Many if not most of these are defined by their intended *function*—what it is they (normally) accomplish. A table, for example, is a kind of furniture suitable for placing objects on a stable flat surface so they can be used by one or more seated humans. A shoe is a covering for a foot that affords it protection when standing, walking, or running. Tables and shoes were once crafted by the hands of skilled laborers, but since the Industrial Revolution are usually machine-made. But as long as a piece of furniture functions as a table, or a piece of footwear functions as a shoe, then however it was made, that is what it is—a table or a shoe.

In contrast, consider what makes something a footprint. Suppose I mold a cast of a foot, which I turn into a footprint-stamping machine. If my device is well constructed, I can go around stamping impressions in the dirt, and pretty much everybody who encounters them later will be convinced what they're seeing are footprints. But they're not footprints—they're replicas, imitations, simulations—fakes.

Now, suppose instead I simply walk across the same dirt surface, my own feet forming impressions along my path. Then let the rain fall and the wind blow, until just the faintest traces remain—only an expert tracker could identify them as human footprints. Faded and distorted though they may be, those lingering marks in the dirt are indeed still footprints. And unlike the far more perfect shapes left by my footprint-stamper, the weather-beaten traces of impressions created by my actual feet are authentic.

A footprint is an example of a concept defined first and foremost by its *origin*. Of course, the most familiar notion of authenticity concerns the origin of a work of art—was this painting rendered by the hand of the master, or by a meticulous forger?[6] If the latter, the painting's value—and very likely its beauty in the eye of its beholder—is diminished. Being a footprint similarly depends on origin—the basic requirement is that the mark must have been made by a foot. The foot may be that of some nonhuman animal, it may be stunted or misshapen, but the impression it leaves is a footprint. Unlike a shoe, which is defined by its intended function, a footprint is defined by how it came to be—how it was *generated*, not by what (if anything) it may be used for.

The key question we'll ponder in this chapter is very simple: Is a poem more like a shoe or a footprint?

————

A number of influential approaches to literary criticism apparently come down on the side of the shoe. Advocates of the New Criticism (following such influential thinkers as I. A. Richards and T. S. Eliot) argued that a work of literature should be considered a kind of found object, like a message in a bottle washed up on the beach. It doesn't matter who (if anyone) wrote it, what thoughts and emotions triggered the writing, or what the author intended it to mean. The critic is to simply examine the finished work, considering whether and how it may impact a reader and perhaps how it resembles or differs from other works. Does the shoe fit? Is the stitching strong enough to last? Does its style project taste, with a touch of novelty? Then it's a fine shoe.

The New Criticism, as I noted earlier, has not aged well. (Such is the typical fate of movements dubbed "New"!) However, the plethora of rival approaches to literary criticism that arose in the twentieth century— inexorably drawn to the suffix *-ism*, as in deconstructionism, feminism, and Marxism—have yet more firmly ignored the psychological process of creation.[7] In its stead they favor analyses (or in the case of deconstructionism, what might more aptly be called antianalyses) of the text itself, perhaps with reference to global sociological factors that provide an interpretive context. The goal of a literary deconstructionist, one might say, is to demonstrate that although the poem might appear to be a shoe, it really is a collage of leather, rubber, and glue. No footprints here.

It seems fair to conclude that leading contemporary schools of literary criticism have no use for our ideal Poet, the Ancient Mariner with his "strange power of speech"; nor for real poets with their griefs and joys and bewilderments, their compulsions and flirtations with madness. These approaches provide no room for consideration of all that bears on the psychology of creativity—analogy and conceptual combination, the control and default networks, neurotransmitters and openness to experience. The loss is theirs.

Of course, some literary theorists have recognized the psychological basis for creative work. As we pointed out in chapter 5, a core idea has been articulated by Harold Bloom, and Owen Barfield before him: "consciousness is to poetry what marble is to sculpture: the material that is being worked." As I put it in chapter 2, a metaphor reflects an effort to "recreate some image of our own inner experience inside the consciousness of another human being." Or to state the same point using the analogy that dominates this chapter, a poem is a kind of footprint—an impression made by the consciousness of the Poet on that of the Reader.

Suppose, then, that we consider the poem as a footprint, defined in part by how it was generated. I say "in part" because it would be foolish for the critic to ignore the poem as a text—a finished work that may well serve functions for the reader that its author never anticipated. The reader as well as the author has psychological work to do. But to redress the imbalance in the approaches to literary criticism over the past century, let's consider what may be termed *neurocognitive criticism*—analysis of the psychological and neural mechanisms that transform the consciousness of the author into an imprint on the consciousness of the reader.[8] A poem has its structure and its functions, to be sure. But it also has its origins, the generative process by which the brain enables creative cognition—and this is where we must look to assess its authenticity.

The approach of neurocognitive criticism has a natural affinity for *biographical* criticism. In modern times the effort to understand poetic creation by biographical analysis began with Samuel Johnson's *Lives of the Most Eminent English Poets* (completed in 1781 after decades of effort), which examined the lives and work of dozens of poets, mainly from the eighteenth century. The contemporary critic Harold Bloom has continued to develop this tradition.[9] In essence, biographical criticism operates by literary detective work—the critic makes use of whatever can be discovered about the lives of authors, while tracing literary and other cultural influences.

Biography is inherently individual, but the interpretation of a life and its achievements (and failures) requires some sense of what is general about human psychology—ideas about how personality and cognitive propensities influence the creative process. The early biographical critics, much like jurors presented with facts about people's actions connected to a crime, simply applied their lay understanding of human nature to form conjectures about how and why particular poets created their works. In the past century, ideas originating in psychology—primarily psychoanalytic concepts derived from Freud and Jung—were sometimes incorporated into biographical criticism. In particular, the notion of unconscious influences on poetic creation became more prominent. But this early marriage between literary criticism and psychology has been shaky. For example, Harold Bloom professed to find a Shakespearean reading of Freud more enlightening than the reverse.

By the twenty-first century, the idea that psychoanalysis is all there is to psychology (or somehow represents it) is indefensible. Some clients may benefit from psychoanalytic therapy, but as an intellectual project psychoanalysis appears to be at an impasse. Some of its core ideas persist—as we saw in earlier chapters, notions of the unconscious and archetypes continue to be explored in cognitive psychology and neuroscience. But psychoanalysis (despite the pretensions of its originators) did not adopt the scientific method. Although the movement once seemed to offer a way to integrate the methods of the humanities with scientific psychology, that vision was a mirage. Psychoanalysis provides no real help in bridging to science.

Neurocognitive criticism is proposed as a second marriage of literary criticism (particularly the biographical approach) with a branch of psychology—this time, with the kind of research on literary psychology and neuroscience we encountered in previous chapters. As I've emphasized, this field is a work in progress—its theories are subject to change without notice. Further advances in neuroimaging technology, for example, are likely to trigger new ideas about how the unconscious aspects of the mind contribute to creativity. Whereas psychoanalysis proffered its received wisdom for adoption by literary critics, scientific psychology can only tender its tentative and fluid ideas. This is as it must be—science is alive and still growing.

———

"Arise to birth with me, my brother"—so begins Neruda's ode to the pre-Columbian peoples of the Andes. In the final poem of a sequence called "The Heights of Macchu Picchu," the poet writes from an intense empathetic bond with those who labored as slaves to build what was to become the lost city of the Incas. They are his brothers, who in his poem are born again.

The Chilean poet Pablo Neruda visited that lost (but rediscovered) city in 1943 and wrote the sequence soon afterward. For the poet it was a period of midlife anguish triggered by the confluence of personal and historical upheaval. Approaching age forty, Neruda had previously lived in Asia for many years, where he witnessed the oppression of the common people by poverty and colonialism. His close friend, the poet Federico García Lorca, had been executed during the Spanish Civil War. Neruda's first marriage had disintegrated and his daughter had died. World War II was now raging. Neruda had become a communist and would remain a left-wing radical until his death in 1973 (under suspicious circumstances following a right-wing coup in Chile).

Out of his earlier life, out of the turmoil of the times, out of his imaginative vision of an ancient city hidden on a mountaintop, Neruda drew strange power of speech. He gave it to long-dead slaves, to those who had been scourged and crucified and forgotten: "I come to speak for your dead mouths." He created authentic poetry.

There is much to be said about the psychological forces that create poets and poems. From the perspective of biographical and neurocognitive criticism, poetry is first of all an expression of life—life in general, and the poet's life in particular. As he so often did, Leonard Cohen found a particularly apt metaphor: "Poetry is just the evidence of a life. If your life is burning well, poetry is just the ash."[10]

Besides the other vagaries of life, poets (like writers and artists of all sorts) are molded by the influences of other poets. The poetic voice of Elizabeth Bishop, to take one example, emerged in part from her friendships with fellow poets Marianne Moore and Robert Lowell.[11] Sometimes (perhaps more often) the greatest influences are not contemporaries, but forerunners with whom the budding poet feels an affinity. Much like the cross-generational tensions within families, poets often have a complex attitude to those they most admire among their precursors. Emerging poets may in essence apprentice themselves to someone dead, as if trying to bring their mentor back to life by offering themselves as a kind of replacement (consider the bonds linking both Langston Hughes and Hart Crane back to Walt Whitman). The great mystery of creativity is how the old is recombined to give birth to the new.

At a later stage of development, a poet must in some way separate from mentors, living or dead, and speak in his or her own voice—a voice at least partly acquired from those very same mentors. Harold Bloom calls it the *agon*—the struggle—that a writer wages against those influences that have served as invaluable guides.[12] Sometimes the agon is with a poet's earlier self, as when at midcareer a radical shift in style is ventured. For poets there are many paths, often tortuous ones, that lead to authenticity.

Biographical and neurocognitive criticism emphasize close examination of the processes by which poems come to be. The idea that authenticity derives from the origin of a work has a particularly poignant implication for poetry translation (see chapter 9).[13] A translator may aspire to create a poem as good as the original—perhaps even better—but it will never be as authentic. The notion of authenticity as it applies to poets, and human beings in general, raises many questions. Perhaps the most important was asked by the eighteenth-century poet Edward Young: "Born originals, how comes it to pass that we die copies?"[14]

But for now I will leave that path of exploration and instead confront the starkest challenge facing the approach I've advocated. Between shoe and footprint, I've claimed poetry is more like the latter. This position raises a question that goes beyond the human: Can neurocognitive criticism—can poetry itself—survive artificial intelligence?

————

"Time—a few centuries here or there—means very little in the world of poems." There is something reassuring about Mary Oliver's words. Especially in an era of rapid change, there is comfort to be had in those things that move slowly. But oceans rise and mountains fall; nothing stays the same. Not even the way poetry is made.

The disappearance of the author in twentieth-century literary criticism can perhaps be traced back to the surrealist movement and its game of "exquisite corpse" (chapter 10).[15] The surrealists believed that a poem can emerge not only from the unconscious mind of an individual, but from the collective mind of many individuals working in consort—even, or perhaps especially, if each individual has minimal knowledge of what the others are doing. Soon the idea of making art from recycled objects emerged. In the realm of literature, this approach took the form of *found poetry*. To create a found poem, one or more people collect bits of text encountered anywhere at all, and with a little editing stitch the pieces together to form a collage-like poem. Examining this generative activity, it may be difficult to identify who if anyone is the "poet" who writes the found poem (or for that matter, to be confident that "writing" is an apt name for the process). Still, even if no one's consciousness guided the initial creation of the constituent phrases, one or more humans will have exercised their sensitivity and discrimination in selecting the bits to include, and the way these pieces are ordered and linked to form a new whole. The author (or authors) at a minimum must do the work of a careful reader. Can the human be pushed still further into the background, or even out of the picture?

The most radical technological advance of the twentieth century might seem to have nothing at all to do with the writing of poetry. If we make a list of the great leaps that led to modern civilization—control of fire, agriculture, the wheel, electricity, and perhaps a few more—the most recent addition is a machine that uses electrons to do computation. The first functioning digital computers were constructed midcentury by Alan Turing and a few others. Over the next not-quite-a-century-yet, computers became enormously faster and more powerful, began to process information in parallel rather than just sequentially, and were linked together into a vast worldwide network known as the internet. Along the way, these devices enabled the creation of artificial versions of a trait previously found only in biological life forms, most notably humans—intelligence.

Artificial intelligence (AI) is in the process of changing the world and its societies in ways no one can fully predict.[16] In the near term, autonomous vehicles will largely replace human drivers. Various present-day human occupations will go the way of scribe and blacksmith. Machine vision can already scour the internet to identify and retrieve images of your face. Machine learning can take the traces of your activities on social media and infer your race, creed, and political views—information very helpful in suggesting new movies and music you may like, or in deciding whether you're a potential enemy of the state. Computer programs are making financial and medical decisions. They could readily (in a practical if not moral sense) make decisions to kill suspected enemies (of some country, or perhaps some computer) located thousands of miles away. Their death warrants could be executed by swarms of lethal AI-guided drones. Meanwhile (and here no real AI is even required), the near-instantaneous dissemination of what is technically called information enables crackpot ideas and evil ideologies to find mass audiences. On the hazier side of the present horizon, there may come a tipping point at which AI surpasses the general intelligence of humans. (In various specific domains, notably mathematical calculation, the intersection point was passed decades ago.) Many people anticipate this technological moment, dubbed the *Singularity*, as a kind of

Second Coming—though whether of a savior or of Yeats's rough beast is less clear. Perhaps by constructing an artificial human, computer scientists will finally realize Mary Shelley's vision.

Of all the actual and potential consequences of AI, surely the least significant is that AI programs are beginning to write poetry. But that effort happens to be the AI application most relevant to our theme. And in a certain sense, poetry may serve as a kind of canary in the coal mine—an early indicator of the extent to which AI promises (threatens?) to challenge humans as artistic creators. If AI can be a poet, what other previously human-only roles will it slip into?

So, what is the current state of AI and computer-generated poetry? This is a less central question than might be supposed. Especially in this time of rapid AI advances, the current state of the artificial poetic arts is merely a transitory benchmark. We need to set aside the old stereotype that computer programs simply follow fixed rules and do what humans have programmed them to do, and so lack any capacity for creativity. Computer programs can now learn from enormous sets of data using methods called *deep learning*. What the programs learn, and how they will behave after learning, is very difficult (perhaps impossible) to predict in advance. The question has arisen (semiseriously) whether computer programs ought to be listed as coauthors of scientific papers reporting discoveries to which they contributed.[17] There is no doubt that some forms of creativity are within the reach, and indeed the grasp, of computer programs.

But what about poetry? To evaluate computer-generated poetry, let's pause to remind ourselves what makes a text work as a poem. A successful poem combines compelling content (what Coleridge called "good sense") with aesthetically pleasing wordplay (metaphor and other varieties of symbolism), coupled with the various types of sound similarities and constraints of form we surveyed in chapter 9.

In broad strokes, an automated approach to constructing poems can operate using a generate-then-select method. First, lots of candidate texts are produced, out of which some (a very few, or just one) are then selected as winners worth keeping. Roughly, computer programs can be very prolific in generating, but (to date) have proved less capable at selecting. At the risk of caricature, the computer poet can be likened to the proverbial monkey at the typewriter, pounding out reams of garbage within which the occasional Shakespearean sonnet might be found—with the key difference that the computer operates far more rapidly than any monkey (or human) could. To be fair, the program's search can be made much less random than the monkey's typing. Current computer poetry programs usually bring in one or more humans to help in selecting poetic gems embedded in vast quantities of computer-generated ore. An important question, of course, is whether an authentic creator requires some ability to evaluate their own creations. Perhaps, as Oscar Wilde argued, there is a sense in which an artist must act as their own critic—or not be a true artist at all.[18]

One use of computers is simply to provide a platform for human generation and selection. The internet makes it easy for large groups of people to collaborate on projects. The kind of collective poetry writing encouraged by the surrealists has evolved into crowdsourcing websites that allow anyone to edit an emerging collective poem. Each contributor gets to play a bit part as author/editor. No doubt some people enjoy participating in the creation of poems by crowdsourcing. It's less clear whether Sylvia Plath would have associated this activity with "the most ingrown and intense of the creative arts."

But can computers write poetry on their own, or even make substantial contributions as partners with humans? Not surprisingly, computers are better able to generate and select poems that impose minimal constraints—the less sense and the less form the text requires, the easier for a machine to generate it. A cynic might suggest that the extremes of twentieth-century free verse set the stage for AI poets by lowering the bar. (I'm reminded of an old Chinese saying, "A blind cat can catch a dead mouse.") If that classic line of surrealism, "The exquisite corpse shall drink the new wine," strikes you as a fine contribution to poetry, then AI is ready to get to work—there are plenty more quasi-random associations to be found by brute search.

As another example, since the 1960s computers have been creating poems in the form of haiku in English. Defined in the crudest possible way, an English haiku consists of words that total seventeen syllables. (I will not take up the question of why anyone would imagine this to be an interesting form.) Rather than actually composing haiku, some computer programs simply look for found poems of seventeen syllables. One program retrieved this haunting gem from the electronic pages of the *New York Times*:[19]

> We're going to start
> winning again, believe me.
> We're going to win.

The current state-of-the-art AI poets can actually generate text, rather than just retrieve it. The techniques vary, but most are founded on a mathematical discipline not typically viewed as poetic—statistics. The "big data" available to current AI systems includes massive electronic text corpora, such as Google News (which at the moment contains upward of 100 billion word tokens, ever-growing). Recall those constraints that govern language (chapter 5)—the rules of syntax, the semantics of word meanings, the sounds described by phonology, the knowledge about context and social situations that constitutes pragmatics. All of those constraints, plus the linguistic choices and styles of individual writers, collectively yield the actual text produced by human writers—which accumulates as electronic data available for AI systems.

This massive body of text can be described by complex distributional statistics—"You shall know a word by the company it keeps."[20] Quite amazingly, machine learning equipped with advanced statistics can recover all sorts of hidden regularities by analyzing how words are distributed in texts.[21] These methods can determine that *dog* and *cat* are very similar in meaning, that *run* and *running* are variants of the same verb, and that *king* and *queen* are related in the same way as *man* and *woman*.

Closer to poetry, machine learning can identify words that are often linked metaphorically. As discussed in chapter 3, many metaphors are conventional. Legions of writers have generated expressions that make use of such common metaphors, leaving traces in the patterns of co-occurrence among words in texts. Armed with statistical analyses of text corpora, AI has entered the humanities. Machine learning can help identify features of word meaning that predict the rated goodness of literary metaphors and the historical period in which texts were written.[22] New tools for writers are becoming available—besides having access to an automated thesaurus and rhyming dictionary, a poet may be able to enlist a computerized metaphor suggester.[23] The statistics of word patterns have entered into debates about Shakespeare's possible collaborations.[24] A basic program for anticipating the next word a person will type can allow a human to select among possible "Shakespearean" continuations of a sentence, thereby creating a sort of parody of a sonnet by the immortal bard.[25] A program that can find associates linking a target topic with a metaphorical source, and render them into approximate English (with some aid from a human), was able to produce a text that begins:[26]

> My marriage is an emotional prison
> Barred visitors do marriages allow
> The most unitary collective scarcely organizes so much
> Intimidate me with the official regulation of your prison
> Let your sexual degradation charm me. ...

It's easy to dismiss AI poetry on the grounds that it has so far failed to produce any good poems. Coleridge would doubtless have seen current AI poetry as the operation of fancy—mechanical recombination of elements—rather than the active imagination. But the fact that AI programs have yet to reach the level of human *makars* is not conclusive evidence that AI can never do so. For the moment, let's grant AI poets the benefit of the doubt, and assume that (with human guidance) they will continue to improve in generating humanlike texts. If an AI were to compose a text that a human could appreciate as a poem, would that poem be authentic?

———

To assess the implications of a potential AI poet, let's start by looking at AI as applied to more basic tasks, asking our entering question: shoe or footprint? For example, suppose we have a six-legged robot that can move around an open environment, climb stairs, and so on. Does it walk? Of course it does. What walking *means* is to use leglike appendages to traverse the solid surfaces of an environment. Walking is fundamentally defined by success in achieving its function.

Suppose further than our robot uses camera eyes to detect objects in its environment—it can avoid bumping into them and can report what kinds of objects they are. Can our robot see? Of course it can—vision is the use of information from reflected light to recognize objects and determine their locations. Once again, the definition is based on function. We don't need to inquire as to how the robot's vision system works, or whether its eyes are humanlike in any important way. The function of vision has been achieved.

In fact, the philosophical doctrine that has generally guided cognitive science and AI is called *functionalism*. Intelligence is fundamentally defined as the achievement of certain functions. There is certainly a further question as to whether the robot/computer is accomplishing these functions in a humanlike manner. Very roughly, cognitive scientists aim to develop humanlike computer models (see chapters 6 and 8), whereas pure AI researchers just want to get the job done. But in general, functionalism grants that walking is walking, and vision is vision, regardless of the physical nature of the entity performing those functions. An eye can be built out of rods and cones or from photodiodes—as long as that eye serves the critical function of translating light into information about external objects, the entity using it has sight. From the perspective of functionalism, intelligence, like a shoe, is to be judged by what it accomplishes.

We can ask parallel questions as we consider major cognitive functions one by one. Perception? Attention? Memory? Reasoning? Decision making? Problem solving? For each it seems a functional definition is compelling. If an AI can look at a chessboard, attend to the critical pieces, remember similar positions encountered in previous games, and choose a winning move, then that AI is playing chess. And indeed, ever since 1997 when the computer program Deep Blue bested the human world champion, AI has reigned as the emperor of chess over all players on earth.

So far, the shoe fits AI just fine. But on the way to poetry we're forced to go further and dive into the murkiest depths of the philosophy of mind. What about understanding? Emotion? Consciousness? Can these aspects of the human mind—all arguably central to poetry and other art forms—be given a strictly functional definition?

The most vexed topic of all is the nature of consciousness.[27] Many aspects of this concept—the ability to focus or shift attention, to evaluate one's own mental states, to perform self-regulation, and to make decisions—appear amenable to functional definitions. Cognitive scientists create computer simulations of these human capabilities, and AI programs certainly exhibit forms of them. But the aspect of consciousness that seems most important—the phenomenal sense of a rose being red, the night sky overwhelming, a loss heartbreaking—has so far defied scientific understanding.

This has been called the Hard Problem of consciousness—a more accurate term would be the Intractable Problem.[28] Before its stony face every sensible philosophical position seems to sink into absurdity. Consider: if consciousness has a purely functional definition—the capacity for self-regulation, let's say—then a thermostat is at least minimally conscious. Absurd. If functionalism falters, suppose we substitute *materialism*—the doctrine that everything in the natural world (including the subjective experience of an individual) is some form of physical matter. Could it be that consciousness is not only dependent on neural activity, but actually *is* neural activity? Then a neurosurgeon should be able to open up a living brain and see the consciousness inside it. Absurd. So it might seem we're left with the famous *dualism* of Descartes—matter (brain included) is one kind of thing, and consciousness is something else altogether. But then the obvious correlations between neural activity and states of consciousness would appear to be some sort of odd coincidence. And how could a poet's ethereal consciousness reach across the dark unfathomable chasm[29] to cause an emerging poem to be scribbled on paper—an event situated firmly in the realm of matter? All absurd.

The only indisputable statement to be made about consciousness is that no consensus exists among philosophers, psychologists, neuroscientists, and AI researchers. Some neuroscientists believe they are on the threshold of providing a materialist account of consciousness, and some AI researchers believe machines will inevitably acquire consciousness as an emergent property when they reach some critical level of complexity. For what it's worth (which I freely admit to be very little), I have no faith in these claims. The complexity argument seemed plausible a half century ago when computers were in their infancy. Today, consider a simple thought experiment: which is more complex, the internet (including every computer attached to it), or the brain of a frog? The internet, I would say. And which is more likely to have some sort of inner experience, the internet or the frog? I'll put my money on the amphibian.

If every available philosophical account of consciousness appears to be absurd, logic leaves us with two possibilities: at least one of these accounts isn't truly absurd after all (we just need to clarify things), or the correct account awaits an insight humankind has yet to be granted. Though I remain officially agnostic, for the purpose of the specific question that presently concerns us—can AI write authentic poetry?—the preponderance of evidence leads me to answer "no." AI has no apparent path to inner experience, which I (and many others) take to be the ultimate source of authentic poetry. A major corollary of this conclusion deserves to be stated: Inner experience can't be defined as a computational process.[30]

What AI has already accomplished is spectacular, and its further advances will continue to change the world. But for all the functions an AI can potentially achieve—the ability to converse intelligently with humans in their natural languages, to interpret their emotions based on facial expression and tone of voice, even to create new artistic works that give humans pleasure—an intelligent program will fall short of authenticity as a poet. AI lacks what is most needed to place the footprints of its own consciousness on another mind—inner experience. The absence of inner experience also means that AI lacks what is most needed to *appreciate* poetry—a sense of poetic truth (see chapter 11).

Alan Turing proposed a rather lighthearted "imitation game," which became known as the *Turing test*.[31] The basic idea is that a computer and a human are placed out of view, and we're allowed to pass them questions and receive their answers. If we're unable to reliably distinguish the computer from the human, then the computer has passed the test, and we must admit it's capable of human thinking. The original test was supposed to be open-ended—we can ask the contestants anything. For the computer to pass would therefore imply that general intelligence has been mechanized. But the idea can be relaxed to assess specific capabilities. In popular culture the Turing test is loosely taken as any way of checking whether a computer program can convince a person that the program has emulated some human capability.

The problem with a Turing test of this sort is that people can be fooled so easily. Understanding, empathy, and other manifestations of sincerity can be faked (by human charlatans as well as by well-designed AI)—and faked on an industrial scale. Decades of exposure to science fiction androids in movies have prepared people to accept AI-guided robots as intelligent humanoids with genuine feelings. Real robots can now be used to provide playmates for children, companions for the elderly, therapists for the distraught, and sex partners for the lovelorn. Some people have become attached to their robot vacuum cleaners. In 2010, the headline for an article posted to the internet read "People's Emotional Attachment to Roombas Bodes Well For Inevitable Sex Robot Industry."[32] By 2017 this prediction was being fulfilled, generating intriguing issues of a pseudomoral nature. An internet headline read, "Sex Robot Molested At Electronics Festival, Creators Say."[33] One of the engineers who helped to develop "Samantha," the alleged victim, lamented, "I think people have just become over-excited and treated her like a sex doll. She isn't a sex doll, she is a robot with AI."

Passing various Turing tests—that is, faking humanity—is a core aim of current AI. A powerful new tool at AI's disposal is called *adversarial learning*.[34] A pair of programs work together as learning partners (more like sparring partners). One program, the Generator, produces a humanesque output, say a verbal response to a question. The second program, the Discriminator, then tries to decide whether the answer was produced by a computer or a human. If the Discriminator correctly reports the response was computer-generated, this feedback will allow the Generator to improve itself—so next time its output will better imitate what a human might say. Whereas if the Discriminator is tricked by the Generator, then the Discriminator will learn to pay closer attention next time to any subtle verbal tics that betray computer-generated responses. And so the cycle continues, until a very smart Generator can reliably convince a very smart Discriminator that the responses of the former were produced by a living, breathing person. Notice the ironic knife twist here—as adversarial learning advances as a training tool for AI, humans will not even be necessary for administering a Turing test. A good Discriminator will do the job faster, more reliably, and for less money.

A near-term goal of AI is that we humans will be happier as we spend our time talking to a polite humanlike chatbox that dishes out "customer service" over the phone or internet. On the horizon, those so-called friends we collect on social media will include a sprinkling of like-minded chatboxes. That romantic prospect you connect with on a dating site may not be the attractive man/woman you long for—may not even be human, in the old-fashioned literal sense. AI—and the Age of Inauthenticity—is upon us.

Turning back to poetry, it remains to be seen whether AI poems will eventually go beyond intended or unintended parody and trigger emotional responses in human readers that run deeper than wry amusement. Considered as texts, will AI poems reach some level confusable with human greatness, or will poetry created without inner experience inevitably press in vain against some inherent limit? Current AI poets are in essence mining the metaphors that humans have already formed and planted in texts—in the view of Robert Frost, "The richest accumulation of the ages is the noble metaphors we have rolled up."[35] Could AI create genuinely novel metaphors, rather than only variations of those we humans have come up with already? Borges thought that truly new metaphors still await discovery. New variations of old metaphors can be very beautiful, he acknowledged, "and only a few critics like myself would take the trouble to say, 'Well, there you have eyes and stars and there you have time and the river over and over again.' The metaphors will strike the imagination. But it may also be given to us—and why not hope for this as well?—it may also be given to us to invent metaphors that do not belong, or that do not yet belong, to accepted patterns."[36]

————

We began this chapter at the "Heights of Macchu Picchu," passed through poetry as the ash of a life well-burned, then plunged to murky depths where intelligence and authenticity move along separate paths. To close let's return to human poetry and listen to intelligence and authenticity rejoined. I will say nothing about this poem, except to observe that the final line—meaningless out of its context—is perhaps the most devastating in English poetry. And to ask—where did *that* come from?

"Mid-Term Break" by Seamus Heaney

I sat all morning in the college sick bay
Counting bells knelling classes to a close.
At two o'clock our neighbours drove me home.

In the porch I met my father crying—
He had always taken funerals in his stride—
And Big Jim Evans saying it was a hard blow.

The baby cooed and laughed and rocked the pram
When I came in, and I was embarrassed
By old men standing up to shake my hand

And tell me they were "sorry for my trouble."
Whispers informed strangers I was the eldest,
Away at school, as my mother held my hand

In hers and coughed out angry tearless sighs.
At ten o'clock the ambulance arrived
With the corpse, stanched and bandaged by the nurses.

Next morning I went up into the room. Snowdrops
And candles soothed the bedside; I saw him
For the first time in six weeks. Paler now,

Wearing a poppy bruise on his left temple,
He lay in the four-foot box as in his cot.
No gaudy scars, the bumper knocked him clear.

A four-foot box, a foot for every year.[37]

"At Woodward's Gardens" by Robert Frost

A boy, presuming on his intellect,
Once showed two little monkeys in a cage
A burning-glass they could not understand
And never could be made to understand.
Words are no good: to say it was a lens
For gathering solar rays would not have helped.
But let him show them how the weapon worked.
He made the sun a pin-point on the nose
Of first one, then the other, till it brought
A look of puzzled dimness to their eyes
That blinking could not seem to blink away.
They stood, arms laced together, at the bars,
And exchanged troubled glances over life.
One put a thoughtful hand up to his nose
As if reminded—or as if perhaps
Within a million years of an idea.
He got his purple little knuckles stung.
The already known had once more been confirmed
By psychological experiment;
And that were all the finding to announce
Had the boy not presumed too close and long.
There was a sudden flash, a monkey snatch,
And the glass was the monkeys', not the boy's.
Precipitately they retired back-cage
And instituted an investigation
On their part, though without the needed insight.
They bit the glass and listened for the flavor,
They broke the handle and the binding off it;
Then, none the wiser, frankly gave it up,
And having hid it in their bedding straw

Against the day of prisoners' ennui,
Came dryly forward to the bars again
To answer for themselves: Who said it mattered
What monkeys did or didn't understand?
They might not understand a burning-glass.
They might not understand the sun itself.
It's knowing what to do with things that counts.[1]

In this final chapter we return to the questions that first motivated this book. Robert Frost was on to something important when he said, "Poetry is simply made of metaphor. So also is philosophy, and science, too." Maud Bodkin also drew a connection from poetry to science: "Perhaps every science must start with metaphor and end with algebra; and perhaps without the metaphor there would never have been any algebra."[2]

What does this perspective imply for the role that poetry plays (or might play) in people's lives? In a 1930 address at Amherst College, Frost gave his thoughts about "education by poetry." Education *by* poetry, in Frost's view, has aims that extend beyond education *in* poetry. He emphasized ways engagement with poetry might teach skills important to a person's life. Frost warned against an education that failed to instill "taste and judgment" in people—without which "they don't know when they are being fooled by a metaphor, an analogy, a parable. And metaphor is, of course, what we are talking about. Education by poetry is education by metaphor."[3]

In these times (and here I write from my vantage point in early twenty-first-century America, and as a professor of psychology, not English), education by poetry appears to be barely an idea. There is widespread concern about the perceived failings of our education system, but the focus is on what is called STEM (science, technology, engineering, and mathematics)— the kind of knowledge that drives progress in burgeoning fields such as neuroscience (chapter 7) and computer science (chapter 14). What is valued most highly is "hard" knowledge and the technical skills demanded by high-paying professions. Time on the human scale is finite, and school-time more so—in the zero-sum game of formal education, time devoted to acquiring the "soft" knowledge of the humanities tends to be peeled away to create a bit more elbow room for STEM education. And poetry is tucked away in a small corner of the humanities.

I have no quarrel with STEM education (indeed, this is a topic on which I've done research).[4] And I foresee no easy fix for the finitude of time. But

it's worth taking another look at what education by poetry might mean—
and why it might be valuable—as we close in on a century since Frost laid
out his thoughts about it.

―――――

Frost raised an intriguing idea about a skill that might be acquired from
poetry: a sharpened ability to critically evaluate metaphors. Recall how the
psychologist Amos Tversky (chapter 3) warned that metaphors can obscure
rather than illuminate: "A metaphor is a cover-up." Given that Tversky's
self-refuting denunciation illustrates why his own proposed remedy—ban
metaphor!—is doomed, perhaps a more realistic educational objective is to
improve critical thinking as applied to metaphor.

Back in 1893, the American humanist Charles Eliot Norton laid out
another central aim of education by literature (and poetry in particular): to
cultivate the imagination.

> The imagination is the supreme intellectual faculty, and yet it is of all the one which
> receives least attention in our common systems of education. The reason is not far
> to seek. The imagination is of all the faculties the most difficult to control, it is the
> most elusive of all, the most far-reaching in its relations, the rarest in its full power.
> But upon its healthy development depend not only the sound exercise of the facul-
> ties of observation and judgment, but also the command of the reason, the control
> of the will, and the quickening and growth of the moral sympathies. The means for
> its culture which good reading affords is the most generally available and one of the
> most efficient.[5]

Notice that among the human capacities that may depend on the
"healthy development" of the imagination, Norton includes "the quicken-
ing and growth of the moral sympathies." The phrasing now seems quaint,
the idea more so. Still, the possibility that poetry could play a role in fostering a kind of "moral sympathy"—what we would probably call *empathy*—is
worth considering.

We meet Professor Norton as this book is nearing its end—indulge me as
I relate a little story about the web of connections to him (a symptom of my
own apophenia, perhaps—see chapter 13). I first encountered Norton just
over two months ago. My family spent Father's Day of 2017 on Salt Spring
Island, British Columbia, where we have a house by the ocean. The island
village of Ganges is graced by an excellent used bookstore (Black Sheep
Books). I have a weakness for old books, and on this occasion my wife and
children bought me one as my present. It was volume II of a five-volume

series called *Heart of Oak Books*, a collection of poems and stories edited by
Norton, intended for young children. I was drawn to the book by its time-
faded red binding and its title—it alludes to the wood used to build British
warships back in the age of sail (the same wood that gave my family its
name).

I began reading the book at bedtime to my seven-year-old son Dylan,
whom we met briefly back in chapter 12. Somewhat to my surprise (for the
children of the twenty-first century and the iPad seem far removed from
those of the nineteenth and its books!), it became one of his favorites. The
collection opens with a poem by William Blake; Shakespeare, Wordsworth,
and Tennyson (among other poets) also contribute. The remaining selections are mostly fairy tales. These generally are still familiar, though the Vic-
torian diction of the renderings gives them a vaguely archaic flavor—"Jack
and the Beanstalk," "Cinderella," "The Sleeping Beauty in the Wood," "Puss
in Boots." Norton's description of imagination—the "supreme intellectual
faculty," "most elusive," "most far-reaching," "most difficult to control"—
is found in his preface to this collection.

Then I stumbled on a small volume of essays by Jorge Luis Borges. The
book was published in 2000, but originated in 1967–1968 as the Charles
Eliot Norton Lectures that Borges gave at Harvard (where Norton was a
professor of art). This honorary lectureship is awarded annually to a person
chosen to speak about "poetry in the broadest sense." A list of the luminaries who have given these lectures since the inception of the series in
1925 includes quite a number of names we've encountered in these pages—
besides Borges, we have T. S. Eliot, Robert Frost, Lionel Trilling, Northrup
Frye, and Harold Bloom. The list itself led me to a book by Trilling—like
that of Borges, it was based on his Harvard lectures. I belatedly added a few
quotes taken from the Borges and the Trilling volumes to these pages—
anything one writes rings more true after discovering that someone smarter
has already said it better. And so it seems that over the course of a century
and more since his death in 1908, the ghost of Professor Norton has quietly
woven an elaborate intellectual web—into which *The Spider's Thread* was
drawn.

Between Frost and Norton, we have identified three potential aims of
education by poetry: development of critical thinking, imagination, empathy. These capacities are interconnected, but I place imagination in the center of the three (as Coleridge might have done two centuries ago). Before we

consider whether poetry might in some way further these educational aims, it's worth asking how important the capacities targeted actually are. Any question about educational value crudely comes in two flavors, pragmatic and idealistic. The pragmatic question is: Will this help me earn a living? The idealistic is: Will this help me live a life that means something, at least to me? Of course, it's best to marry the two questions—will this help me find a job that lets me do something I find meaningful? But sometimes the two questions must have different answers.

I take it to be self-evident that any, or better yet all three, of critical thinking, imagination, and empathy are likely to contribute to building a meaningful life. But will they help to find a job? Each of these capacities is, as Norton recognized, both elusive and difficult to control. This is good news for the young of the twenty-first century. If you think back to our survey of current AI in the previous chapter, many of the occupations of your parents are in imminent danger of being taken over by extremely smart computers and robots. But in the near term (with a bit of luck, in the working lives of at least another generation), the human mind will remain the central imaginative engine for creative work. Many of the people who develop future AI and other new technologies will have advanced skills of the hard variety—mathematics, engineering, neuroscience, for example. But some (and the very best will combine both sorts) will bring the soft skills of imagination to bear on creating the future. Metaphor finds its natural home in poetry, but travels far.

Another question that arises is whether poetry (or literature in general—in this chapter I don't make much of a distinction) offers any advantages over other activities that might benefit imagination or creativity. After all, Norton was writing before the invention of movies, videogames, virtual realities, and similar forms of immersive entertainment and experience. There is currently great interest in the development of behavioral or neural interventions specifically targeting improvement of cognitive functioning ("brain training"). Although such interventions have so far produced little if any practical benefit, they are demonstrably superior to education by poetry when judged by success in financing overhyped start-up companies.[6]

There is no doubt that most people today, most of the time, prefer high-tech media to poetry. Still, there are reasons to suppose that poetry has its own strengths as a means of education. There's an obvious sense in which the written word leaves more to the imagination than do multisensory media. The lack of direct sensory detail, and consequently greater cognitive demands imposed on the reader, may well make literature a particularly effective mode of exercising the imagination. And of course, reading literature involves the imaginative use of *language*, a medium for mental representation that is unique in many ways (including at the neural level). Metaphors may be explored in other media, but nowhere are they as pervasive as in poetry, nor as deeply embedded in language.

One more preliminary question about education by poetry needs to be addressed. Whose education is to be the focus—Poet or Reader? As we considered the writing of poetry throughout this book, we found a great deal of overlap between the mental activities of poets and of other creators. Recent research on creativity paints an intriguing picture of the delicate interplay between the control and default networks, between the intellect and personality traits. We saw hints that expertise in writing poetry is accompanied by refined interleaving of neural activity in multiple brain areas. Although more research is needed, it seems plausible that progress as a poet may alter neural pathways in ways that support a wider range of creative endeavors.

But this doesn't mean everyone should become a poet. People differ in the language skills and other capacities required to write poetry. In addition, poets and other creators have repeatedly emphasized that intrinsic motivation is essential. Not everyone—perhaps not anyone on every day—wants or needs to be a poet. As I write this, I harbor grave doubt that if I were to find myself marooned on Bukowski's desert island, I would pass the time scratching words in the sand. Happily, writing poetry and drinking oneself to death are not the only choices life offers (at least to most of us). Robert Frost again: "I only want people to write poetry if they want to write poetry. I have never encouraged anyone to write poetry that did not want to write it, and I have not always encouraged those who did want to write it. That ought to be one's own funeral. It is a hard, hard life, as they say."[7]

Few today have heard of Franz Xaver Kappus. A young cadet in the Austro-Hungarian Army in 1902, Kappus was torn between pursuit of a military career and a longing to become a poet. He ventured to write to ask the advice of Rainer Maria Rilke, an Austrian poet (and son of an army officer) he greatly admired. Over the next few years Rilke wrote back with a series of ten letters, which eventually were published as *Letters to a Young Poet*.[8] These letters offer the experienced poet's insights into the nature of poetry and its creation, interwoven with thoughts on love, sex, and life in general. Throughout the correspondence Rilke is kind and encouraging in a general way, but he never advocates that young Kappus become a poet. Like so many others, Rilke claims that such a path must begin with a drive emanating from within. "Nobody can counsel and help you, nobody. There is only one single way. Go into yourself. ... This above all—ask yourself in the stillest hour of your night: *must* I write?" Rilke's emphasis on the need for intrinsic motivation is entirely consistent with what was said in previous chapters. He goes on to say that "a work of art is good if it has sprung from necessity. In this nature of its origin lies the judgment of it: there is no other." The psychological origin of a poem determines its authenticity.

Toward the end of his final letter, Rilke gives his blessing to the course Kappus in fact took: to continue his military career. Poetry, Rilke intimates, is no substitute for living "in a rough reality being solitary and courageous." For better or worse, what Rilke really wrote were "letters from a master poet," addressed to someone on a different path. But by publishing Rilke's letters, Kappus created his own small but significant role in the history of poetry.

So, for those who may go on to become poets—you've been duly warned. My own bit of practical advice: Keep your day job!

Now, let's consider the less hazardous route to education by poetry— what might be gained by reading it? In passing from writing to reading, we are *not* entering a lesser realm. Borges once again: "I think of myself as being essentially a reader. As you are aware, I have ventured into writing; but I think that what I have read is far more important than what I have written. For one reads what one likes—yet one writes not what one would like to write, but what one is able to write."[9]

In the later nineteenth century, San Francisco was home to a small zoo located in an amusement park called Woodward's Gardens. Out of a small incident set there (whether real or imagined I don't know), Robert Frost created a parable for modern times. His poem, like one of Aesop's fables, includes animals as characters. But Frost's animals are not endowed with humanlike speech and wit—they're just two ordinary zoo monkeys. The human traits belong to a very human character—a boy out for a bit of fun. He carries a technological instrument—a burning-glass—intended for such benign purposes as starting a campfire. The monkeys are incapable of understanding how the tool works, but the boy, with his human intellect and creativity, is quick to realize its potential as a weapon. He uses the glass to annoy the monkeys by aiming a beam of sunlight at the nose of each in turn. The monkeys have no idea what's going on, but one of them puts a paw to its nose, intercepting the beam and its concentrated heat. This action precipitates my favorite lines in the poem:

> The already known had once more been confirmed
> By psychological experiment. ...

And so the episode would have ended, except the boy carelessly gets too close to the cage and lingers there too long—allowing the monkeys to snatch away his toy. The monkeys proceed to bite and otherwise manipulate their prize, but learn nothing about what it is or how it works. Still, they seem to vaguely sense it's safer to keep this dangerous thing for themselves, and so they hide it away. Frost concludes with the moral of his parable:

> They might not understand a burning-glass.
> They might not understand the sun itself.
> It's knowing what to do with things that counts.

Of course, this bit of poetic wisdom (like the poetic justice of the stolen plaything) is not directed to the monkeys, but to the boy. And he—clever but thoughtless (and a tad heartless)—stands as a concrete universal representing the entire human race. In how many different ways (the reader is invited to ponder) can humans manage to pluck the fruits of their prodigious intellects, exploiting each new technology to mess things up? When the world ends, whether with a bang or a whimper, the monkeys will not be the ones to blame.

We've been educated by poetry.

————

The educational benefits of poetry are best achieved by stealth. Long ago Norton advised, "The training should begin very early. ... The reading lesson should never be hard or dull; nor should it be made the occasion for instruction in any specific branch of knowledge. The essential thing is that ... the child should like what he reads or hears read. ... He should be led on by pleasure from step to step."[10] Nursery rhymes tap into the natural human responses to rhythm, rhyme, and the other varieties of verbal sound play out of which poems can be built (chapter 9). The sounds of a human language readily give rise to meaning—the acoustic resonance of words

paves the way for the analogical resonance of poetry. A great deal of meaning is conveyed by Lewis Carroll's nonsense poem, "Jabberwocky":[11]

'Twas brillig, and the slithy toves
   Did gyre and gimble in the wabe:
All mimsy were the borogoves,
   And the mome raths outgrabe.

"Beware the Jabberwock, my son!
   The jaws that bite, the claws that catch!
Beware the Jubjub bird, and shun
   The frumious Bandersnatch!"

Poetry is governed by the yin-yang of magic and reason. Though the
ratio varies from one poem to another, a reader's early encounters should
be with poems that showcase the magic—"poetry as enchantment."[12] For
example, Coleridge knew how a poem can cast a spell:

Weave a circle round him thrice,
And close your eyes with holy dread
For he on honey-dew hath fed,
And drunk the milk of Paradise.[13]

And T. S. Eliot knew how simple repetition can create an incantation,
which he used to set up a punchline destined to become a timeless allusion:

This is the way the world ends
This is the way the world ends
This is the way the world ends
Not with a bang but a whimper.[14]

Education by poetry depends, of course, on some sort of education *in*
poetry. Many middle-class North American children arrive in the fourth
grade with little sense of what makes a poem different from ordinary prose.[15]
In particular, they may not have learned that poems typically carry symbolic meaning. Is it possible to actually teach the concept of symbolism?
The developmental psychologist Joan Peskin devised and tested a method
to guide children and adolescents (ranging in age from about eleven to
seventeen years) through the process of expressing ideas and emotions by
means of poetic symbols.[16] Across three grades, a matched class of students
was assigned to either an experimental or a control condition. All students
completed an initial and final test of their ability to interpret symbolic
poetry. In between (in two lessons each lasting about an hour and a half), a

teacher led the experimental group through three interventions that were intended to help them grasp the analogical nature of poetic symbols. For the same length of time, the same teacher taught a matched control group to interpret poetry, with lessons directed at techniques that poets use to appeal to the emotions and imagination.

Peskin and her collaborators focused on symbols related to the cyclic seasons—a central Jungian archetype. In the first of three interventions, each class assigned to the experimental condition was shown a visual depiction of the wheel of the seasons, something like the one shown in figure 15.1. The picture conveyed both the cyclic progression and the two opposing pairs (spring and autumn, summer and winter). The wheel also listed some of the concepts conventionally associated with each season, such as spring with joy, summer with fulfillment, autumn with nostalgia, and winter with despair. The class was asked to brainstorm additional words that seemed to belong with each season. Then the students practiced relating poems to the wheel.

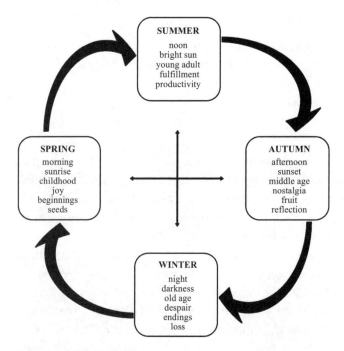

Figure 15.1
The wheel of the seasons: A support for teaching children about symbols in poetry

In the second intervention, students in the experimental group were encouraged to use Venn diagrams to highlight the overlap between the source and target concepts in a metaphor, such as the commonalities between a falling leaf and feelings of loneliness or isolation.

Then in the third intervention, students were given practice in identifying the source and target analogs within very short poems in the Imagist style. As mentioned in chapter 9, Ezra Pound developed this style based in part on the influence of classical Chinese poetry. The students began with a famous poem consisting of a single couplet:

"In a Station of the Metro" by Ezra Pound

The apparition of these faces in the crowd;
Petals on a wet, black bough.[17]

The first line in this poem can be interpreted as the target. The second line, which uses symbolic elements to describe faces emerging from the dark subway, constitutes the source analog. After discussing several Imagist couplets, students wrote a few of their own two-line image metaphors. Working in small groups, the students then physically separated the two lines of their compositions and scrambled them. Afterward the groups worked to connect the separated lines to reconstruct the original poems, discussing the source and target mappings.

On the final test, when compared to students in the control group, those who had been guided to connect poems and metaphors with the symbolism afforded by the seasons and with analogical source-target relations were better able to find plausible symbolic interpretations of poems. They also seemed to derive more enjoyment from reading the poem. It's as if their lesson had provided the key to a locked door, opening up a new way of understanding poetry—and perhaps fostering a new sensitivity to analogical resonance between metaphors and their own experiences.

As we saw in previous chapters, poetry is rooted not only in symbolism but also in sound, and more specifically in the nuances of the human voice. Dana Gioia has drawn attention to the ways appreciation of a poem can be enhanced by oral performance. If a poem is uttered aloud (ideally from memory, or else by oral reading), the performer gains the opportunity to literally feel like the poet. The emotional impact of a poem is linked to its prosody, to the intensity of the voice, the way the lips move, the way the arms gesture, the way the entire body lifts up and sinks back with the rhythm. No longer a reader only, but also a creator, the performer has the opportunity to form what cognitive scientists call a *generative model* of the poet—an internal representation of how the poem might have arisen from the consciousness of its author. Or perhaps one might say, from the consciousness of some *possible* author—for a poem typically admits of multiple readings, not only in its interpretation but in its rendering into speech. How the poem first came into being may not be as important as how the performer recreates it.

One advantage of education by poetry is that it's likely to last. When aging goes well, it may sometimes be true that "bodily decrepitude is wisdom," [18] but the losses loom larger than any gains. Advanced age leads to cognitive decline, especially in the kind of fluid intelligence required to cope with novel and complex information. However, the crystalized intelligence that underlies language comprehension tends to be preserved. This is especially true for those older adults who have acquired strong vocabularies and high verbal fluency through a lifetime of reading.[19] Moreover, older people comprehend metaphors (at least relatively simple ones) in much the same way younger people do—focusing on what the source and target have in common, while backgrounding irrelevancies.[20] And for young and old alike, poetry may make it a little easier to live "in a rough reality being solitary and courageous."

———

Critical thinking, imagination, empathy—these are three general skills that reading poetry might credibly help to develop. Let's first consider empathy, which is a kind of emotional imagination—the ability to share in the emotions of someone else. Empathy should not be confused with morality—there is no reason to think that poets or their readers are on average more or less moral than people in general. You might suppose, perhaps, that poets naturally espouse antiwar positions. But the oldest great poem of western literature, Homer's *Iliad*, celebrates the glories of warriors and their battles. Plenty of later poems have followed suit. A character in a play by the French writer Jean Giraudoux cynically observed, "As soon as war is declared it will be impossible to hold the poets back. Rhyme is still the most effective drum."[21]

Even if poetry serves to build empathy, human decency will not be assured—the ability to anticipate someone's emotional reactions can be used to devise exquisitely personalized tortures.[22] Nonetheless, the capacity to appreciate the feelings of others *does* play a key role in human moral reasoning—though an attitude of benevolence is also required, as well as some dispassionate reasoning. The first moral argument a young child can be expected to grasp is "How would that make *you* feel?"

The philosopher Ted Cohen argued that the ability to imagine oneself as another person is necessary both to appreciate literature and to be morally aware. To take another's point of view is much the same psychological process regardless of whether that other is a real person or a fictional character. Identification of the self with another is a form of comparison—and at least a cousin of metaphor. The power of poetry in fostering emotional identification was highlighted almost two centuries ago by Percy Bysshe Shelley: "The great secret of morals is love; or a going out of our nature, and an identification of ourselves with the beautiful which exists in thought, action, or person, not our own. A man, to be greatly good, must imagine intensely and comprehensively; he must put himself in the place of another and of many others; the pains and pleasure of his species must become his own. The great instrument of moral good is the imagination; and poetry administers to the effect by acting upon the cause."[23]

Psychologists have begun to investigate the possible connections between reading literature and various skills related to social understanding. For example, people who read fiction show gains in laboratory tests of empathy and theory of mind.[24] A neuroimaging study found that reading a passage identified as fiction (rather than as fact) tends to jointly activate the control and default networks.[25] Moreover, a neuroimaging study found that reading prose or poetry of an emotional nature activated brain areas associated with emotional responses to music.[26] Because poetry is generally more emotion-laden than prose, this effect was more pronounced for poetry. In addition, reading poems tended to activate the brain's default network. In much the same way as a poet turns inward when composing, readers of poetry also may enter a kind of reverie.

To grasp a metaphor is to make an imaginative leap from one domain to another. The core psychological processes used to understand metaphors—analogy and conceptual combination—contribute to creative thinking in general. The impact of metaphor on imaginative thinking may be especially strong because multiple processes are evoked at once. New meanings can be created on the spot by metaphorical plurisigns, enhanced by analogical resonance between concepts linked by sound-based couplings.

A metaphor does its work by breaking down old concepts and recreating them in new configurations. As Shelley argued, the language of a poet "is vitally metaphorical; that is, it marks the before unapprehended relations of things and perpetuates their apprehension, until the words which represent them, become, through time, signs for portions or classes of thoughts."

A full appreciation of metaphor also requires critical thinking—the ratio of reason to magic is based on a balance between the two poles of poetry. On the one hand, the cooperative principle encourages Coleridge's "willing suspension of disbelief." It's as if the poet says to the reader, "Consider *this* as a serious possibility—let's travel together and see where the path takes us." And off we go in the spirit of poetic lightness, taking one thing as something else altogether, just to see where the metaphor leads. But there comes a point where the path ends, or at least becomes too indistinct to follow. As I. A. Richards emphasized, "There is no whole to any analogy, we use as much of it as we need; and, if we tactlessly take any analogy too far, it breaks down."[27] This is what Frost (and Tversky) warned against—the danger of being fooled by a metaphor.

A difficult question is how a receptive but critical reader is to negotiate between the willing suspension of disbelief and the need to recognize a metaphor's limits. This is where the coherence principle plays an important role. In a good science fiction story, much of what is true of the actual world no longer holds, but the imaginary world has its own internal coherence. Similarly, a metaphor invites us to see one thing as another, but some type of coherence is supposed to emerge from this new vision. Furthermore, if one ventures to transport some perceived poetic truth back to the actual world, all the constraints of this world become relevant in evaluating whether a literal truth has been discovered.

As I was perusing the internet looking for information about "At Woodward's Gardens," I came across a website where it was argued that Frost's parable warns against the use of medical knowledge to invent birth control pills. It seems the analogy being drawn was that the benign use of a burning-glass is like medical knowledge, and its misuse to torment caged animals is like creating a contraceptive device. But regardless of one's attitude to birth control, this proposed mapping is nonsensical. A burning-glass is a piece of technology, not a form of abstract knowledge. Birth control pills are also a technological innovation. But unlike the boy's burning-glass, birth control pills were not created for one purpose and then used for another—contraception was their intended function in the first place. This reader's interpretation seems to simply take a prior belief—"contraception is bad"—and identify it with the bad act described in the poem, without any serious attempt to build a coherent overall mapping. The result looks like miseducation by poetry.

The critical evaluation of metaphors is particularly important for those who might wish to follow Bodkin's suggested path of science—from metaphor to mathematical model.[28] As a metaphor moves from the realm of poetry—"the sun pours down like honey"—into that of science—"light and fluids both propagate by wave motion"—it must be refined into a tighter, less emotional, more coherent conception. Much is lost, and much gained.

In present-day America the norms of objective truth are under constant attack. Competing ideologies are replacing any sense of a shared reality. People are all too willing to suspend disbelief—in preposterous claims that no conceivable evidence could manage to debunk. The coherence principle has been debased into blind faith in entrenched preconceptions. In political discourse, the cooperative principle has been replaced by the assumption that those who disagree with us are bald-faced liars. Empathy is reserved for those who belong to the right tribe.

Of all the remedies that might be proposed for the current retreat from the ideals of the Enlightenment, few would appear less credible than education by poetry. But there we have it—critical thinking, imagination, empathy—intertwined within wordplay that activates some of the same neural circuitry as music. Reason is a hallmark of human intelligence, but without imagination and emotion it feels dry and lifeless. Imagination and emotion kindle a kind of magic in our inner experience, but magical thinking run amok sinks to folly soon enough. So—read poetry, and find your ratio of reason to magic.

———

I began this book aiming to say something approximately right, rather than precisely wrong, about metaphor in poetry. I hope I've managed that much, but I'm keenly aware that many mysteries still surround metaphor and its connections to the mind, the brain, and poetry. Metaphor, like the gossamer threads that Whitman's spider was flinging into empty space, aims to establish a first connection between regions previously separate. If the threads catch, if the ductile anchor holds, the task of weaving a web still remains.

The spider's web is another metaphor, perhaps several. However dense the weave, the web creates not a wall but a net, with spaces that let light pass through it. Earlier we encountered a passage from Coleridge (end of chapter 4) that seemed to anticipate Whitman: "On St. Herbert's Island, I saw a spider with most beautiful legs, floating in the air on his back by a single thread which he was spinning out." This beautiful spider was Coleridge just past thirty, throwing out his "hints and first thoughts." By the time Coleridge was in his midfifties, suffering from depression and a worsening opium addiction, the spider he saw was darker: "As we advance in years, the World, that *spidery* Witch, spins its threads narrower and narrower, still closing in on us, till at last it shuts us up ... and well if there be sky-lights, and a small opening left for the Light from above."[29]

Two centuries on, we still need that small opening. Let Leonard Cohen leave us with a benediction:

> Ring the bells that still can ring
> Forget your perfect offering
> There is a crack, a crack in everything
> That's how the light gets in.[30]

3. The entire poem is available at https://www.poetryfoundation.org/poems-and -poets/poems/detail/43347 (also see the opening of chapter 13).

4. The entire poem is available at https://www.poemhunter.com/poem/counting -the-mad.

5. The quote is from Nagel (1986, p. 3).

6. I later discovered that this name is shared with a short story by Ryūnosuke Akutagawa, published a century ago. The story is a parable in which the Buddha offers a spider's thread to a sinner as a chance for redemption—a line that lets him try to pull himself up out of hell to paradise. See https://isistatic.org/journal-archive/ ma/01_02/ryunosuke.pdf.

7. The quote is from Kierkegaard (1843/1971); for the reminding I thank Dušan Stamenković.

Chapter 3

1. This poem was written in 1959. All lines from "Metaphors" are from *Crossing the Water* (1971) by Sylvia Plath. Published by Faber and Faber Ltd. Copyright © 1960 by Ted Hughes. Reprinted by permission of HarperCollins Publishers, USA, and by permission of publishers Faber and Faber Ltd. in all other territories.

2. The quote is from Aristotle's *Poetics* (c. 335 BCE).

3. The quote is from an article by Michael Lewis, "A Bitter Ending: Daniel Kahneman, Amos Tversky, and the Limits of Collaboration," in *The Chronicle of Higher Education*, January 29, 2017, https://www.chronicle.com/article/A-Bitter-Ending/ 238990?key=.

4. See the concluding paragraphs of *Tractatus Logico-Philosophicus* (1922).

5. A classic treatment of ambiguity is that of William Empson (1930), a student of I. A. Richards. Also see Ullmann (1962/1979, chap. 7) and Tuggy (1993).

6. The poem is available at https://www.poetryfoundation.org/poems-and-poets/ poems/detail/45087.

7. The terms *target* and *source* correspond to what Richards (1936) called the *tenor* and *vehicle* of a metaphor. Although Richards's terms often appear in discussions of metaphor, I adopt the terms more commonly used in psychological work on analogy (Gick & Holyoak, 1980), as well as in discussions of metaphor from the perspective of cognitive linguistics (e.g., Lakoff, 1987; Lakoff & Turner, 1989).

8. Although amazingly little is known with any certainty about the life of Shakespeare, there is a serious possibility that Sonnet 18 is addressed to a male (known only as the "Fair Youth"). Shakespeare was nonetheless married. Given the

connection between creativity and openness to experience (discussed in chapter 13), it would not be surprising if the greatest poet in the English language were bisexual.

9. See Wheelwright (1968, chap. 6).

10. The quote is from Ricœur (1977, p. 96).

11. See Zeki (2004).

12. These observations come from a lecture titled "The Metaphor" that the great Argentine writer delivered at Harvard in 1967, published in Borges (2000).

13. See Lakoff and Johnson (1980; also Johnson, 1987). The idea that many metaphors are commonly used in everyday communication was anticipated by Embler (1966, in the chapter "Metaphor in Everyday Speech") and by Reddy (1979). An even earlier forerunner was the Serbian mathematician Mihailo Petrović (1933/1967).

14. The quote is from Black (1979, p. 20).

15. Keysar et al. (2000) provided evidence from psycholinguistic experiments that words used with their conventional meanings do *not* routinely activate conceptual mappings in the process of being understood (see also Glucksberg & McGlone, 1999).

16. See Lakoff and Turner (1989; also Turner, 1987; Kövecses, 2009). Regarding the distinction between metaphorical and literal meaning, Lakoff and Turner generally favored the term *nonmetaphorical* over *literal*. In addition to metaphor, they also highlighted the importance of metonymy in thought and language.

17. For defenses of the psychological distinction between literal and metaphorical language, see Kittay (1987, especially pp. 19–22) and Stern (2000, pp. 176–187). Many literal word meanings have a metaphorical history (i.e., their current dictionary meaning arose from a metaphorical usage that later became conventional; Barfield, 1928/1964).

18. The concept of a concrete universal was developed by the German philosopher Hegel in his book *The Science of Logic*, first fully published in 1816.

19. Sartre's 1949 quotation is cited by Ullmann (1962/1979, p. 216).

20. Hugo's quote is from *Les Misérables* (1862).

21. Retrieved from https://www.theguardian.com/world/2009/feb/05/us-airways -crash-transcript.

22. For a broad discussion of distributed cognition see Hutchins (1995).

23. See Pinker (1994) for an engaging introduction to language and its acquisition.

24. The metaphor of *resonance* has often been applied to metaphor (e.g., Beardsley, 1958, p. 147; Black, 1979, p. 26; and much more recently, El Refaie, 2015). Ricœur

(1977, p. 215) used the term *reverberation* to express the same basic idea, which is also anticipated by Apter's (1982) conception of *cognitive synergy*.

25. The idea that metaphor involves a network of relationships was articulated by Goodman (1968, especially pp. 71–74), extending earlier suggestions by Richards (1936) and Black (1962a).

26. Theories of analogy use the term *mapping* in a way that roughly corresponds to what Black (1962a) called the *ground* of a metaphor.

27. For a review of research on analogical thinking as a general cognitive activity, see Holyoak (2012).

28. For a discussion see Kennedy (2008).

29. Gabrielle Starr (2013) provides an illuminating discussion of the similarities and differences among aesthetic responses to poetry, painting, and music.

Chapter 4

1. This poem, written in 1797, was downloaded from https://www.poetryfoundation.org/poems-and-poets/poems/detail/43991.

2. See Black (1962a, p. 27).

3. Important exceptions include Turner (1987), Lakoff and Turner (1989), Gibbs (1994), and Miall (2006).

4. The details of Coleridge's life and work are largely drawn from the two-volume biography by Holmes (1989, 1998) and from a biography of Dorothy Wordsworth by Wilson (2008).

5. This quote from Coleridge appears in a letter to William Godwin dated November 19, 1801, retrieved from http://inamidst.com/coleridge/letters/letter422.

6. The quote from Wordsworth appears in Wilson (2008, p. 85).

7. The quote from William Hazlitt appears in the 1875 article "William Hazlitt" in *Littell's Living Age*, Vol. 125, p. 261 (Boston: Littell and Gay).

8. The quote is from Aristotle's *Poetics* (c. 335 BCE).

9. A recent critic observed that "the egomania of Wordsworth exalts his own poetic mind over any other source of splendor" (Bloom, 1994, p. 28).

10. As an aside, Coleridge never met Percy Shelley, though he did meet Byron and Keats. However, Shelley was very familiar with Coleridge's writings, which had a considerable influence on his own famous essay on poetry (Shelley, 1821/1840).

11. The quote is from Richards (1924/1948, p. 140).

12. The quote is from Coleridge, dated July 12, 1827, appearing in *Specimens of the Table Talk of S. T. Coleridge*, retrieved from http://www.gutenberg.org/ebooks/8489. Though Coleridge used the phrase to characterize an ideal for a poem, it arguably applies to any kind of good literary writing, prose as well as poetry. Writing is described as "poetic" when it uses compressed symbolic language to evoke ideas and emotions. The nebulous border between prose and poetry is like that between freezing drizzle and snow—see Howard Nemerov's poem that serves as the epigraph for this book.

13. The quote is from a letter from Coleridge to John Thelwall dated December 17, 1796, retrieved from https://archive.org/details/cu31924104096536.

14. This quote is from Coleridge (1817).

15. The quote is from Richards (1924/1948, p. 131).

16. This quote is from Eliot's essay "The Music of Poetry" (1942; included in Eliot, 1957, p. 31).

17. This quote is from Richards (1936, p. 94).

18. The quote is from Coleridge (1817).

19. This term appears in Coleridge (1817).

20. The quote is from Coleridge (1817).

21. This quote is from Coleridge, appearing in *The Friend, I*, p. 451 (1809–1810).

22. The quote that follows is from a letter to James Gillman in 1827 (quoted by Hawkes, 1972, pp. 54–55). The word *syntaxis* is an archaic form of *syntax*.

23. The origin of this saying is unknown.

24. New Criticism as it developed in America was related to an earlier movement termed Russian Formalism. For a comprehensive anthology of papers illustrating different perspectives on literary criticism, see Rivkin and Ryan (2017).

25. This chapter title appears in Richards (1924/1948).

26. See Richards (1929). For a brief review of later psychological studies of how people actually read poems, see Goodblatt (2001).

27. See Hardcastle (2005).

28. This quote is from Richards (1924/1948, p. 181).

29. See Ogden and Richards (1923/1989).

30. The quote is from Richards (1936, p. 131).

31. See Goodblack and Glicksohn (2010).

32. The most detailed discussion appears in Richards (1936, chaps. 6–7).

33. The quote is from Richards (1936, p. 119). Richards used the terms *tenor* and *vehicle*, for which I have substituted *target* and *source* (terms from the literature on analogy).

34. The quote that follows is from Goodman (1968, p. 80).

35. See Black (1962a, 1962b, 1979).

36. The quote is from Black (1962a, p. 37).

37. This phrase is a chapter title in Richards (1936).

38. The quote is from Black (1962b, pp. 236–237).

39. See Black (1979, pp. 22–23).

40. This quote is from Black (1962a, p. 43).

41. For discussions of the terms *focus, frame,* and *strong metaphor,* see Black (1979). Bloom (2011) discusses his related notion of inevitability.

42. See Goodman (1968, especially pp. 71–80).

43. Eliot's remarks, written in 1929, appear in Eliot, Dickey, Formichelli, & Schuchard (2015, pp. 704–705). The term *allegory* has suffered from being linked to particularly heavy-handed displays of metaphorical correspondences, notably in older works with Christian themes. The classic example is *Pilgrim's Progress*, where the main character, who metaphorically represents the followers of Christ, is named "Christian." I use the term more broadly to refer to extended metaphors, especially those that involve narrative. This more general sense has a long tradition in literary criticism (for example, see Fletcher, 1964).

44. Eliot's poem is available at https://www.poetryfoundation.org/poetrymagazine/poems/detail/44212.

45. This passage from Coleridge's notebooks was written in 1803, appearing in *Anima Poetae* (p. 32). It was retrieved from https://archive.org/details/animapoetae from00colegoog.

Chapter 5

1. This poem is from Koon Woon's collection *Water Chasing Water* (2013). Copyright © 2013 by Koon Woon. Reprinted with permission of the author.

2. The quote is from Paul Ricœur (1977, p. 195).

3. A notable contribution to this field was a book by Maud Bodkin (1934), which emphasized insights arising from the theories of Freud and especially Jung. My use

of "Ancient Mariner" as an analogy for the idealized Poet and Reader was inspired by Bodkin's discussion of that poem.

4. The quote is from James (1892).

5. Coleridge's poem is available at https://www.poetryfoundation.org/poems-and -poets/poems/detail/43997.

6. Of course, the Guest was actually a listener, and indeed poetry began and continues as an oral tradition, but reading dominates in the literate world.

7. See Sikora, Kuiken, and Miall (2011).

8. The quote is from an entry in her journal from 1958 (Plath, 2000, p. 444).

9. See Thrash et al. (2017).

10. The quotation is from Bloom (2011, p. 28), who in turn acknowledges Barfield (1928/1964, appendix I) for describing consciousness as the fundamental material underlying the creation of poetry.

11. See James (1892).

12. Psychological evidence indicates that psychological distance increases when we imagine ourselves to be further away from something in time or space, or place ourselves in some imagined counterfactual situation. Moreover, psychological distance is correlated both with distinct patterns of neural responses and variations in cognitive judgments and emotional responses. For an overview of "construal-level theory," see Trope and Liberman (2010).

13. Recent research indicates that cognition and emotion are closely coupled at both the behavioral and the neural level (see Ellsworth, 2013; Pessoa & Pereira, 2013).

14. Nelson Goodman (1968) discusses variations in syntactic and semantic "density" across different types of representations used in art and in language.

15. In contrast, compositional semantics is concerned with the meanings of larger linguistic units, such as sentences. For an overview of classical linguistic analyses of semantics, see Ullmann (1962/1979).

16. Key writings on the pragmatics of language include Austin (1962), Grice (1957, 1975, 1989), and Searle (1975). For an overview, see Clark (1996).

17. See Grice (1975).

18. See especially Grice (1957).

19. Goodman (1968) argues that metaphor expresses meaning in a more continuous manner than does literal language—more akin to a picture (though not necessarily visual). This is why rich metaphors resist being fully paraphrased.

20. This quote is from Cohen (2008, p. 1).

21. The *Book of Odes* (*Shijing*) is a classic compendium of poetry composed between roughly 1100 and 600 BCE. The quoted passage is taken from Kao and Mei (1978, p. 319).

Chapter 6

1. This poem is from *New and Collected Poems: 1975–2015* (2016). Copyright © 2016 by Jay Parini. Reprinted with permission of Beacon Press, Boston.

2. This quote is from Eliot (1928, p. x).

3. The quote is from Kounios and Beeman (2015, p. 9).

4. The collection is by Cohen (1993).

5. For detailed examples and analyses of types of conceptual blending see Turner (1996) and Fauconnier (1997).

6. The quote is from his 1948 essay "The Effects of Analogy," which appears in Stevens (1951, pp. 117–118). Max Black (1962b) and Mary Hesse (1963) describe how analogy relates to the concept of models, which is central to science. Analogy and metaphor are salient varieties of what Arthur Koestler (1964) called *bisociation*, a concept he viewed as fundamental to creativity. Literary theorists influenced by Jungian psychology have related analogy to archetypal patterns in literature. Joseph Campbell (1949) wrote a classic treatment of myths as archetypal patterns. Northrup Frye examined the role of analogy in literature in his essay "Archetypal Criticism: Theory of Myths" (in Frye, 1957; also see Bodkin, 1934, and Fletcher, 1964). Holyoak (1982) explored connections between work on analogy within the modern tradition of cognitive science and the interpretation of literature.

7. The quote is from Tate (1953, p. 78).

8. The quote is from Black (1962a, p. 42).

9. For a general introduction to the concept of psychological coherence, see Thagard (2000); for discussion of the role of coherence in analogical reasoning, see Holyoak and Thagard (1995).

10. The initial studies were conducted by Gick and Holyoak (1980, 1983). For a review of psychological studies of analogy and similar forms of relational reasoning, see Holyoak (2012).

11. See Duncker (1945).

12. This idea was proposed by Gick and Holyoak (1980). Our subsequent study (Gick & Holyoak, 1983) provided the first experimental demonstration that comparing multiple examples of story problems to one another promotes acquisition of a

more abstract schema, which in turn increases spontaneous transfer to further new cases that fit the schematized pattern. Many later studies have confirmed this basic finding (e.g., Catrambone & Holyoak, 1989; Loewenstein, Thompson, & Gentner, 2003).

13. Thagard and Shelley (2001) discussed the emotional impact of analogies, and Goode, Dahl, and Moreau (2010) provided experimental evidence that emotional analogies can influence consumer decisions. People's commonsense understanding of the political analogy between Saddam Hussein and Hitler was investigated by Spellman and Holyoak (1992).

14. Syntactic constraints (also called *structural constraints*) were emphasized by Gentner (1983). Syntactic constraints support an approximate isomorphism between two representations: elements that play parallel roles in corresponding propositions should map to one another, ideally in a one-to-one fashion (Holland, Holyoak, Nisbett, & Thagard, 1986). Holyoak (1985) posited the importance of pragmatic constraints that focus attention on important elements of the analogs. Holyoak and Thagard (1989) proposed a computational model in which the three types of constraints work together within a constraint network. Spellman and Holyoak (1996) experimentally investigated the joint effects of multiple types of constraints. The three types are discussed more extensively by Holyoak and Thagard (1995).

15. A classic introduction to artificial neural networks that have the properties of constraint networks is provided by Rumelhart, McClelland, and the PDP Research Group (1986).

16. For an overview, see Holyoak (2012).

17. For a demonstration of implicit analogy operating in problem solving, see Schunn and Dunbar (1996).

18. The classic demonstration of semantic priming is due to Meyer and Schvaneveldt (1971).

19. See Spellman, Holyoak, and Morrison (2001; also Estes & Jones, 2006, 2009; Mather, Jones, & Estes, 2014; Popov & Hristova, 2017). Relational priming is closely related to conceptual combination (see below).

20. Kintsch and van Dijk (1978) developed a theory of how coherence operates in story understanding.

21. For an overview of work on the role of story coherence in jury decision making, see Pennington and Hastie (1993). Holyoak and Simon (1999) showed how coherence shifts arise in the course of making decisions about legal cases, and Simon (2012) discusses how coherence-based reasoning influences actual decision making in courts of law.

22. For evidence of coherence shifts in everyday decision making, see Simon, Krawczyk, and Holyoak (2004). Russo (2014) provides a general review of how preferences are constructed on the fly as decisions are being made.

23. Holyoak and Powell (2016) review evidence that people's moral judgments involve coherence-based reasoning.

24. The role of coherence in aesthetic judgments was emphasized by Beardsley (1958).

25. Many researchers have made important contributions to understanding conceptual combination, as well as related mental activities such as judging similarity and forming new concepts. Major early papers include those by Greg Murphy (1988) and by Edward Wisniewski and colleagues (Wisniewski & Gentner, 1991; Wisniewski & Love, 1998; Wisniewski & Bassok, 1999), as well as by Gagne and Shoben (1997). For an overview of work on this and related topics, see Murphy (2002).

26. Medin and Shoben (1988) showed that people consider gray more similar to black for cloud color but more similar to white for hair color.

27. Papers on property-based and relation-based interpretations of noun-noun combinations include Wisniewski and Love (1998) and Bassok and Medin (1997).

28. Simmons and Estes (2008) found such individual differences in a task requiring similarity judgments.

29. Lynott and Connell (2010) showed that prosody influences conceptual combination for noun-noun pairs. Their experiments also demonstrated that most individuals generate a mix of property-based and relation-based interpretations (for different examples).

30. Their theory of how conceptual combination is guided by coherence constraints is described in papers by Costello and Keane (2000, 2001).

31. This poem is the most important surviving work of literature in Old English. The quote is from a translation by Seamus Heaney (2000).

32. Evidence that conceptual combination does not necessitate full-blown analogical reasoning is summarized by Keane and Costello (2001). Estes and Glucksberg (2000) describe how property transfer could be achieved by a relatively simple cognitive process.

Chapter 7

1. This poem by the renowned nineteenth-century American poet was retrieved from https://www.poemhunter.com/poem/the-brain-is-wider-than-the-sky.

2. A special case of metonymy in which a part is used to refer to the whole (e.g., "gray beard" for an older man) is termed *synecdoche*. For a discussion of the relationship between metaphor and metonymy, see Lodge (1977, part 2).

3. I can only sketch the barest outline of the complexities that arise in understanding the human brain and how it supports thinking and feeling. A good preliminary introduction is the online resource *Brain Facts* (2012), published by the Society for Neuroscience (http://www.brainfacts.org/about-neuroscience/brain-facts-book). For an overview with a more detailed discussion of the methods used to study the neural basis for thinking, see Morrison and Knowlton (2012).

4. For an interesting neuropsychological study on this topic, see Johnstone et al. (2012).

5. This estimate is taken from a paper by Herculano-Houzel (2009). In addition to neurons, *glial* cells (which do not communicate via electrical impulses) also play important roles in memory and cognition (see Fields et al., 2014).

6. This process is called Hebbian learning, first proposed by the psychologist Donald Hebb (1949), who coined the rhyming adage. For a general overview, including limitations of Hebbian learning, see McClelland (2006).

7. For an overview see Beversdorf (2013).

8. For example, see Lombardo et al. (2011).

9. This quote is from the preface to *Lyrical Ballads* (2nd ed., 1800), retrieved from http://www.online-literature.com/wordsworth/lyrical-ballads-vol1.

10. See, for example, a study by Just et al. (2010).

11. The best evidence for the role of the anterior temporal lobe as a semantic hub comes from studies of patients who suffer from degenerative brain damage in that area. These people have serious problems in understanding word meanings (for a review see Patterson et al., 2007). A study by Peelen and Caramazza (2012) focuses on the role of the anterior temporal lobe in processing more abstract aspects of word meanings.

12. For a good overview of research on the functions of the rostrolateral PFC, see Burgess and Wu (2013).

13. See Semendeferi et al. (2001).

14. For an overview and interpretation of the role of the rostrolateral PFC and its associated networks in analogical reasoning, see Knowlton et al. (2012).

15. See Aichelburg et al. (2016).

16. For reviews see Beeman and Chiarello (1998) and Jung-Beeman (2005).

17. For a broad review of what is known about the neural underpinnings of the pragmatic functions of language, including metaphor comprehension, see Stemmer (2017).

18. A classic study was performed by Brownell et al. (1990).

19. The coarse-coding hypothesis was described by Beeman and Chiarello (1998).

20. For a general introduction to the cognitive neuroscience of creativity, see Kounios and Beeman (2015). Kasparian (2013) provides a nuanced review of the roles played by the two hemispheres in different tasks involving comprehension of metaphors and other figurative expressions.

21. For evidence of the role of the alpha frequency band in creative thinking, see Lustenberger et al. (2015).

22. For an overview see Duncan (2010). For evidence of the involvement of the rostrolateral PFC in both analogical reasoning and retrieval of episodic memories, see Westphal et al. (2016).

23. See Zanto and Gazzaley (2013).

24. Finn et al. (2015) report a study linking the connectivity of the frontoparietal network to levels of what is called *fluid* intelligence—the ability to reason about novel situations.

25. For evidence see Silvia and Beaty (2012) and Beaty and Silvia (2013).

26. For an overview see Buckner et al. (2008).

27. See Gusnard et al. (2001).

28. For discussions of these functions of the medial PFC, see Kouneiher et al. (2009) and Passingham et al. (2010).

29. See Vessel et al. (2013).

30. Smallwood et al. (2011) report evidence that spontaneous thinking is accompanied by reduced attention to perceptual inputs.

31. This quote from Hugo appears in Bachelard (1969, p. 12).

32. The quote is from Poe's story "Eleonora" (1848/1975, p. 645).

33. Oliver (1994) describes some of the activities that can foster the writing of poems.

34. This study was conducted by Oppezzo and Schwartz (2014). An important footnote on their findings: you have to actually *walk* outdoors to get the greatest benefit—being rolled along in a wheelchair isn't enough.

35. See Christoff et al. (2009), Smallwood et al. (2011), and Beaty et al. (2016) for discussions of how the control and default networks may cooperate to guide internally directed thought. Westphal et al. (2016) present evidence that the two networks also cooperate when people try to recall memories tied to specific contexts.

36. Giambra (1995) was the first to point out that people often consciously decide to initiate mind wandering.

Chapter 8

1. This poem is from Mary Oliver's collection *Why I Wake Early* (2004). Copyright © 2004 by Mary Oliver. Reprinted by permission of the Charlotte Sheedy Literary Agency Inc.

2. In an elaboration of the discussion in this chapter, Holyoak and Stamenković (2018) present a detailed assessment of psychological theories of metaphor comprehension.

3. For those interested in finding examples of metaphors, for research or other purposes, a number of good sources are included in the bibliography. For examples of literary metaphors, see Katz et al. (1988), Sommer and Weiss (1996), Turner (1987), and Lakoff and Turner (1989). For other types of examples, sources include Cardillo et al. (2010), Dancygier and Sweetser (2014), Gentner and Clement (1988), Knowles and Moon (2006), and Lakoff and Johnson (1980).

4. This metaphor (doubtless intended to amuse psychology nerds) comes courtesy of Cardillo et al. (2010).

5. For work on the emotional impact of literary reading see Oatley (1994, 2016) and Miall and Kuiken (2002). Bohrn et al. (2013) examine the neural correlates of aesthetic judgments about proverbs.

6. These famous lines conclude "The Road Not Taken." Retrieved from https://www.poetryfoundation.org/resources/learning/core-poems/detail/44272.

7. For a version of the alternative "literal first" view, see Searle (1979).

8. This study was reported by Glucksberg, Gildea, and Bookin (1982).

9. An important early study on the role of context in metaphor comprehension was reported by Ortony et al. (1978).

10. For relevant evidence see Blasko and Connine (1993).

11. Ortony et al. (1978) were early proponents of this view; also see Giora (1997).

12. It might also be noted that, almost universally, modern researchers have *not* traced their views to Coleridge (but see Kittay, 1987, for one of the scholarly exceptions).

13. These are the opening lines of "Fern Hill," retrieved from https://www.poets .org/poetsorg/poem/fern-hill.

14. See Tourangeau and Sternberg (1981, 1982) and Gentner and Clement (1988).

15. See Glucksberg and Keysar (1990) and Kintsch (2000).

16. See Bowdle and Gentner (2005).

17. For example, Gentner et al. (2001) use the terms *comparison* and *alignment* (the process of finding relational correspondences) interchangeably in claiming that analogy provides the primary basis for metaphor. Glucksberg (2003) appears to accept this equivalence (though he argues for an alternative theory of metaphor processing). In priming experiments, Wolff and Gentner (2000) showed that early metaphor processing is symmetrical across the source and target roles. They argued on this basis that metaphor processing must begin with comparison, and hence alignment. However, this interpretation ignores the possibility that comparison may occur without alignment. In fact, evidence suggests that in making speeded similarity judgments, early comparison does *not* make use of relational correspondences (Goldstone & Medin, 1994).

18. For evidence of remarkably sophisticated comparisons by honeybees, see Avarguès-Weber and Giurfa (2013).

19. For a review of evidence that high-level relational reasoning is a specifically human ability, see Penn, Holyoak, and Povinelli (2008).

20. For evidence concerning the time course of relational processing, see Goldstone and Medin (1994) and Kroger, Holyoak, and Hummel (2004).

21. Waltz et al. (1999) provided evidence that reasoning with multiple relations is severely impaired by damage to the prefrontal cortex. Knowlton et al. (2012) sketch a neural model of analogical reasoning.

22. Vartanian (2012) and Hobeika et al. (2016) report careful meta-analyses of neuroimaging studies of analogy that support this conclusion. One of the best-controlled studies was performed by Bunge et al. (2009).

23. This study was reported by Green et al. (2012; also see Green et al., 2010). For a more general discussion of the role of the rostrolateral PFC in creative cognition, see Green (2016). Green et al. (2017) report evidence that electrical stimulation of this brain area can help people find creative solutions to verbal analogy problems.

24. A neuroimaging study of conceptual combination was reported by Baron et al. (2010).

25. These meta-analyses of metaphor processing were reported by Bohrn et al. (2012), Rapp et al. (2012), and Vartanian (2012).

26. This famous nonevent is from the short story "Silver Blaze" by Sir Arthur Conan Doyle.

27. For a study directed at metaphor production, see Benedek et al. (2014).

28. This hypothesis was initially proposed (Bowdle & Gentner, 2005) based in part on evidence that for novel metaphors, people prefer the simile form ("A mind is like a kitchen") over the corresponding nominal form ("A mind is a kitchen"), whereas the preferred form reverses for conventional metaphors ("Faith is [like] an anchor"). Bowdle and Gentner argued that since similes highlight comparison, and (contrary to our earlier discussion) comparison is equivalent to analogical mapping, this preference reversal implies that analogy is used for novel metaphors. However, later work by Jones and Estes (2006) showed that the changes in preferred form were due to a confounding between novelty and aptness. A more compelling interpretation of the evidence is that people prefer the nominal form for *apt* metaphors. It is simply the case that conventional metaphors in everyday use tend to be better (more apt) than novel ones constructed for use in psychology experiments. For further discussion, see Glucksberg and Haught (2006).

29. This study was reported by Cardillo et al. (2012).

30. This finding is consistent with predictions based on a proposal by Giora (1997).

31. For an early demonstration of the role played by the rostrolateral PFC in solving nonverbal problems that require integration of multiple relations, see Christoff et al. (2001).

32. An early version of this computational approach to word meaning was Latent Semantic Analysis (Landauer & Dumais, 1997). A more recent algorithm for extracting meaning vectors from large text corpora is Word2vec (Mikolov, Yih, & Zweig, 2013). Some work has been done on learning relations from pairs of words represented using such vectors (Lu et al., 2012).

33. The model is described by Kintsch (2000; see also Kintsch, 2001, as well as Kintsch & Bowles, 2002).

34. For discussions of metaphorical asymmetries, see Ortony (1979) and Glucksberg and Keysar (1990).

35. This interference effect was demonstrated by McGlone and Manfredi (2001). Interestingly, priming irrelevant information in the target did *not* slow down processing of the metaphor (another example of target-source asymmetry). See also Glucksberg, McGlone, and Manfredi (1997).

36. See Gernsbacher, Keysar, Robertson, and Werner (2001).

37. The example is due to Gibbs (1994, p. 215).

38. For evidence see Chiappe and Chiappe (2007).

39. Holyoak (1982) discussed how analogy relates to extended metaphors and literary interpretation in general.

40. For a discussion of the binding problem and its implications for computational models of analogical reasoning, see Doumas and Hummel (2012) and Halford et al. (1998, 2014).

41. The linguist Samuel Levin (1977) proposed a theory of metaphor based on property transfer, somewhat similar in spirit to Kintsch's model. Interestingly, Levin noted (p. 103) that his theory is unable to explain metaphors of Aristotle's proportional type. Likewise, Kintsch (2000, p. 264) acknowledged the limitations of his model as an account of literary metaphors. Without analogy, it is possible to go a considerable distance toward understanding metaphor, but that road ends well short of the intended destination.

42. For general overviews, see Gentner (2010), Halford, Wilson, and Phillips (2010), and Holyoak (2012).

43. Examples include LISA (*Learning and Inference with Schemas and Analogies*; see Hummel & Holyoak, 1997, 2003) and DORA (*Discovery Of Relations by Analogy*; Doumas, Hummel, & Sandhofer, 2008).

44. Kintsch and van Dijk (1978) proposed a model of text coherence. For evidence that analogical reasoning using texts proceeds in sequential pieces, guided by text coherence, see Kubose, Holyoak, and Hummel (2002).

45. The term *coupling* was introduced by Levin (1962) in his analysis of linguistic structures that operate in poetry. As we will see in chapter 9, couplings can be generated by phonological similarities of words as well as by parallels between their positions within a poem.

46. This version is in modern English, with line breaks added. The entire "Meditation XVII" can be found at http://www.online-literature.com/donne/409.

Chapter 9

1. Du Fu, one of the greatest Chinese poets, lived during the Tang dynasty. My translation appears in a bilingual selection of poems by Du Fu and his equally illustrious contemporary, Li Bai (Holyoak, 2007).

2. Valéry draws this analogy in his essay "Poetry and Abstract Thought" (Valéry, 1958, p. 70).

3. This is the final line of "Among School Children" by Yeats.

4. The primacy of meaning or "gist" relative to verbatim wording in memory for prose has been demonstrated in many psychological experiments (e.g., Bransford & Franks, 1971; Sachs, 1967; Sulin & Dooling, 1974).

5. See Apter (1982).

6. For experimental evidence that people remember the exact words more accurately for poetry than ordinary prose, see Tillman and Dowling (2007) and Lea et al. (2008). Of course, literary prose can also produce highly memorable and quotable phrases and sentences. Consider the opening of Tolstoy's *Anna Karenina*: "All happy families are alike; each unhappy family is unhappy in its own way."

7. These lines begin Dylan Thomas's poem of the same name, which is included in his collected poems (Thomas, 1971).

8. Winifred Nowottny (1962) wrote a classic book on language as it is used in poetry. More recent general discussions of poetry and the constraints that govern it include those by Oliver (1994), Steele (1999), Parini (2008), and Gioia (2016). Parts of this section are adapted from Holyoak (2006).

9. The quote is from Yeats's essay "The Symbolism of Poetry" (in Yeats, 1903, p. 243).

10. For more detailed discussion of this example, see Oliver (1994, pp. 19–24).

11. For a general introduction to universals of poetry, with a focus on the role of meter, see Turner and Pöppel (1983).

12. For an experimental demonstration see Obermeier et al. (2013).

13. The entire poem (written around 1851) can be found at https://www.poetry foundation.org/poems-and-poets/poems/detail/43588.

14. This study was conducted by Hannon and Johnson (2005).

15. A study by Escoffier, Herrmann, and Schirmer (2015) provides relevant evidence.

16. For a discussion of work on neural synchrony (very rapid rhythmic brain activity) as it relates to sensory awareness, see Engel and Singer (2001).

17. This study was conducted by Foster and Valentine (2001).

18. The quote is from Yeats (1903, p. 247).

19. This quote by Eliot is from his essay "Reflections on *vers libres*," first published in *The New Statesman* (1917); available at https://www.newstatesman.com/culture/culture/2013/05/t-s-eliot-reflections-vers-libre.

20. For an illuminating discussion of the development of contemporary poetic styles, see Steele (1990).

21. This quote is from "The Music of Poetry" (1942; included in Eliot, 1957, p. 31).

22. The quote is from Oliver (1994, p. 10).

23. The *almost* sets aside poems based on the visual arrangement of words on a page. I only refer to poetry based fundamentally on speech sounds (which, aggregated over the course of history, is virtually all of it).

24. For an overview of rhythm in poetry, especially free verse, see Hrushovski (1960).

25. This estimate has been defended by Cowan (2001) as a downward revision of the "magical number seven" proposed by Miller (1956).

26. See McGlone and Tofighbakhsh (2000).

27. See Rubin (1995).

28. The classic summary of Jakobson's view is as follows: *"The poetic function projects the principle of equivalence from the axis of selection into the axis of combination"* (Jakobson, 1960, p. 358; italics in original). In Jakobson's overarching approach (called *structural linguistics*), the structure of a sentence is treated as two axes. The axis of selection refers to a choice from among alternative words that might fill each grammatical position (e.g., the head noun might be *dog* rather than *cat*, which are in this sense "equivalent" as possible alternatives; similarly, *barked* and *jumped* would be among the alternative selections for the main verb). The axis of combination refers to the integration of the words selected for each position to form a grammatical and meaningful sentence. In poetry, Jakobson argues that nonsyntactic cues (notably, phonological properties such as meter, rhyme, and alliteration) create "equivalences" (or "couplings," to use the less misleading term introduced by Levin, 1962) between words occupying *different* positions within a sentence (or larger text).

29. The full poem is available at https://www.poets.org/poetsorg/poem/night -funeral-harlem.

30. The full poem, "Acquainted with the Night," is available at https://www. poemhunter.com/poem/acquainted-with-the-night/.

31. Kao and Mei (1978) discuss the role of historical allusions in classical Chinese poetry.

32. This example appears in Roethke (2006).

33. See, for example, Kao and Mei (1978). The translated lines, from Li Bai's poem "Sending Off a Friend," are discussed in their article (p. 289).

34. A book by Christine Brooke-Rose (1958) surveys the syntactic forms that metaphors can take in poetry (also see Perrine, 1971).

35. This poetic metaphor (the most used and abused example in the vast literature on the topic) is from *Romeo and Juliet* (act 2, scene 2). Other examples of metaphors presented here are from "The Thin Man" (Donald Justice), "The Voice of the Ancient Bard" (William Blake), "Endymion" (John Keats), "Blood and the Moon" (W. B.

Yeats), and "Sonnet VII" (John Milton). The lines by Tomas Tranströmer conclude "An Artist in the North" (Tranströmer, 1987, p. 86). This translation from the Swedish is by May Swenson.

36. The examples here are from "Absalom and Achitophel" (John Dryden), "The Thin Man" (Donald Justice), "The Tower" (W. B. Yeats), and "A Grief Ago" (Dylan Thomas).

37. For a very clear exposition of the form and meaning of this poem, see Hawkes (1967, pp. 200–202).

38. This quote is from Pound's essay "Elizabethan Classicists II" (Pound, 1917, p. 135). For a discussion of how Pound's translations of classical Chinese poetry influenced twentieth-century poetry in English, see Xie (1999).

39. See Bloom (2011).

40. See K. Holyoak (2012).

Chapter 10

1. This poem was written in 1919 and included in the poet's 1921 collection, *Michael Robartes and the Dancer*.

2. The quote is from an article by the reporter Nick Tabor (2015).

3. Yeats's key symbol was actually a "double gyre," similar in form to two cones with one inverted inside the other. His basic idea of an intertwined duality has much in common with the meaning of the yin-yang symbol (see chapter 1). Many books have been written about the origins of Yeats's poetic symbols, of which I have found that by Kathleen Raines (1986) to be particularly insightful. Yeats himself described his symbolic gyre in *A Vision* (1925), a barely readable prose effort to explain his system of poetic symbols. As summarized in a contemporary review, "The misapplication on this scale in the field of psychology and history of one of the first intellects of our time is probably the price that our time has to pay for the possession of a great poet" (Wilson, 1929). Take this example as a valuable caution— the bridge from poetry to psychology is perilous to cross (in either direction).

4. Useful discussions of symbols in classical Chinese poetry include articles by Cranmer-Byng (1917) and Kao and Mei (1978), as well as many works by the great scholar and translator Burton Watson (e.g., Watson, 1971).

5. For example, see Jung (1934/1953).

6. The quote is from Yeats's essay "Symbolism in Painting" (1903, p. 227; first published in 1898).

7. The quoted lines are from the lyrics of Bowie's 1969 song.

8. The quote is from Richards (1934/1962, p. 217).

9. This essay was written in 1901 and appears in Yeats (1903; the quotes are from p. 29).

10. This question has been addressed in great detail in a thoughtful book by James Olney (1980), who summarizes the points of correspondence between the views of Yeats and Jung (pp. 6–7). In a nutshell, Olney concludes that although the two knew of each other, they never met, and each developed his ideas independently of the other. However, a common cause can be identified: both the poet and the psychologist were influenced by the classical Platonic tradition in philosophy. Thus many minds indeed flowed into one another, primarily through the medium of books. Though the two men arrived at their remarkably similar positions separately, priority of publication goes to the poet. Yeats's essay "Magic" was written in 1901 and published in 1903, whereas Jung's notion of the collective unconscious was first introduced in 1912 (see Wimsatt & Brooks, 1957, p. 599n6).

11. The quote is from an essay by Jung originally published in 1933, reprinted in a book edited by Ghiselin (1952, p. 208).

12. Major works in the Jungian tradition related to the interpretation of literature include books by Bodkin (1934), Frye (1957), and Campbell (1949).

13. Common criticisms include that the approach embraces stereotypes of women (notably in Jung's concept of the *anima*), and that it fails to highlight how literature is influenced by history and culture. For a collection of papers that reconsider Jungian literary analysis, see the volume edited by Baumlin, Baumlin, and Jensen (2004).

14. Yeats made this point anecdotally in his essay "Magic" (Yeats, 1903). Jung proposed an elaborate theory of dream interpretation (Jung, 1948/1974).

15. The quote is from Frye (1957, p. 118).

16. This poem was first published in 1794 in the collection *Songs of Experience*, retrieved from https://www.poetryfoundation.org/poems-and-poets/poems/detail/43682.

17. The quoted lines are from his poem "Crazy Jane Talks with the Bishop," published in 1933. The entire poem is available at https://www.poetryfoundation.org/poems-and-poets/poems/detail/43295.

18. The quote is from an interview with Plath published in Orr (1966, p. 169).

19. I can't resist noting Harold Bloom's (2011) acerbic comment that all of Poe's writings are greatly improved by French translation. His opinion oddly complements Eliot's suggestion that Mallarmé is better read in English. It seems that despite all the risks involved, translation of poetry may sometimes yield benefits even for bilingual readers.

20. The original poem was first published in 1887. This translation from the French is by Henry Weinfield (Mallarmé, 1994, p. 42). Weinfield also provides an extensive commentary on Mallarmé's poetry, including this example (pp. 183–185). The present discussion is largely based on that of Weinfield.

21. The quotation is from Eliot's essay "The Music of Poetry," first published in 1942 (Eliot, 1957).

22. The famous line is from his *Poésies*, published in 1870.

23. This translation from the French is by Cicely Buckley (Éluard, 1995, p. 63). The original poem was first published in 1929.

24. This translation is by Buckley (Éluard, 1995, p. 151).

25. This is the second of a six-part sequence composed between 1921 and 1926 (Crane, 2001). Hart Crane, "Voyages: II," from *The Complete Poems of Hart Crane*, edited by Marc Simon. Copyright © 1933, 1958, 1966 by Liveright Publishing Corporation. Copyright © 1986 by Marc Simon. Used by permission of Liveright Publishing. For an erudite explication of the poem see Bloom (2004).

26. The quote from Hart Crane is from an article by Monroe and Crane (1929).

Chapter 11

1. This poem was written in 1945 (Hughes, 1994). "I, Too" is from *The Collected Poems of Langston Hughes*, Arnold Rampersad, Editor, with David Roessel, Associate Editor, copyright © 1994 by the Estate of Langston Hughes. Used by permission of Alfred A. Knopf, an imprint of the Knopf Doubleday Publishing Group, a division of Penguin Random House LLC. All rights reserved. Other rights by permission of Harold Ober Associates Incorporated.

2. This point was emphasized by Barfield (1928/1964). In basic sensation, sensory adaptation is ubiquitous across all modalities (for a review see Webster, 2012).

3. Indeed, as Starr (2013) points out, all experiences with art are events. Poetry and music unfold over time; eye movements over a painting or sculpture trace the shifting gaze of the viewer. Starr argues that the imagery of motion, broadly construed, is a central component of aesthetic experience.

4. The typical properties of oral versus written communications are described by Clark and Brennan (1991).

5. The full poem is available at https://www.poetryfoundation.org/poems-and-poets/poems/detail/44464.

6. This idea is from Mill's essay "What Is Poetry?," written in 1833 (https://www.uni-due.de/lyriktheorie/texte/1833_mill1.html).

7. The quote is from a lecture Borges gave in 1968 (Borges, 2000, p. 117).

8. For a translation of Du Fu's poem see K. Holyoak (2012, p. 30).

9. The theory of politeness is based on the work of Brown and Levinson (1978).

10. The entire poem is available at https://www.poetryfoundation.org/poems-and -poets/poems/detail/49303.

11. The imagery of "the sailors, caresses of Atlantic and Caribbean love" takes us back to Hart Crane's "Voyages: II," discussed at the end of chapter 10.

12. The entire poem is available at https://www.poetryfoundation.org/poems-and-poets/poems/detail/44477.

13. Rhetorical beauty at least contributes to the *appearance* of truth, in that aphorisms are judged as more credible if they rhyme (e.g., "Woes unite foes" carries a stronger punch than does "Troubles unite enemies"). This bias has been dubbed the "Keats heuristic" (McGlone & Tofighbakhsh, 1999).

14. This is part IV of the poem, which was first published in 1917. The entire poem is available at https://www.poemhunter.com/poem/thirteen-ways-of-looking-at-a -blackbird.

15. The discussion in this section, including the concept of poetic lightness, is largely based on Wheelwright (1968). Wheelwright argued forcefully against an idea associated with I. A. Richards (1929), who seemed to deny that poetry can make meaningful assertions.

16. In fact, there have been serious academic discussions regarding the closely related question of whether simplicity (akin to beauty) necessarily corresponds to probability (akin to truth) as an organizational principle governing human perception (Chater, 1996).

17. The quote is from Starr (2013, p. 16).

18. This point was emphasized by Harap (1933).

19. The quote is from Wheelwright (1968, p. 192).

20. The quote is from Borges (2000, p. 31).

21. This is part II of his poem "Thirteen Ways of Looking at a Blackbird."

22. The quote is from Wilde's 1891 essay "The Truth of Masks."

Chapter 12

1. This translation from the original Polish is by Clare Cavanaugh. Adam Zagajewski, "Mysticism for Beginners," is from *Without End: New and Selected Poems*.

2. The quote that follows is taken from her essay "The Process of Making Poetry," first published in 1930 and reprinted in Ghiselin (1952, p. 110). Besides Lowell and Spender (see below), notable introspective accounts of the process of poetry composition include Edgar Allan Poe's (1846) discussion of his poem "The Raven," and a book by Paul Valéry (1958). I. A. Richards, who composed as well as criticized poetry, wrote an essay describing the origin of one of his poems (Richards, 1960). Fehrman (1980) discussed several case studies of the creative process involving well-known poets.

3. The quote is from a lecture that Borges gave in 1967 (Borges, 2000, p. 16).

4. The quote is from Spender's essay "The Making of a Poem," first published in 1946 and reprinted in Ghiselin (1952, p. 114).

5. The chapter title is a phrase from a novel by Samuel Johnson, *The History of Rasselas, Prince of Abissinia*, written in 1759.

6. For a broad discussion of what makes motivation intrinsic rather than extrinsic, see Kruglanski et al. (2018).

7. Love has been a consistent theme of poetry over the centuries, which surely has proved effective on occasion as an aid in seduction. For what it's worth, psychologists have recently shown that women (at least in China) rate photographs of men paired with a metaphor that compliments a woman's appearance as more attractive (Gao et al., 2017).

8. The quote is from a letter that Charles Bukowski wrote to John William Corrington, January 17, 1961 (Bukowski, 1995, p. 6).

9. For an excellent anthology of poetry by women over the course of history, see Barnstone and Barnstone (1992).

10. Coleridge drew this analogy in his *Biographia Literaria* (1817).

11. The full poem, written in 1939, can be found at https://www.poemhunter.com/poem/long-legged-fly.

12. For a scientific analysis of the motion of water striders and of tiny robots that emulate them, see Koh et al. (2015).

13. The quotes that follow are from Lowell's essay, reprinted in Ghiselin (1952, p. 110).

14. Many of the activities of the unconscious mind involve processes collectively referred to as "System 1." These processes are evolutionarily primitive and can lead to systematic biases in judgment and decision making (see Kahneman, 2011).

15. The classic statement is that of Wallas (1926).

16. This is a line from a poem called "All That Is Gold Does Not Glitter," which appears in *The Fellowship of the Ring* by J. R. R. Tolkien.

17. The quote is from Richards (1936, p. 125).

18. For evidence see Verhaeghen et al. (2014).

19. See Seli et al. (2016) for a discussion of differences between intentional and unintentional mind wandering.

20. This study of the relation between deliberate mind wandering and an aspect of mindfulness was reported by Seli, Carriere, and Smilek (2015).

21. See Smallwood (2013).

22. The literary theorist Owen Barfield discussed the oscillation of two modes of thinking involved in poetic creation, arguing that these oscillations can occur across a wide range of timescales. Barfield speculated that if the frequency of oscillation were to approach infinity, the poet would be "creating out of full self-consciousness" (1928/1964, p. 110).

23. See Schacter et al. (2007).

24. See Schooler et al. (2011). Baird et al. (2012) report that an incubation period is particularly effective when the person is assigned an undemanding task that permits mind wandering, rather than being required to perform a demanding task or allowed to simply rest.

25. This study was reported by Cai et al. (2009).

26. The quote is from Gaston Bachelard (1969, p. 63).

27. The classic psychoanalytic proposals are presented in Freud (1900/1980) and Jung (1948/1974). Lakoff (1997) discusses the connections between metaphor and dream symbols.

28. See for example Barrett (2001). Chapter 3 in her book describes a number of cases in which dreams appear to have contributed to literary creativity. For example, after the evening of ghost stories described in chapter 4, Mary Shelley had a dream that became the seed of *Frankenstein*.

29. This poem appears in Holyoak (2010).

30. For a review see Kounios and Beeman (2009).

31. One study (Liu et al., 2012) investigated the neural activity that accompanies improvisation of freestyle rap, a genre that combines elements of poetry and music. Here we describe a later study (Liu et al., 2015) that focused on the composition and revision of poetry by novices and experts.

32. For discussions of the importance of mental imagery in creative thinking, see Shepard (1978) and Starr (2013).

33. The quotes that follow are from Spender's essay (1946/1952, pp. 118, 115–116).

Chapter 13

1. "In a Dark Time," copyright © 1960 by Beatrice Roethke, Administratrix of the Estate of Theodore Roethke; from *The Collected Poems of Theodore Roethke* (1974). Used by permission of Doubleday, an imprint of the Knopf Doubleday Publishing Group, a division of Penguin Random House LLC. All rights reserved.

2. The quote is from an interview by Peter Orr (Orr, 1966, p. 172).

3. The quote is from an interview by Orr (1966, p. 106).

4. The quote is from an entry in her journal from 1958 (Plath, 2000, p. 442).

5. See Csikszentmihalyi (1990).

6. The quote is from Spender (1946/1952, p. 124).

7. See Ulrich et al. (2014).

8. See for example Lemogne et al. (2012).

9. The quote is from an entry in Plath's journal written in 1950 (Plath, 2000, p. 17).

10. Systematic study of writing as therapy was pioneered by Pennebaker (1997).

11. Her admonition is from a letter that Bishop wrote to Lowell on March 21, 1972; quoted by Kalstone (1989, p. 241).

12. As an example of work showing the detrimental impact of schizophrenia on metaphor comprehension, see Mossaheb et al. (2014).

13. This paper was first published as Nagel (1974). The day after I wrote this conjecture (that people could never intuit the inner experience of a bat, since we lack a sense of echolocation), I stumbled on a magazine article talking about the latest developments in the burgeoning field of neuroengineering. One current project involves using ultrasound to calculate the distance of objects and then vibrating a person's finger at different frequencies—generating a novel sense of echolocation! So, perhaps I'm simply wrong about the impossibility of appreciating the hypothetical poetry of superintelligent bats. We can no longer assume that the "human condition" is immutable (see chapter 14).

14. This study was reported by Kennet et al. (2014). Mednick (1962) was the first to propose that creativity involves finding remote associative connections.

15. The quote is from Richards (1924/1948, p. 181).

16. See for example DeYoung et al. (2012).

17. See a study by Kaufman et al. (2010).

18. See Watson (2003).

19. For suggestive evidence see Silvia and Beaty (2012).

20. For an investigation of the connection between apophenia and the tendency toward schizophrenia (schizotypy), see Fyfe et al. (2008).

21. The relationship of the dopamine system to personality traits is discussed by DeYoung (2013); the link to bipolar disorder by Ashok et al. (2017); and the link to schizotypy and schizophrenia by Brisch et al. (2014).

22. For detailed discussions of how openness and intelligence relate to each other and to creativity, see DeYoung et al. (2012, 2014).

23. See Kaufman et al. (2016).

24. For reviews of studies examining the linkage between creativity and various forms of mental illness across disciplines, see Simonton (2014) and Barrantes-Vidal (2014); for case studies of poets in particular see Kaufman (2001).

25. Critics have often warned that poetry should not be overly intellectual or explicitly philosophical. For example, Lewis (1946, p. 160) cautioned that "the long course of literary activity is strewn with the wreckages of artists lured to their doom by the siren songs of intellectual truth." For more on the nature of poetic truth, see chapter 11.

26. This is the title of a volume of collected poems by Norman Finkelstein (2016).

27. See Carson (2011).

28. For reviews of work relating creativity to mental illness, see Beaussart et al. (2014) and Fink et al. (2014).

29. Macaulay's quote is from his 1825 essay "Milton" (quoted by Wimsatt & Brooks, 1957, p. 414).

30. The quote is from Richards (1924/1948, p. 185).

31. However, it has been suggested that depression may have adaptive value as an extended analysis of personal problems (Andrews & Thomson, 2009).

32. The case of Nash was made famous by the biography *A Beautiful Mind* (Nassar, 1998) and a movie of the same title.

33. See Kaufman (2001).

34. The quote is from Plath (1963, p. 237).

35. The quote is from an entry in her journal from 1951 (Plath, 2000, pp. 49–50).

Chapter 14

1. The original Spanish version of this poem, composed after the poet visited the ancient Incan mountain fortress in 1943, was first published in 1946. Pablo Neruda, "Heights of Macchu Picchu: XII" ["Rise up and be born with me, brother"], from *The Essential Neruda: Selected Poems*. Translation copyright © 2004 by Mark Eisner. Reprinted with the permission of The Permissions Company, Inc., on behalf of City Lights Publishers, www.citylights.com.

2. The authenticity of this quote is undeniable, established beyond doubt by the wide range of successful people to whom it has been misattributed (Jean Giraudoux, Groucho Marx, and George Burns, to name a few). Doubtless all those who have stolen it have done so with the utmost sincerity, as have I.

3. See Trilling (1971).

4. The quote is from Wilde's 1891 essay "The Critic as Artist."

5. The quote is from Bloom (1994, p. 16).

6. For a cogent argument that an aesthetic difference in a work of art need not require a perceptual difference, see the chapter "Art and Authenticity" in Goodman (1968).

7. For a comprehensive overview see Rivkin and Ryan (2017).

8. Several scholars (foreshadowed by Turner and Pöppel, 1983) have recently advanced versions of the basic idea that psychological and neural evidence (particularly concerning the reader's response to a text) can augment literary analyses. Cave (2016) argued that cognitive science can help to understand the appreciation of literature, and Hogan (2014) emphasized that neural evidence is also relevant. Jacobs (2015) developed *neurocognitive poetics* as an approach to modeling the ways cognition and emotion impact literary reading. Starr (2013) presents a neurocognitive approach to understanding aesthetic experiences elicited by painting, music, and poetry. In the sense intended here, neurocognitive criticism emphasizes literary writing in addition to reading, and draws attention to the potential synergy between neurocognitive theories and biographical criticism.

9. See Bloom (1994, 2011).

10. The quote is from an interview with Cohen published in *Look* magazine, "Songs Sacred and Profane" by Ira Mothner (June 10, 1969).

11. See Kalstone (1989).

12. See Bloom (2011).

13. This idea is implicit in Borges's essay "Word-Music and Translation," based on a lecture delivered in 1968 (Borges, 2000).

14. The quote is from Young's 1759 essay, "Conjectures on Original Composition."

15. This odd occurrence was announced by Roland Barthes (1977) in his essay "The Death of the Author."

16. The philosopher of science Margaret Boden has written multiple books over four decades in which she has examined AI and its implications for the human mind. Her first major treatment of the topic was published in 1977, and the most recent in 2016. The latter book is an excellent introduction to current AI approaches to creativity. Whenever in this chapter a note might be expected but seems missing, Boden (2016) very likely provides the background. In addition, Boden (2004) discusses creativity in general, including the role of AI.

17. Bohannon (2017) surveys recent projects in which AI has aided scientific discoveries. Other articles in the same issue of *Science* magazine (July 7, 2017) describe specific examples in greater detail.

18. This position is defended in his 1891 essay "The Critic as Artist."

19. This electronically found haiku was found again (by me) at http://haiku .nytimes.com/post/162051428038/were-going-to-start-winning-again-believe-me -we.

20. The quote is from the linguist John Firth (1957, p. 11).

21. For example, see Mikolov et al. (2013). This line of work has much in common with the computational models of conceptual combination I discussed in chapter 8.

22. See Jacobs and Kinder (2017).

23. This possibility is based on work such as that of Gervás (2016).

24. For example, see Fox et al. (2012).

25. Such a program is described on the website of J. Nathan Matias: http:// natematias.com/portfolio/DesignArt/Swift-SpeareStatisticalP.html.

26. This program, called Stereotrope, is described by Veale (2013). The quoted lines appear on p. 157.

27. For reviews of neuroscientific theories of consciousness see Lau and Rosenthal (2011) and Block (2009).

28. The name is due to the philosopher David Chalmers (1995). The conceptual difficulties posed by phenomenological experience were described earlier by other philosophers, notably Thomas Nagel (1974, 1986).

29. This phrase characterizing the mind-body problem can be traced to Alvarado Middleditch, MD, in his 1882 book with the breathtaking title *Homes and Home Life: How to Obtain Good Health, Long Life, and Happy Homes. Also, the Physical, Intellectual*

and Moral Training of Children; Home Government; The Care of the Sick; What to Do in Cases of Accident, Etc. (p. 555).

30. This conclusion is consistent with that of the famous "Chinese room" argument proposed in 1980 by the philosopher John Searle (see Searle, 1999). This argument takes the form of a parable in which a person who only speaks English goes through computational steps to take questions in Chinese and respond in Chinese, but does not thereby acquire or exhibit any understanding of Chinese. See Searle (1997) for his views specifically on consciousness.

31. See Turing (1950).

32. Retrieved from https://gizmodo.com/5483750/peoples-emotional-attachment -to-roombas-bodes-well-for-inevitable-sex-robot-industry.

33. Retrieved from https://www.huffingtonpost.com/entry/samantha-sex-robot -molested_us_59cec9f9e4b06791bb10a268.

34. For example see Kannan and Vinyals (2016).

35. The quote is from Frost (1931/2007, p. 108).

36. The quote (from a Harvard lecture of 1967) appears in Borges (2000, p. 41).

37. This poem was first published in the collection *Death of a Naturalist* (Heaney, 1966). Seamus Heaney, "Mid-Term Break" from *Opened Ground: Selected Poems 1966– 1996*. Copyright © 1998 by Seamus Heaney. Used by permission of Faber and Faber Ltd. (UK) and by Farrar, Straus & Giroux, LLC, http://www.fsgbooks.com. All rights reserved.

Chapter 15

1. This poem was first published in *Poetry* magazine (April 1936).

2. The quote is from Bodkin (1934, p. 242). As an aside, one scientific topic in which theories have often begun as metaphors is human memory (see Roediger, 1980).

3. The quote is from Frost (1931/2007, p. 103).

4. For example, see Richland, Zur, and Holyoak (2007).

5. The quote is from Norton (1893, p. v).

6. For a critical assessment of recent efforts to develop cognitive training programs, see Simons et al. (2016).

7. The quote is from Frost (1931/2007, p. 108).

8. These letters (in German) were first published in 1929. See Rilke (1934/1993). The quotes are from the first letter and the tenth (last).

9. The quote is from his lecture "A Poet's Creed," delivered in 1968 (Borges, 2000, pp. 97–98).

10. The quote is from Norton (1893, p. iii).

11. The complete poem, first published in 1871, is available at https://www .poetryfoundation.org/poems/42916/jabberwocky.

12. The phrase is from Gioia (2016).

13. These are the final lines of "Kubla Khan" (see the opening of chapter 4).

14. These lines (italics in original) conclude "The Hollow Men" by T. S. Eliot, first published in 1925. The complete poem is available at https://allpoetry.com/The -Hollow-Men.

15. See Peskin (2010) for a study of changes in children's poetic literacy from fourth grade through high school.

16. This work is reported in Peskin et al. (2010) and Peskin and Wells-Jopling (2012).

17. This poem was first published in 1913 in *Poetry* magazine. It can be found at https://www.poets.org/poetsorg/poem/station-metro.

18. This phrase is from the poem "After Long Silence" by W. B. Yeats. The complete poem is available at https://www.poemhunter.com/poem/after-long-silence.

19. See Federmeier et al. (2002).

20. See Newsome and Glucksberg (2002).

21. This quote is drawn from a 1935 play by Giraudoux, translated into English as *Tiger at the Gates* (more literally, "The Trojan War Will Not Take Place").

22. The psychologist Paul Bloom (2016) has argued that empathy does not provide a firm basis for moral judgments, at least in the absence of dispassionate reasoning (but for a critical discussion, see Zaki, 2017).

23. This quote (and the one that follows) is from Shelley (1821/1840).

24. See Oatley (2016).

25. This study was reported by Altmann et al. (2014).

26. See Zeeman et al. (2013). In addition, Wassiliwizky et al. (2017) found that the emotional impact of a poem is particularly intense at points of closure (the ends of stanzas or of the entire poem), and when an imagined listener is being addressed.

27. The quote is from Richards (1936, p. 133).

28. The same basic idea was developed in greater detail by Max Black (1962b) and Mary Hesse (1963).

29. The quote is from a letter dated February 21, 1825, that Coleridge wrote to an unknown correspondent (Coleridge, 1971, p. 414).

30. These lines are from Cohen's song "Anthem," released on an album in 1992.

References

Aichelburg, C., Urbanski, M., Thiebaut de Schotten, M., Humbert, F., Levy, R., & Volle, E. (2016). Morphometry of left frontal and temporal poles predicts analogical reasoning abilities. *Cerebral Cortex*, 26, 915–932.

Altmann, U., Bohrn, I. C., Lubrich, O., Menninghaus, W., & Jacobs, A. M. (2014). Fact *vs* fiction—how paratextual information shapes our reading processes. *Social Cognitive and Affective Neuroscience*, 9, 22–29.

Andrews, P. W., & Thomson, J. A. (2009). The bright side of being blue: Depression as an adaptation for analyzing complex problems. *Psychological Review*, 116, 620–654.

Apter, M. (1982). Metaphor as synergy. In D. S. Miall (Ed.), *Metaphor: Problems and perspectives* (pp. 55–70). Brighton, UK: Harvester Press.

Aristotle. (c. 335 BCE). *Poetics*. http://classics.mit.edu/Aristotle/poetics.3.3.html.

Ashok, A. H., Marques, T. R., Jauhar, S., Nour, M. M., Goodwin, G. M., Young, A. H., et al. (2017). The dopamine hypothesis of bipolar affective disorder: The state of the art and implications for treatment. *Molecular Psychiatry*, 22, 666–679.

Austin, J. L. (1962). *How to do things with words*. London: Oxford University Press.

Avarguès-Weber, A., & Giurfa, M. (2013). Conceptual learning by miniature brains. *Proceedings of the Royal Society B: Biological Sciences*, 280, 20131907. doi:10.1098/rspb.2013.1907.

Bachelard, G. (1969). *The poetics of reverie: Childhood, language, and the cosmos* (D. Russell, Trans.). Boston: Beacon Press. (Original French edition, 1960.)

Baird, B., Smallwood, J., Franklin, M. F., Mrazek, M. D., Kam, J., & Schooler, J. W. (2012). Mind-wandering facilitates incubation. *Psychological Science*, 23, 1117–1122.

Barfield, O. (1928/1964). *Poetic diction: A study in meaning*. New York: McGraw-Hill.

Barnstone, A., & Barnstone, W. (Eds.). (1992). *A book of women poets: From antiquity to now*. New York: Schocken.

Baron, S. G., Thompson-Schill, S. L., Weber, M., & Osherson, D. (2010). An early stage of conceptual combination: Superimposition of constituent concepts in left anterolateral temporal lobe. *Cognitive Neuroscience*, 1, 44–51.

Barrantes-Vidal, N. (2014). Creativity and the spectrum of affective and schizophrenic psychoses. In J. C. Kaufman (Ed.), *Creativity and mental illness* (pp. 169–204). Cambridge: Cambridge University Press.

Barrett, D. (2001). *The committee of sleep: How artists, scientists, and athletes use dreams for creative problem-solving—and how you can too*. New York: Crown/Random House.

Barthes, R. (1977). The death of the author. In *Image music text* (S. Heath, Trans.). London: Fontana Press.

Bassok, M., & Medin, D. L. (1997). Birds of a feather flock together: Similarity judgments with semantically rich stimuli. *Cognitive Psychology*, 36, 311–336.

Baumlin, J. S., Baumlin, T. F., & Jensen, G. H. (Eds.). (2004). *Post-Jungian criticism: Theory and practice*. Albany: State University of New York Press.

Beardsley, M. C. (1958). *Aesthetics: Problems in the philosophy of criticism*. New York: Harcourt, Brace.

Beaty, R. E., Benedek, M., Silvia, P. J., & Schacter, D. L. (2016). Creative cognition and brain network dynamics. *Trends in Cognitive Sciences*, 20, 87–95.

Beaty, R. E., & Silvia, P. J. (2013). Metaphorically speaking: Cognitive abilities and the production of figurative language. *Memory & Cognition*, 41, 255–267.

Beaussart, M. L., White, A. E., Pullaro, A., & Kaufman, J. C. (2014). Reviewing recent empirical findings on creativity and mental illness. In J. C. Kaufman (Ed.), *Creativity and mental illness* (pp. 42–59). Cambridge: Cambridge University Press.

Beeman, M. (1998). Coarse coding and discourse comprehension. In M. Beeman & C. Chiarello (Eds.), *Right hemisphere language comprehension: Perspectives from cognitive neuroscience* (pp. 255–284). Mahwah, NJ: Erlbaum.

Beeman, M., & Chiarello, C. (1998). Complementary right- and left-hemisphere language comprehension. *Current Directions in Psychological Science*, 7, 2–8.

Benedek, M., Beaty, M., Jauk, E., Koschutnig, K., Fink, A., Dunst, B., et al. (2014). Creating metaphors: The neural basis of figurative language production. *NeuroImage*, 90, 99–106.

Beversdorf, D. Q. (2013). Pharmacological effects on creativity. In O. Vartanian, A. S. Bristol, & J. C. Kaufman (Eds.), *Neuroscience of creativity* (pp. 151–173). Cambridge, MA: MIT Press.

Black, M. (1962a). Metaphor. In M. Black (Ed.), *Models and metaphors* (pp. 38–47). Ithaca, NY: Cornell University Press.

Black, M. (1962b). Models and archetypes. In M. Black (Ed.), *Models and metaphors* (pp. 219–243). Ithaca, NY: Cornell University Press.

Black, M. (1979). More about metaphor. In A. Ortony (Ed.), *Metaphor and thought* (pp. 19–41). Cambridge: Cambridge University Press.

Blasko, D. G., & Connine, C. M. (1993). Effects of familiarity and aptness on metaphor processing. *Journal of Experimental Psychology: Learning, Memory, and Cognition*, 19, 295–308.

Block, N. (2009). Comparing the major theories of consciousness. In M. Gazzaniga (Ed.), *The Cognitive Neurosciences IV* (pp. 1111–1122). Cambridge, MA: MIT Press.

Bloom, H. (1994). *The Western Canon: The books and school of the ages*. New York: Harcourt Brace.

Bloom, H. (2004). The art of reading poetry. In H. Bloom (Ed.), *The best poems of the English language: From Chaucer through Frost* (pp. 1–29). New York: HarperCollins.

Bloom, H. (2011). *The anatomy of influence: Literature as a way of life*. New Haven, CT: Yale University Press.

Bloom, P. (2016). *Against empathy: The case for rational compassion*. New York: Ecco/ HarperCollins.

Boden, M. A. (1977). *Artificial intelligence and natural man*. New York: Basic Books.

Boden, M. A. (2004). *The creative mind: Myths and mechanisms* (2nd ed.). London: Routledge.

Boden, M. A. (2016). *AI: Its nature and future*. Oxford: Oxford University Press.

Bodkin, M. (1934). *Archetypal patterns in poetry: Psychological studies of imagination*. London: Oxford University Press.

Bohannon, J. (2017). The cyberscientist. *Science*, 357, 18–21.

Bohrn, I. C., Altmann, U., & Jacobs, A. M. (2012). Looking at the brains behind figurative language: A quantitative meta-analysis of neuroimaging studies of metaphor, idiom, and irony processing. *Neuropsychologica*, 50, 2669–2683.

Bohrn, I. C., Altmann, U., Lubrich, O., Menninghaus, W., & Jacobs, A. M. (2013). When we like what we know: A parametric fMRI analysis of beauty and familiarity. *Brain and Language*, 124, 1–8.

Borges, J. L. (1968). *Conversations with Jorge Luis Borges (interviews by Richard Burgin)*. New York: Holt, Rinehart and Winston.

Borges, J. L. (2000). *This craft of verse (the Charles Eliot Norton Lectures 1967–1968)*. Cambridge, MA: Harvard University Press.

Bowdle, B., & Gentner, D. (2005). The career of metaphor. *Psychological Review*, 112, 193–216.

Bransford, J. D., & Franks, J. J. (1971). The abstraction of linguistic ideas. *Cognitive Psychology*, 2, 331–350.

Brisch, R., Saniotis, A., Wolf, R., Bielau, H., Bernstein, H.-G., Steiner, J., et al. (2014). The role of dopamine in schizophrenia from a neurobiological and evolutionary perspective: Old fashioned, but still in vogue. *Frontiers in Psychiatry*, 5, 47. doi:10.3389/fpsyt.2014.00047.

Brooke-Rose, C. (1958). *A grammar of metaphor*. London: Secker & Warburg.

Brown, P., & Levinson, S. C. (1978). *Politeness: Some universals in language usage*. New York: Cambridge University Press.

Brownell, H. H., Simpson, T. L., Bihrle, A. M., Potter, H. H., & Gardner, H. (1990). Appreciation of metaphoric alternative word meanings by left and right brain-damaged patients. *Neuropsychologia*, 28, 375–383.

Bruner, J. (1986). *Actual minds, possible worlds*. Cambridge, MA: Harvard University Press.

Buckner, R. L., Andrews-Hanna, J. R., & Schacter, D. L. (2008). The brain's default network: Anatomy, function, and relevance to disease. *Annals of the New York Academy of Sciences*, 1124, 1–38.

Bukowski, C. (1995). In S. Cooney (Ed.), *Living on luck: Selected letters 1960s–1970s* (Vol. 2). Santa Rosa, CA: Black Sparrow Press.

Bunge, S. A., Helskog, E. H., & Wendelken, C. (2009). Left, but not right, rostrolateral prefrontal cortex meets a stringent test of the relational integration hypothesis. *NeuroImage*, 46, 338–342.

Burgess, P. W., & Wu, H.-C. (2013). Rostral prefrontal cortex (Brodmann area 10): Metacognition in the brain. In D. T. Stuss & R. T. Knight (Eds.), *Principles of frontal lobe function* (2nd ed.). New York: Oxford University Press.

Cai, D. J., Mednick, S. A., Harrison, E. M., Kanady, J. C., & Mednick, S. C. (2009). REM, not incubation, improves creativity by priming associative networks. *Proceedings of the National Academy of Sciences of the United States of America*, 106, 10130–10134.

Campbell, J. (1949). *The hero with a thousand faces*. New York: Pantheon Books.

Cardillo, E. R., Schmidt, G. L., Kranjec, A., & Chatterjee, A. (2010). Stimulus design is an obstacle course: 560 matched literal and metaphorical sentences for testing neural hypotheses about metaphor. *Behavior Research Methods*, 42, 651–664.

Cardillo, E. R., Watson, C. E., Schmidt, G. L., Kranjec, A., & Chatterjee, A. (2012). From novel to familiar: Tuning the brain for metaphors. *NeuroImage*, 59, 3212–3221.

Carson, S. H. (2011). Creativity and psychopathology: A shared vulnerability model. *Canadian Journal of Psychiatry*, 56, 144–153.

Catrambone, R., & Holyoak, K. J. (1989). Overcoming contextual limitations on problem-solving transfer. *Journal of Experimental Psychology: Learning, Memory, and Cognition*, 15, 1147–1156.

Cave, T. (2016). *Thinking with literature*. Oxford: Oxford University Press.

Chalmers, D. J. (1995). Facing up to the problem of consciousness. *Journal of Consciousness Studies*, 2, 200–219.

Chater, N. (1996). Reconciling simplicity and likelihood principles in perceptual organization. *Psychological Review*, 103, 566–581.

Chiappe, D. L., & Chiappe, P. (2007). The role of working memory in metaphor production and comprehension. *Journal of Memory and Language*, 56, 172–188.

Christoff, K., Gordon, A. M., Smallwood, J., Smith, R., & Schooler, J. W. (2009). Experience sampling during fMRI reveals default network and executive system contributions to mind wandering. *Proceedings of the National Academy of Sciences of the United States of America*, 106, 8719–8724.

Christoff, K., Prabhakaran, V., Dorfman, J., Zhao, Z., Kroger, J. K., Holyoak, K. J., et al. (2001). Rostrolateral prefrontal cortex involvement in relational integration during reasoning. *NeuroImage*, 14, 1136–1149.

Clark, H. H. (1996). *Using language*. New York: Cambridge University Press.

Clark, H. H., & Brennan, S. E. (1991). Grounding in communication. In L. B. Resnick, J. M. Levine, & S. D. Teasley (Eds.), *Perspectives on socially shared cognition* (pp. 127–149). Washington, DC: American Psychological Association.

Cohen, L. (1993). *Stranger music: Selected poems and songs*. Toronto: McClelland & Stewart.

Cohen, T. (2008). *Thinking of others: On the talent for metaphor*. Princeton, NJ: Princeton University Press.

Coleridge, S. T. (1817). *Biographia literaria*. London: Rest Fenner. http://www.gutenberg.org/ebooks/6081.

Coleridge, S. T. (1971). In E. L. Griggs (Ed.), *Collected letters of Samuel Taylor Coleridge* (Vol. 5). Oxford: Clarendon Press.

Costello, F. J., & Keane, M. T. (2000). Efficient creativity: Constraint-guided conceptual combination. *Cognitive Science*, 24, 299–349.

Costello, F. J., & Keane, M. T. (2001). Testing two theories of conceptual combination: Alignment versus diagnosticity in the comprehension and production of combined concepts. *Journal of Experimental Psychology: Learning, Memory, and Cognition*, 27, 255–271.

Cowan, N. (2001). The magical number 4 in short-term memory: A reconsideration of mental storage capacity. *Behavioral and Brain Sciences*, 24, 87–185.

Crane, H. (2001). In M. Simon (Ed.), *Complete poems of Hart Crane*. New York: Liveright.

Cranmer-Byng, L. (1917). Chinese poetry and its symbols. *The Lotus Magazine, 8*, 357–360, 363.

Csikszentmihalyi, M. (1990). *Flow: The psychology of optimal experience*. New York: Harper & Row.

Dancygier, B., & Sweetser, E. (2014). *Figurative language*. Cambridge: Cambridge University Press.

DeYoung, C. G. (2013). The neuromodulator of exploration: A unifying theory of the role of dopamine in personality. *Frontiers in Human Neuroscience*, 7, 762. doi:10.3389/fnhum.2013.00762.

DeYoung, C. G., Grazioplene, R. G., & Peterson, J. B. (2012). The Openness/Intellect trait domain as a paradoxical simplex. *Journal of Research in Personality*, 46, 63–78.

DeYoung, C. G., Quilty, L. C., Peterson, J. B., & Gray, J. R. (2014). Openness to experience, intellect, and cognitive ability. *Journal of Personality Assessment*, 96, 46–52.

Doumas, L. A. A., & Hummel, J. E. (2012). Computational models of higher cognition. In K. J. Holyoak & R. G. Morrison (Eds.), *The Oxford handbook of thinking and reasoning* (pp. 52–66). New York: Oxford University Press.

Doumas, L. A. A., Hummel, J. E., & Sandhofer, C. M. (2008). A theory of the discovery and predication of relational concepts. *Psychological Review*, 115, 1–43.

Duncan, J. (2010). The multiple-demand (MD) system of the primate brain: Mental programs for intelligent behavior. *Trends in Cognitive Sciences*, 14, 172–179.

Duncker, K. (1945). On problem solving. *Psychological Monographs*, 58 (whole no. 270).

Eliot, T. S. (1928). Introduction (pp. vii-xxv). In E. Pound, *Selected poems* (T. S. Eliot, Ed.). London: Faber & Gwyer.

Eliot, T. S. (1933). *The uses of poetry*. London: Faber and Faber.

Eliot, T. S. (1957). *On poetry and poets*. New York: Farrar, Straus and Cudahy.

Eliot, T. S, Dickey, F., Formichelli, J., & Schuchard, R. (Eds.). (2015). *The complete prose of T. S. Eliot: The critical edition: Literature, politics, belief 1927–1929*. Baltimore: Johns Hopkins University Press.

Ellsworth, P. C. (2013). Appraisal theory: Old and new questions. *Emotion Review*, 5, 125–131.

El Refaie, E. (2015). Cross-modal resonances in creative multimodal metaphors: Breaking out of conceptual prisons. In M. J. Pinar Sanz (Ed.), *Multimodality and cognitive linguistics* (pp. 13–26). Amsterdam: John Benjamins.

Éluard, P. (1995). *Ombres et soleil (Shadows and sun): Selected writings of 1913–1952* (C. Buckley, Trans.). Durham, NH: Oyster River Press.

Embler, W. (1966). *Metaphor and meaning*. DeLand, FL: Everett/Edwards.

Empson, W. (1930). *Seven types of ambiguity*. London: Chatto and Windus.

Engel, A. K., & Singer, W. (2001). Temporal binding and the neural correlates of sensory awareness. *Trends in Cognitive Sciences*, 5, 16–25.

Escoffier, N., Herrmann, C. S., & Schirmer, A. (2015). Auditory rhythms entrain visual processes in the human brain: Evidence from evoked oscillations and event-related potentials. *NeuroImage*, 111, 267–276.

Estes, Z., & Glucksberg, S. (2000). Interactive property attribution in concept combination. *Memory & Cognition*, 28, 28–34.

Estes, Z., & Jones, L. L. (2006). Priming via relational similarity: A COPPER HORSE is faster when seen through a GLASS EYE. *Journal of Memory and Language*, 138, 89–101.

Estes, Z., & Jones, L. L. (2009). Integrative priming occurs rapidly and uncontrollably during lexical processing. *Journal of Experimental Psychology: General*, 138, 112–130.

Fauconnier, G. (1997). *Mappings in thought and language*. Cambridge: Cambridge University Press.

Federmeier, K. D., McLennan, D. B., De Ochoa, E., & Kutas, M. (2002). The impact of semantic memory organization and sentence context on spoken language processing by younger and older adults: An ERP study. *Psychophysiology*, 39, 133–146.

Fehrman, C. (1980). *Poetic creation: Inspiration or craft?* (K. Petherick, Trans.). Minneapolis: University of Minnesota Press. (Original Swedish version published 1974.)

Fields, R. D., Araque, A., Johansen-Berg, H., Lim, S.-S., Lynch, G., Nave, K.-A., et al. (2014). Glial biology in learning and cognition. *Neuroscientist*, 20, 426–431.

Fink, A., Benedek, M., Unterrainer, H.-F., Papousek, I., & Weiss, E. M. (2014). Creativity and psychopathology: Are there similar mental processes involved in creativity and psychosis-proneness? *Frontiers in Psychology*, 5, 1211. doi:10.3389/psyg.2014.01211.

Finkelstein, N. (2016). *The ratio of reason to magic: New & selected poems*. Loveland, OH: Dos Madres Press.

Finn, E. S., Shen, X., Scheinost, D., Rosenberg, M. D., Huang, J., Chun, M. M., et al. (2015). Functional connectome fingerprinting: Identifying individuals using patterns of brain connectivity. *Nature Neuroscience*, 18, 1664–1671.

Firth, J. R. (1957). A synopsis of linguistic theory 1930–1955. In J. R. Firth (Ed.), *Studies in Linguistic Analysis (special volume of the Philological Society)*. Oxford: Blackwell.

Fletcher, A. (1964). *Allegory: The theory of a symbolic mode*. Ithaca, NY: Cornell University Press.

Foster, N. A., & Valentine, E. R. (2001). The effect of auditory stimulation on autobiographical recall in dementia. *Experimental Aging Research*, 27, 215–228.

Fox, N., Ehmoda, O., & Charniak, E. (2012). *Statistical stylometrics and the Marlowe-Shakespeare authorship*. Proceedings of the Georgetown University Roundtable on Language and Linguistics (GURT), 363–371. http://cs.brown.edu/research/pubs/theses/masters/2012/ehmoda.pdf.

Freud, S. (1900/1980). *The interpretation of dreams*. New York: Avon.

Frost, R. (1931/2007). Education by poetry: A meditative monologue. In M. Richardson (Ed.), *The collected prose of Robert Frost*. Cambridge, MA: Belknap Press of Harvard University Press.

Frost, R. (1946/2007). The constant symbol. In M. Richardson (Ed.), *The collected prose of Robert Frost*. Cambridge, MA: Belknap Press of Harvard University Press.

Frye, N. (1957). *Anatomy of criticism: Four essays*. Princeton, NJ: Princeton University Press.

Fyfe, S., Williams, C., Mason, O. J., & Pickup, G. J. (2008). Apophenia, theory of mind and schizotypy: Perceiving meaning and intentionality in randomness. *Cortex*, 44, 1316–1325.

Gagliano, A., Paul, E., Booten, K., & Hearst, M. A. (2016). Intersecting word vectors to take figurative language to new heights. In *Proceedings of the Fifth Workshop on Computational Linguistics for Literature, NAACL-HLT 2016* (pp. 20–31). San Diego: Association for Computational Linguistics.

Gagne, C. L., & Shoben, E. J. (1997). Influence of thematic relations on the comprehension of modifier-noun combinations. *Journal of Experimental Psychology: Learning, Memory, and Cognition*, 23, 71–87.

Gao, Z., Gao, S., Xu, L., Zheng, X., Ma, X., Luo, L., et al. (2017). Women prefer men who use metaphorical language when paying compliments in a romantic context. *Scientific Reports*, 7, 40871. doi:10.1038/srep40871.

Gentner, D. (1983). Structure-mapping: A theoretical framework for analogy. *Cognitive Science*, 7, 155–170.

Gentner, D. (2010). Bootstrapping the mind: Analogical processes and symbol systems. *Cognitive Science*, 34, 752–775.

Gentner, D., Bowdle, B., Wolff, P., & Boronat, C. (2001). Metaphor is like analogy. In D. Gentner, K. J. Holyoak, & B. N. Kokinov (Eds.), *The analogical mind: Perspectives from cognitive science* (pp. 199–253). Cambridge, MA: MIT Press.

Gentner, D., & Clement, C. (1988). Evidence for relational selectivity in the interpretation of analogy and metaphor. In G. H. Bower (Ed.), *Advances in the psychology of learning and motivation* (Vol. 22, pp. 307–358). New York: Academic Press.

Gernsbacher, M. A., Keysar, B., Robertson, R. R., & Werner, N. K. (2001). The role of suppression and enhancement in understanding metaphors. *Journal of Memory and Language*, 45, 433–450.

Gervás, P. (2016). Constrained creation of poetic forms during theme-driven exploration of a domain defined by an N-gram model. *Connection Science*, 28, 111–130.

Giambra, L. M. A. (1995). A laboratory method for investigating influences on switching attention to task-unrelated imagery and thought. *Consciousness and Cognition*, 4, 1–21.

Gibbs, R. W., Jr. (1994). *The poetics of mind: Figurative thought, language, and understanding*. Cambridge: Cambridge University Press.

Gick, M. L., & Holyoak, K. J. (1980). Analogical problem solving. *Cognitive Psychology*, 12, 306–355.

Gick, M. L., & Holyoak, K. J. (1983). Schema induction and analogical transfer. *Cognitive Psychology*, 15, 1–38.

Gildea, P., & Glucksberg, S. (1983). On understanding metaphor: The role of context. *Journal of Verbal Learning and Verbal Behavior*, 22, 577–590.

Gioia, D. (2016). *Poetry as enchantment*. Bismarck, ND: Wiseblood Books.

Giora, R. (1997). Understanding figurative and literal language: The graded salience hypothesis. *Cognitive Linguistics*, 8, 183–206.

Glucksberg, S. (2003). The psycholinguistics of metaphor. *Trends in Cognitive Sciences*, 7, 92–96.

Glucksberg, S., Gildea, P., & Bookin, H. B. (1982). On understanding nonliteral speech: Can people ignore metaphors? *Journal of Verbal Learning and Verbal Behavior*, 21, 85–98.

Glucksberg, S., & Haught, C. (2006). On the relation between metaphor and simile: When comparison fails. *Mind & Language*, 21, 360–378.

Glucksberg, S., & Keysar, B. (1990). Understanding metaphorical comparisons: Beyond similarity. *Psychological Review, 97,* 3–18.

Glucksberg, S., & McGlone, M. S. (1999). When love is not a journey: What metaphors mean. *Journal of Pragmatics, 31,* 1541–1558.

Glucksberg, S., McGlone, M. S., & Manfredi, D. (1997). Property attribution in metaphor comprehension. *Journal of Memory and Language, 36,* 50–67.

Goldstone, R. L., & Medin, D. L. (1994). Time course of comparison. *Journal of Experimental Psychology: Learning, Memory, and Cognition, 20,* 29–50.

Goodblack, C., & Glicksohn, J. (2010). Conversations with I. A. Richards: The renaissance in cognitive literary studies. *Poetics Today, 31,* 387–432.

Goodblatt, C. (2001). Adding an empirical dimension to the study of poetic metaphor. *Journal of Literary Semantics, 30,* 167–180.

Goode, M. R., Dahl, D. W., & Moreau, C. P. (2010). The effect of experiential analogies on consumer perception and attitudes. *Journal of Marketing Research (JMR), 42,* 274–286.

Goodman, N. (1968). *Languages of art: An approach to a theory of symbols.* Indianapolis: Bobbs-Merrill.

Green, A. E. (2016). Creativity, within reason: Semantic distance and dynamic state creativity in relational thinking and reasoning. *Current Directions in Psychological Science, 25,* 28–35.

Green, A. E., Kraemer, D. J., Fugelsang, J. A., Gray, J. R., & Dunbar, K. N. (2010). Connecting long distance: Semantic distance in analogical reasoning modulates frontopolar cortex activity. *Cerebral Cortex, 20,* 70–76.

Green, A. E., Kraemer, D. J., Fugelsang, J. A., Gray, J. R., & Dunbar, K. N. (2012). Neural correlates of creativity in analogical reasoning. *Journal of Experimental Psychology: Learning, Memory, and Cognition, 38,* 264–272.

Green, A. E., Spiegel, K. A., Giangrande, E. J., Weinberger, A. B., Gallagher, N. M., & Turkeltaub, P. E. (2017). Thinking cap plus thinking zap: tDCS of frontopolar cortex improves creative analogical reasoning and facilitates conscious augmentation of state creativity in verb generation. *Cerebral Cortex, 27,* 2628–2639.

Grice, P. (1957). Meaning. *Philosophical Review, 66,* 377–388.

Grice, P. (1975). Logic and conversation. In P. Cole & J. L. Morgan (Eds.), *Syntax and semantics,* Vol. 3: *Speech acts* (pp. 41–58). New York: Academic Press.

Grice, P. (1989). *Studies in the way of words.* Cambridge, MA: Harvard University Press.

Gusnard, D. A., Akbudak, E., Shulman, G. L., & Raickle, M. E. (2001). Medial frontal cortex and self-referential mental activity: Relation to a default mode of brain function. *Proceedings of the National Academy of Sciences of the United States of America*, 98, 4259–4264.

Halford, G. S., Wilson, W. H., Andrews, G., & Phillips, S. (2014). *Categorizing cognition: Conceptual coherence in the foundations of psychology.* Cambridge, MA: MIT Press.

Halford, G. S., Wilson, W. H., & Phillips, S. (1998). Processing capacity defined by relational complexity: Implications for comparative, developmental, and cognitive psychology. *Behavioral and Brain Sciences*, 21, 803–831.

Halford, G. S., Wilson, W. H., & Phillips, S. (2010). Relational knowledge: The foundation of higher cognition. *Trends in Cognitive Sciences*, 14, 497–505.

Hannon, E. E., & Johnson, S. P. (2005). Infants use meter to categorize rhythms and melodies: Implications for musical structure learning. *Cognitive Psychology*, 50, 354–377.

Harap, L. (1933). What is poetic truth? *Journal of Philosophy*, 30, 477–488.

Hardcastle, J. (2005). Of dogs and martyrs: Sherrington, Richards, Pavlov and Vygotsky. *Changing English*, 12, 31–42.

Hawkes, D. (1967). *A little primer of Tu Fu.* London: Oxford University Press.

Hawkes, T. (1972). *Metaphor.* London: Methuen.

Heaney, S. (1966). *Death of a naturalist.* London: Faber and Faber.

Heaney, S. (2000). *Beowulf.* New York: Farrar, Straus and Giroux.

Hebb, D. O. (1949). *The organization of behavior.* New York: Wiley.

Herculano-Houzel, S. (2009). The human brain in numbers: A linearly scaled-up primate brain. *Frontiers in Human Neuroscience*, 3(31). doi:10.3389/neuro.09.031.2009.

Hesse, M. B. (1963). *Models and analogies in science.* London: Sheed and Ward.

Hobeika, L., Diard-Detoeuf, C., Garcin, B., Levy, R., & Volle, E. (2016). General and specialized brain correlates for analogical reasoning: A meta-analysis of functional imaging studies. *Human Brain Mapping*, 37, 1953–1969.

Hogan, P. C. (2014). Literary brains: Neuroscience, criticism, and theory. *Literature Compass*, 11, 293–304.

Holland, J. H., Holyoak, K. J., Nisbett, R. E., & Thagard, P. R. (1986). *Induction: Processes of inference, learning, and discovery.* Cambridge, MA: MIT Press.

Holmes, R. (1989). *Coleridge: Early visions, 1772–1804.* London: Harper Perennial.

Holmes, R. (1998). *Coleridge: Darker reflections, 1804–1834.* London: Harper Perennial.

Holyoak, K. J. (1982). An analogical framework for literary interpretation. *Poetics*, 11, 105–126.

Holyoak, K. J. (1985). The pragmatics of analogical transfer. In G. H. Bower (Ed.), *The psychology of learning and motivation* (Vol. 19, pp. 59–87). New York: Academic Press.

Holyoak, K. (2006). What should a poem be like? In N. H. McAlister (Ed.), *Rhyme and reason: Modern formal poetry.* Port Perry, Ontario, Canada: McAlister.

Holyoak, K. (2007). *Facing the moon: Poems of Li Bai and Du Fu.* Durham, NH: Oyster River Press.

Holyoak, K. (2010). *My minotaur: Selected poems 1998–2006.* Loveland, OH: Dos Madres Press.

Holyoak, K. (2012). *Foreigner: New English poems in Chinese Old Style.* Loveland, OH: Dos Madres Press.

Holyoak, K. J. (2012). Analogy and relational reasoning. In K. J. Holyoak & R. G. Morrison (Eds.), *The Oxford handbook of thinking and reasoning* (pp. 234–259). New York: Oxford University Press.

Holyoak, K. J., & Powell, D. (2016). Deontological coherence: A framework for commonsense moral reasoning. *Psychological Bulletin*, 142, 1179–1203.

Holyoak, K. J., & Simon, D. (1999). Bidirectional reasoning in decision making by constraint satisfaction. *Journal of Experimental Psychology: General*, 128, 3–31.

Holyoak, K. J., & Stamenković, D. (2018). Metaphor comprehension: A critical review of theories and evidence. *Psychological Bulletin*, 144, 641–671.

Holyoak, K. J., & Thagard, P. (1989). Analogical mapping by constraint satisfaction. *Cognitive Science*, 13, 295–355.

Holyoak, K. J., & Thagard, P. (1995). *Mental leaps: Analogy in creative thought.* Cambridge, MA: MIT Press.

Hrushovski, B. (1960). On free rhythms in modern poetry. In T. A. Sebeok (Ed.), *Style in language* (pp. 173–180). Cambridge, MA: Technology Press of the Massachusetts Institute of Technology.

Hughes, L. (1994). In A. Rampersad & D. E. Roessel (Eds.), *The collected poems of Langston Hughes.* New York: Knopf.

Hummel, J. E., & Holyoak, K. J. (1997). Distributed representations of structure: A theory of analogical access and mapping. *Psychological Review*, 104, 427–466.

Hummel, J. E., & Holyoak, K. J. (2003). A symbolic-connectionist theory of relational inference and generalization. *Psychological Review*, 110, 220–264.

Hutchins, E. (1995). *Cognition in the wild*. Cambridge, MA: MIT Press.

Jacobs, A. M. (2015). Neurocognitive poetics: Methods and models for investigating the neuronal and cognitive-affective bases of literature reception. *Frontiers in Human Neuroscience*, 9, 186. doi:10.3389/fnhum.2015.00186.

Jacobs, A. M., & Kinder, A. (2017). "The brain is the prisoner of thought": A machine-learning assisted quantitative narrative analysis of literary metaphors for use in neurocognitive poetics. *Metaphor and Symbol*, 32, 139–160.

Jacobson, R. (1960). Linguistics and poetics. In T. A. Sebeok (Ed.), *Style in language* (pp. 350–375). Cambridge, MA: Technology Press of the Massachusetts Institute of Technology.

James, W. (1892). The stream of consciousness (chap. 11 in *Psychology: A briefer course*). http://psychclassics.yorku.ca/James/jimmy11.htm.

Johnson, M. (1987). *The body in the mind: The bodily basis of meaning, imagination, and reason*. Chicago: University of Chicago Press.

Johnstone, B., Bodling, A., Cohen, D., & Wegrzyn, A. (2012). Right parietal lobe-related "selflessness" as the neuropsychological basis of spiritual transcendence. *International Journal for the Psychology of Religion*, 22, 267–284.

Jones, L. L., & Estes, Z. (2006). Roosters, robins, and alarm clocks: Aptness and conventionality in metaphor comprehension. *Journal of Memory and Language*, 55, 18–32.

Jung, C. G. (1933/1952). Psychology and literature. In B. Ghiselin (Ed.), *The creative process (pp. 208–223)*. Oakland: University of California Press.

Jung, C. G. (1934/1953). (1979). Archetypes of the collective unconscious (R. F. C. Hull, Trans.). H. Read, M. Fordham, & G. Adler (Eds.), *Collected works (Bollingen Series XX)* (Vol. 9). Princeton, NJ: Princeton University Press.

Jung, C. G. (1948/1974). General aspects of dream psychology. In *Dreams* (R. F. C. Hull, Trans.) (pp. 23–66). Princeton, NJ: Princeton University Press.

Jung-Beeman, M. (2005). Bilateral brain processes for processing natural language. *Trends in Cognitive Sciences*, 9, 512–518.

Just, M. A., Cherkassky, V. L., Aryal, S., & Mitchell, T. M. (2010). A neurosemantic theory of concrete noun representation based on the underlying brain codes. *PLoS One*, 5(1), e8622. https://doi.org/10.1371/journal.pone.0008622.

Kahneman, D. (2011). *Thinking, fast and slow*. New York: Farrar, Straus and Giroux.

Kalstone, D. (1989). *Becoming a poet: Elizabeth Bishop with Marianne Moore and Robert Lowell*. New York: Farrar, Straus and Giroux.

Kannan, A., & Vinyals, O. (2016). Adversarial evaluation of dialogue models. In Workshop on Adversarial Training, *Proceedings of NIPS 2016*, Barcelona, Spain. https://arxiv.org/pdf/1701.08198.pdf.

Kao, Y.-K., & Mei, T.-L. (1978). Meaning, metaphor, and allusion in T'ang poetry. *Harvard Journal of Asiatic Studies*, 38, 281–356.

Kasparian, K. (2013). Hemispheric differences in figurative language processing: Contributions of neuroimaging methods and challenges in reconciling current empirical findings. *Journal of Neurolinguistics*, 26, 1–21.

Katz, A., Paivio, A., Marschark, M., & Clark, J. (1988). Norms for 204 literary and 260 nonliterary metaphors on 10 psychological dimensions. *Metaphor and Symbolic Activity*, 3, 191–214.

Kaufman, J. C. (2001). The Sylvia Plath effect: Mental illness in eminent creative writers. *Journal of Creative Behavior*, 35, 37–50.

Kaufman, S. B., DeYoung, C. G., Gray, J. R., Jiménez, L., Brown, J., & Mackintosh, N. (2010). Implicit learning as an ability. *Cognition*, 116, 321–340.

Kaufman, S. B., Quilty, L. C., Grazioplene, R. G., Hirsh, J. B., Gray, J. R., Peterson, J. B., et al. (2016). Openness to Experience and Intellect differentially predict creative achievement in the arts and sciences. *Journal of Personality*, 84, 248–258.

Keane, M. T., & Costello, F. J. (2001). Setting limits on analogy: Why conceptual combination is not structural alignment. In D. Gentner, K. J. Holyoak, & B. N. Kokinov (Eds.), *The analogical mind: Perspectives from cognitive science* (pp. 287–312). Cambridge, MA: MIT Press.

Kennedy, J. M. (2008). Metaphor and art. In R. W. Gibbs (Ed.), *Cambridge handbook of metaphor and thought* (pp. 447–461). New York: Cambridge University Press.

Kennet, Y. N., Anaki, D., & Faust, M. (2014). Investigating the structure of semantic networks in low and high creative persons. *Frontiers in Human Neuroscience*, 9, 407.

Keysar, B., Shen, Y., Glucksberg, S., & Horton, W. S. (2000). Conventional language: How metaphorical is it? *Journal of Memory and Language*, 43, 576–593.

Kierkegaard, S. (1843/1971). *Either/or* (D. Swenson & L. M. Swenson, Trans.). Princeton, NJ: Princeton University Press.

Killingsworth, M. J. (1977). Another source for Whitman's use of "electric." *Walt Whitman Review*, 23, 129–132.

Kintsch, W. (2000). Metaphor comprehension: A computational theory. *Psychonomic Bulletin & Review*, 7, 257–266.

Kintsch, W. (2001). Predication. *Cognitive Science*, 25, 173–202.

Kintsch, W., & Bowles, A. R. (2002). Metaphor comprehension: What makes a metaphor difficult to understand? *Metaphor and Symbol*, 17, 249–262.

Kintsch, W., & van Dijk, T. A. (1978). Toward a model of text comprehension and production. *Psychological Review*, 85, 363–394.

Kittay, E. F. (1987). *Metaphor: Its cognitive force and linguistic structure.* Oxford: Oxford University Press.

Knowles, M., & Moon, R. (2006). *Introducing metaphor.* New York: Routledge.

Knowlton, B. J., Morrison, R. G., Hummel, J. E., & Holyoak, K. J. (2012). A neurocomputational system for relational reasoning. *Trends in Cognitive Sciences*, 16, 373–381.

Koestler, A. (1964). *The act of creation.* London: Hutchinson.

Koh, J.-S., Yang, E., Jung, G.-P., Jung, S.-P., Son, J. H., Lee, S.-I., et al. (2015). Jumping on water: Surface tension–dominated jumping of water striders and robotic insects. *Science*, 349, 517–521.

Kouneiher, F., Charron, S., & Koechlin, E. (2009). Motivation and cognitive control in the human prefrontal cortex. *Nature Neuroscience*, 12, 939–945.

Kounios, J., & Beeman, M. (2009). The *Aha!* moment: The cognitive neuroscience of insight. *Current Directions in Psychological Science*, 18, 210–216.

Kounios, J., & Beeman, M. (2015). *The Eureka factor: Aha moments, creative insight, and the brain.* New York: Random House.

Kövecses, Z. (2002). *Metaphor: A practical introduction.* New York: Oxford University Press.

Kövecses, Z. (2009). Metaphor and poetic creativity: A cognitive linguistic approach. *Acta Universitatis Sapientiae: Philologica*, 1, 181–196.

Kroger, J. K., Holyoak, K. J., & Hummel, J. E. (2004). Varieties of sameness: The impact of relational complexity on perceptual comparisons. *Cognitive Science*, 28, 335–358.

Kruglanski, A. W., Fishbach, A., Woolley, K., Bélanger, J. J., Chernikova, M., Molinario, E., et al. (2018). A structural model of intrinsic motivation: On the psychology of means-ends fusion. *Psychological Review, 125*, 165–182.

Kubose, T. T., Holyoak, K. J., & Hummel, J. E. (2002). The role of textual coherence in incremental analogical mapping. *Journal of Memory and Language*, 47, 407–435.

Lakoff, G. (1987). *Women, fire, and dangerous things: What categories reveal about the mind.* Chicago: University of Chicago Press.

Lakoff, G. (1997). How unconscious metaphorical thought shapes dreams. In D. Stein (Ed.), *Cognitive science and the unconscious* (pp. 89–120). Washington, DC: American Psychiatric Press.

Lakoff, G., & Johnson, M. (1980). *Metaphors we live by*. Chicago: University of Chicago Press.

Lakoff, G., & Turner, M. (1989). *More than cool reason: A field guide to poetic metaphor*. Chicago: University of Chicago Press.

Landauer, T. K., & Dumais, S. T. (1997). A solution to Plato's problem: The latent semantic analysis theory of the acquisition, induction, and representation of knowledge. *Psychological Review*, 104, 211–240.

Laozi. (1972/1997). *Tao Te Ching* (G.-F. Feng & J. English, Trans.). New York: Vintage Books.

Lau, H., & Rosenthal, D. (2011). Empirical support for higher-order theories of conscious awareness. *Trends in Cognitive Sciences*, 15, 365–373.

Lea, R. B., Rapp, D. N., Elfenbein, A., Mitchel, A. D., & Romine, R. S. (2008). Sweet silent thought: Alliteration and assonance in poetry comprehension. *Psychological Science*, 19, 709–716.

Lemogne, C., Delaveau, P., Freton, M., Guionnet, S., & Fossati, P. (2012). Medial prefrontal cortex and the self in major depression. *Journal of Affective Disorders*, 136, e1–e11.

Levin, S. R. (1962). *Linguistic structures in poetry*. The Hague: Mouton.

Levin, S. R. (1977). *The semantics of metaphor*. Baltimore: Johns Hopkins University Press.

Levin, S. R. (1982). Aristotle's theory of metaphor. *Philosophy & Rhetoric*, 15, 24–46.

Lewis, H. D. (1946). On poetic truth. *Philosophy (London, England)*, 21, 147–166.

Liu, S., Chow, H. M., Xu, Y., Erkkinen, M. G., Swett, K. E., Eagle, M. W., et al. (2012). Neural correlates of lyrical improvisation: An fMRI study of freestyle rap. *Scientific Reports*, 2, 834. doi:10.1038/srep00834.

Liu, S., Erkkinen, M. G., Healey, M. L., Xu, Y., Swett, K. E., Chow, H. M., et al. (2015). Brain activity and connectivity during poetry composition: Toward a multidimensional model of the creative process. *Human Brain Mapping*, 36, 3351–3372.

Lodge, D. (1977). *The modes of modern writing: Metaphor, metonymy, and the typology of modern literature*. London: Edward Arnold.

Loewenstein, J., Thompson, L., & Gentner, D. (2003). Analogical learning in negotiation teams: Comparing cases promotes learning and transfer. *Academy of Management Learning & Education*, 2, 119–127.

Lombardo, M. V., Chakrabarti, B., Bullmore, E. T., Baron-Cohen, S., & the MRC AIMS Consortium. (2011). Specialization of right temporo-parietal junction for mentalizing and its relation to social impairments in autism. *NeuroImage*, 56, 1832–1838.

Lowell, A. (1930/1952). The process of making poetry. Reprinted in B. Ghiselin (Ed.), *The creative process (pp. 109–112)* . Oakland: University of California Press.

Lu, H., Chen, D., & Holyoak, K. J. (2012). Bayesian analogy with relational transformations. *Psychological Review*, 119, 617–648.

Lustenberger, C., Boyle, M. R., Foulser, A. A., Mellin, J. M., & Fröhlich, F. (2015). Functional role of frontal alpha oscillations in creativity. *Cortex*, 67, 74–82.

Lynott, D., & Connell, L. (2010). The effect of prosody on conceptual combination. *Cognitive Science*, 34, 1107–1123.

Mallarmé, S. (1994). *Collected poems: A bilingual edition* (H. Weinfield, Trans.). Berkeley: University of California Press.

Mather, E., Jones, L. L., & Estes, Z. (2014). Priming by relational integration in perceptual identification and Stroop colour naming. *Journal of Memory and Language*, 71, 57–70.

McClelland, J. L. (2006). How far can you go with Hebbian learning, and when does it lead you astray? In Y. Munakata & M. H. Johnson (Eds.), *Attention and performance XXI: Processes of change in brain and cognitive development* (pp. 33–69). New York: Oxford University Press.

McGlone, M. S., & Manfredi, D. (2001). Topic-vehicle interaction in metaphor comprehension. *Memory & Cognition*, 29, 1209–1219.

McGlone, M. S., & Tofighbakhsh, J. (1999). The Keats heuristic: Rhyme as reason in aphorism interpretation. *Poetics*, 26, 235–244.

McGlone, M. S., & Tofighbakhsh, J. (2000). Birds of a feather flock conjointly (?): Rhyme as reason in aphorisms. *Psychological Science*, 11, 424–428.

Mead, C. (1914). *Logic: Deductive and inductive* (4th ed.). London: Simpkin, Marshall, Hamilton, Kent & Co. http://www.gutenberg.org/files/18440.

Medin, D. L., & Shoben, E. J. (1988). Context and structure in conceptual combination. *Cognitive Psychology*, 20, 158–190.

Mednick, S. A. (1962). The associative basis of the creative process. *Psychological Review*, 69, 220–231.

Meyer, D. E., & Schvaneveldt, R. W. (1971). Facilitation in recognizing pairs of words: Evidence of a dependence between retrieval operations. *Journal of Experimental Psychology*, 90, 227–234.

Miall, D. S. (2006). *Literary reading: Empirical and theoretical studies*. New York: Peter Lang.

Miall, D. S., & Kuiken, D. (2002). A feeling for fiction: Becoming what we behold. *Poetics*, 30, 221–241.

Mikolov, T., Yih, W. T., & Zweig, G. (2013). Linguistic regularities in continuous space word representations. *HLT-NAACL*, 13, 746–751.

Miller, G. A. (1956). The magical number seven plus or minus two: Some limits on our capacity for processing information. *Psychological Review*, 63, 81–97.

Monroe, H., & Crane, H. (1926). A discussion with Hart Crane. *Poetry*, *29*, 34-41.

Morrison, R. G., & Knowlton, B. J. (2012). Neurocognitive methods in higher cognition. In K. J. Holyoak & R. G. Morrison (Eds.), *The Oxford handbook of thinking and reasoning* (pp. 67–89). New York: Oxford University Press.

Mossaheb, N., Aschauer, H. N., Stoettner, S., Schmoeger, M., Pils, N., Raab, M., et al. (2014). Comprehension of metaphors in patients with schizophrenia-spectrum disorders. *Comprehensive Psychiatry*, 55, 928–937.

Murphy, G. L. (1988). Comprehending complex concepts. *Cognitive Science*, 12, 529–562.

Murphy, G. L. (2002). *The big book of concepts*. Cambridge, MA: MIT Press.

Nagel, T. (1974). What is it like to be a bat? *Philosophical Review*, 83, 435–450.

Nagel, T. (1986). *The view from nowhere*. New York: Oxford University Press.

Nassar, S. (1998). *A beautiful mind*. New York: Simon & Schuster.

Neruda, P. (2004). *The essential Neruda: Selected poems* (M. Eisner, Ed.). San Francisco: City Lights Publishers.

Newsome, M. R., & Glucksberg, S. (2002). Older adults filter irrelevant information during metaphor comprehension. *Experimental Aging Research*, 28, 253–267.

Norton, C. E. (Ed.). (1893). *Heart of oak books* (Vol. II). Boston: Heath.

Nowottny, W. (1962). *The language poets use*. London: Athlone Press.

Oatley, K. (1994). A taxonomy of the emotions of literary response and a theory of identification in fictional narrative. *Poetics*, 23, 53–74.

Oatley, K. (2016). Fiction: Simulation of social worlds. *Trends in Cognitive Sciences*, 20, 618–628.

Obermeier, C., Menninghaus, W., von Koppenfels, M., Raettig, T., Schmidt-Kassow, M., Otterbein, S., et al. (2013). Aesthetic and emotional effects of meter and rhyme in poetry. *Frontiers in Psychology*, 4. doi:10.3389/fpsyg.2013.00010.

Ogden, C. K., & Richards, I. A. (1923/1989). *The meaning of meaning: A study of the influence of language upon thought and of the science of symbolism.* Orlando, FL: Harcourt Brace Jovanovich.

Oliver, M. (1994). *A poetry handbook.* San Diego: Harcourt Brace.

Oliver, M. (2004). *Why I wake early: New poems.* Boston: Beacon Press.

Olney, J. (1980). *The rhizome and the flower: The perennial philosophy—Yeats and Jung.* Berkeley: University of California Press.

Oppezzo, M., & Schwartz, D. L. (2014). Give your ideas some legs: The positive effect of walking on creative thinking. *Journal of Experimental Psychology: Learning, Memory, and Cognition,* 40, 1142–1152.

Orr, P. (Ed.). (1966). *The poet speaks.* New York: Barnes & Noble.

Ortony, A. (1979). Beyond literal similarity. *Psychological Review,* 86, 161–180.

Ortony, A., Schallert, D. L., Reynolds, R. E., & Antos, S. L. (1978). Interpreting metaphors and idioms: Some effects of context on comprehension. *Journal of Verbal Learning and Verbal Behavior,* 17, 465–477.

Parini, J. (2008). *Why poetry matters.* New Haven, CT: Yale University Press.

Parini, J. (2016). *New and collected poems: 1975–2015.* Boston: Beacon Press.

Passingham, R. E., Bengtsson, S. L., & Lau, H. (2010). Medial frontal cortex: From self-generated action to reflection on one's own performance. *Trends in Cognitive Sciences,* 14, 16–21.

Patterson, K., Nestor, P. J., & Rogers, T. T. (2007). Where do you know what you know? The representation of semantic knowledge in the human brain. *Nature Reviews Neuroscience,* 8, 976–987.

Peelen, M. V., & Caramazza, A. (2012). Conceptual object representations in human anterior temporal cortex. *Journal of Neuroscience,* 32, 15728–15736.

Penn, D. C., Holyoak, K. J., & Povinelli, D. J. (2008). Darwin's mistake: Explaining the discontinuity between human and nonhuman minds. *Behavioral and Brain Sciences,* 31, 109–130.

Pennebaker, J. W. (1997). Writing about emotional experiences as a therapeutic process. *Psychological Science,* 8, 162–166.

Pennington, N., & Hastie, R. (1993). The story model for juror decision making. In R. Hastie (Ed.), *Inside the juror: The psychology of juror decision making* (pp. 192–221). New York: Cambridge University Press.

Perrine, L. (1971). Four forms of metaphor. *College English,* 33, 125–138.

Peskin, J. (2010). The development of poetic literature through the school years. *Discourse Processes*, 47, 77–103.

Peskin, J., Allen, G., & Wells-Jopling, R. (2010). The "Educated Imagination": Applying instructional research to the teaching of symbolic interpretation of poetry. *Journal of Adolescent & Adult Literacy*, 53, 498–507.

Peskin, J., & Wells-Jopling, R. (2012). Fostering symbolic interpretation during adolescence. *Journal of Applied Developmental Psychology*, 33, 13–23.

Pessoa, L., & Pereira, M. G. (2013). Cognition-emotion interactions: A review of the functional magnetic resonance imaging literature. In M. D. Robinson, E. Watkins, & E. Harmon-Jones (Eds.), *Handbook of cognition and emotion* (pp. 55–68). New York: Guilford Press.

Petrović, M. (1933/1967). *Metafore i alegorije* [*Metaphors and allegories*]. Belgrade: Srpska književna zadruga.

Pinker, S. (1994). *The language instinct*. New York: Harper Perennial Modern Classics.

Plath, S. (1963). *The bell jar*. London: Heinemann.

Plath, S. (1971). *Crossing the water*. London: Faber and Faber.

Plath, S. (2000). In K. V. Kukil (Ed.), *The unabridged journals of Sylvia Plath 1950–1962*. New York: Anchor Books.

Poe, E. A. (1846). The philosophy of composition. *Graham's Magazine, 28*, 163–167. https://www.eapoe.org/works/essays/philcomp.htm.

Poe, E. A. (1848/1975). *The complete tales and poems of Edgar Allan Poe*. New York: Random House.

Popov, V., & Hristova, P. (2017). The relational luring effect: Retrieval of relational information during associative recognition. *Journal of Experimental Psychology: General*, 146, 722–745.

Pound, E. (1917). Elizabethan classicists II. *The Egoist, 4*(9), 135–136. https://library.brown.edu/pdfs/1308598180212503.pdf.

Raines, K. (1986). *Yeats the initiate: Essays on certain themes in the writings of W. B. Yeats*. Mountrath, Ireland: Dolmen Press.

Rapp, A. M., Mutschler, D. E., & Erb, M. (2012). Where in the brain is nonliteral language? A coordinate-based meta-analysis of functional magnetic resonance imaging studies. *NeuroImage*, 62, 600–610.

Reddy, M. J. (1979). The conduit metaphor: A case of frame conflict in our language about language. In A. Ortony (Ed.), *Metaphor and thought* (pp. 284–297). Cambridge: Cambridge University Press.

Richards, I. A. (1924/1948). *Principles of literary criticism* (3rd ed.). London: Routledge & Kegan Paul.

Richards, I. A. (1929). *Practical criticism: A study of literary judgment.* London: Kegan Paul, Trench, Trubner & Co.

Richards, I. A. (1934/1962). *Coleridge on imagination* (3rd ed.). London: Routledge & Kegan Paul.

Richards, I. A. (1936). *The philosophy of rhetoric.* New York: Oxford University Press.

Richards, I. A. (1960). Poetic process and literary analysis. In T. A. Sebeok (Ed.), *Style in language* (pp. 9–23). Cambridge, MA: Technology Press of the Massachusetts Institute of Technology.

Richland, L. E., Zur, O., & Holyoak, K. J. (2007). Cognitive supports for analogies in the mathematics classroom. *Science, 316,* 1128–1129.

Ricœur, P. (1977). *The rule of metaphor: Multi-disciplinary studies of the creation of meaning in language* (R. Czerny, Trans.). Toronto: University of Toronto Press. (Original French edition titled *La métaphore vive,* 1975.)

Rilke, R. M. (1934/1993). *Letters to a young poet* (M. D. Herter Norton, Trans.). New York: Norton.

Rivkin, J., & Ryan, M. (Eds.). (2017). *Literary theory: An anthology* (3rd ed.). Hoboken, NJ: Wiley-Blackwell.

Roediger, H. L., III. (1980). Memory metaphors in cognitive psychology. *Memory & Cognition, 8,* 231–246.

Roethke, T. (1974). *The collected poems of Theodore Roethke.* New York: Knopf Doubleday.

Rosenthal, M. L. (1996). Introduction: The poetry of Yeats. In W. B. Yeats, *Selected poems and four plays of William Butler Yeats* (pp. xix–xliv) (4th ed., M. L. Rosenthal, Ed.). New York: Scribner.

Rubin, D. C. (1995). *Memory in oral traditions: The cognitive psychology of epic, ballads, and counting-out rhymes.* New York: Oxford University Press.

Rumelhart, D. E., McClelland, J. L., & the PDP Research Group. (1986). *Parallel distributed processing: Explorations in the microstructure of cognition,* Vol. 1: *Foundations.* Cambridge, MA: MIT Press.

Russo, J. E. (2014). The predecisional distortion of information. In E. A. Wilhelms & V. F. Reyna (Eds.), *Neuroeconomics, judgment, and decision making* (pp. 91–110). New York: Psychology Press.

Sachs, J. (1967). Recognition memory for syntactic and semantic aspects of connected discourse. *Perception & Psychophysics, 2,* 437–442.

Schacter, D. L., Addis, D. R., & Buckner, R. L. (2007). Remembering the past to imagine the future: The prospective brain. *Nature Reviews Neuroscience*, 8, 657–661.

Schooler, J. W., Smallwood, J., Christoff, K., Handy, T. C., Reichle, E. D., & Sayette, M. A. (2011). Meta-awareness, perceptual decoupling and the wandering mind. *Trends in Cognitive Sciences*, 15, 319–326.

Schunn, C. D., & Dunbar, K. (1996). Priming, analogy, and awareness in complex reasoning. *Memory & Cognition*, 24, 271–284.

Searle, J. R. (1975). A taxonomy of illocutionary acts. In K. Gunderson (Ed.), *Minneapolis Studies in the Philosophy of Science, Vol. 7: Language, mind, and knowledge* (pp. 344–369). Minneapolis: University of Minnesota Press.

Searle, J. R. (1979). Metaphor. In A. Ortony (Ed.), *Metaphor and thought* (pp. 92–123). Cambridge: Cambridge University Press.

Searle, J. R. (1997). *The mystery of consciousness*. London: Granta Books.

Searle, J. R. (1999). The Chinese room argument. In R. A. Wilson & F. Keil (Eds.), *The MIT encyclopedia of the cognitive sciences* (pp. 115–116). Cambridge, MA: MIT Press.

Seli, P., Carriere, J. S. A., & Smilek, D. (2015). Not all mind wandering is created equal: Dissociating deliberate from spontaneous mind wandering. *Psychological Research*, 79, 750–758.

Seli, P., Risko, E. F., Smilek, D., & Schacter, D. L. (2016). Mind-wandering with and without intention. *Trends in Cognitive Sciences*, 20, 605–617.

Semendeferi, K., Armstrong, E., Schleicher, A., Zilles, K., & Van Hoesen, G. W. (2001). Prefrontal cortex in humans and apes: A comparative study of area 10. *American Journal of Physical Anthropology*, 114, 224–241.

Shelley, P. B. (written in 1821, first published in 1840). A defense of poetry. http://www.gutenberg.org/files/5428/5428-h/5428-h.htm.

Shepard, R. N. (1978). The mental image. *American Psychologist*, 33, 125–137.

Shklovsky, V. (1917/1988). Art as technique. In D. Lodge (Ed.), *Modern criticism and theory (1988)* (pp. 16–30). London: Longman.

Sikora, S., Kuiken, D., & Miall, D. S. (2011). Expressive reading: A phenomenological study of readers' experience of Coleridge's *The Rime of the Ancient Mariner*. *Journal of Aesthetics, Creativity, and the Arts*, 5, 258–268.

Silvia, P. J., & Beaty, R. E. (2012). Making creative metaphors: The importance of fluid intelligence for creative thought. *Intelligence*, 40, 343–351.

Simmons, S., & Estes, Z. (2008). Individual differences in the perception of similarity and difference. *Cognition*, 108, 781–795.

Simon, D. (2012). *In doubt: The psychology of the criminal justice process.* Cambridge, MA: Harvard University Press.

Simon, D., Krawczyk, D. C., & Holyoak, K. J. (2004). Construction of preferences by constraint satisfaction. *Psychological Science,* 15, 331–336.

Simons, D. J., Boot, W. R., Charness, N., Gathercole, S. E., Chabris, C. F., Hambrick, D. Z., et al. (2016). Do "brain-training" programs work? *Psychological Science in the Public Interest,* 17 (suppl.), 103–186.

Simonton, K. D. (2014). The mad (creative) genius: What do we know after a century of historiometric research? In J. C. Kaufman (Ed.), *Creativity and mental illness* (pp. 25–41). Cambridge: Cambridge University Press.

Smallwood, J. (2013). Distinguishing how from why the mind wanders: A process-occurrence framework for self-generated mental activity. *Psychological Bulletin,* 139, 519–535.

Smallwood, J., Brown, K., Baird, B., & Schooler, J. W. (2011). Cooperation between the default mode network and the frontal-parietal network in the production of an internal train of thought. *Brain Research,* 1428, 60–70.

Smallwood, J., Brown, K., Tipper, C., Giesbrecht, B., Franklin, M. S., Mrazek, M. D., et al. (2011). Pupillometric evidence for the decoupling of attention from perceptual input during offline thought. *PLoS One,* 6(3), e18298. https://doi.org/10.1371/journal.pone.0018298.

Smith, E. E., & Osherson, D. N. (1984). Conceptual combination with prototype concepts. *Cognitive Science,* 8, 337–361.

Snow, C. P. (1959/2001). *The two cultures.* Cambridge: Cambridge University Press.

Sommer, E., & Weiss, D. (1996). *Metaphors dictionary.* Detroit: Visible Ink.

Spellman, B. A., & Holyoak, K. J. (1992). If Saddam is Hitler then who is George Bush? Analogical mapping between systems of social roles. *Journal of Personality and Social Psychology,* 62, 913–933.

Spellman, B. A., & Holyoak, K. J. (1996). Pragmatics in analogical mapping. *Cognitive Psychology,* 31, 307–346.

Spellman, B. A., Holyoak, K. J., & Morrison, R. G. (2001). Analogical priming via semantic relations. *Memory & Cognition,* 29, 383–393.

Spender, S. (1946/1952). The making of a poem. Reprinted in B. Ghiselin (Ed.), *The creative process (pp. 112-125).* Oakland: University of California Press.

Starr, G. G. (2013). *Feeling beauty: The neuroscience of aesthetic experience.* Cambridge, MA: MIT Press.

Steele, T. (1990). *Missing measures: Modern poetry and the revolt against meter*. Fayette-ville: University of Arkansas Press.

Steele, T. (1999). *All the fun's in how you say a thing*. Athens: Ohio University Press.

Stemmer, B. (2017). Neuropragmatics. In Y. Huang (Ed.), *Oxford handbook of pragmatics* (pp. 362–379). New York: Oxford University Press.

Stern, J. (2000). *Metaphor in context*. Cambridge, MA: MIT Press.

Stevens, W. (1951). *The necessary angel: Essays on reality and the imagination*. London: Faber and Faber.

Sulfridge, C. (1973). Meaning in Whitman's use of "electric." *Walt Whitman Review*, 19, 151–153.

Sulin, R. A., & Dooling, D. J. (1974). Intrusion of a thematic idea in retention of prose. *Journal of Experimental Psychology*, 103, 255–262.

Tabor, N. (2015). No slouch. *Paris Review*, April 7. https://www.theparisreview.org/blog/2015/04/07/no-slouch/.

Tate, A. (1953). *The forlorn demon: Didactic and critical essays*. Chicago: Regnery.

Thagard, P. (1997). Coherent and creative conceptual combinations. In T. B. Ward, S. M. Smith, & J. Viad (Eds.), *Creative thought: An investigation of conceptual structures and processes* (pp. 129–141). Washington, DC: American Psychological Association.

Thagard, P. (2000). *Coherence in thought and action*. Cambridge, MA: MIT Press.

Thagard, P., & Shelley, C. (2001). Emotional analogies and analogical inference. In D. Gentner, K. J. Holyoak, & B. N. Kokinov (Eds.), *The analogical mind: Perspectives from cognitive science* (pp. 335–362). Cambridge, MA: MIT Press.

Thomas, D. (1971). *The collected poems of Dylan Thomas 1934–1952*. New York: New Directions.

Thrash, T. M., Maruskin, L. A., Moldovan, E. G., Oleynick, V. C., & Belzak, W. C. (2017). Writer-reader contagion of inspiration and related states: Conditional process analyses within a cross-classified writer x reader framework. *Journal of Personality and Social Psychology*, 113, 466–491.

Tillman, B., & Dowling, W. J. (2007). Memory decreases for prose, but not poetry. *Memory & Cognition*, 35, 628–639.

Tourangeau, R., & Rips, L. (1991). Interpreting and evaluating metaphors. *Journal of Memory and Language*, 30, 452–472.

Tourangeau, R., & Sternberg, R. J. (1981). Aptness in metaphor. *Cognitive Psychology*, 13, 27–55.

Tourangeau, R., & Sternberg, R. J. (1982). Understanding and appreciating metaphors. *Cognition*, 11, 203–244.

Tranströmer, T. (1987). *Selected poems 1954–1986*. New York: Ecco Press.

Trilling, L. (1971). *Sincerity and authenticity (the Charles Eliot Norton Lectures 1969–1970)*. Cambridge, MA: Harvard University Press.

Trope, Y., & Liberman, N. (2010). Construal-level theory of psychological distance. *Psychological Review*, 117, 440–463.

Tuggy, D. (1993). Ambiguity, polysemy, and vagueness. *Cognitive Linguistics*, 4, 273–290.

Turing, A. M. (1950). Computing machinery and intelligence. *Mind*, 59, 433–460.

Turner, F., & Pöppel, E. (1983). The neural lyre: Poetic meter, the brain, and time. *Poetry*, 12, 277–309.

Turner, M. (1987). *Death is the mother of beauty: Mind, metaphor, criticism*. Chicago: University of Chicago Press.

Turner, M. (1996). *The literary mind: The origins of thought and language*. New York: Oxford University Press.

Ullmann, S. (1962/1979). *Semantics: An introduction to the science of meaning*. New York: Harper & Row.

Ulrich, M., Keller, J., Hoenig, K., Waller, C., & Grön, G. (2014). Neural correlates of experimentally induced flow. *NeuroImage*, 86, 194–202.

Valéry, P. (1958). *The art of poetry* (D. Folliot, Trans.). New York: Vintage Books.

van Peer, W. (1986). *Stylistics and psychology: Investigations of foregrounding*. London: Croom Helm.

Vartanian, O. (2012). Dissociable neural systems for analogy and metaphor: Implications for the neuroscience of creativity. *British Journal of Psychology*, 103, 302–316.

Veale, T. (2013). Less rhyme, more reason: Knowledge-based poetry generation with feeling, insight and wit. In *Proceedings of the International Conference on Computational Creativity* (pp. 152–159). Sydney: Association for Computational Creativity.

Verhaeghen, P., Joormann, J., & Aikman, S. N. (2014). Creativity, mood, and the examined life: Self-reflective rumination boosts creativity, brooding breeds dysphoria. *Psychology of Aesthetics, Creativity, and the Arts*, 8, 211–218.

Vessel, E. A., Starr, G. G., & Rubin, N. (2013). Art reaches within: Aesthetic experience, the self and the default mode network. *Frontiers in Neuroscience*, 7, 258. doi:10.3389/fnins.2013.00258.

Wallas, G. (1926). *The art of thought*. London: Jonathan Cape.

Waltz, J. A., Knowlton, B. J., Holyoak, K. J., Boone, K. B., Mishkin, F. S., de Menezes Santos, M., et al. (1999). A system for relational reasoning in human prefrontal cortex. *Psychological Science, 10,* 119–125.

Wassiliwizky, E., Koelsch, S., Wagner, V., Jacobsen, T., & Menninghaus, W. (2017). The emotional power of poetry: Neural circuitry, psychophysiology and compositional principles. *Social Cognitive and Affective Neuroscience, 12,* 1229–1240.

Watson, B. (1971). *Chinese lyricism: Shih poetry from the second to the twelfth century.* New York: Columbia University Press.

Watson, D. (2003). To dream, perchance to remember: Individual differences in dream recall. *Personality and Individual Differences, 34,* 1271–1286.

Webster, M. A. (2012). Evolving concepts of sensory adaptation. *F1000 Biology Reports.* doi:10.3410/B4-21.

Westphal, A. J., Reggente, N., Ito, K. L., & Rissman, J. (2016). Shared and distinct contributions of rostrolateral prefrontal cortex to analogical reasoning and episodic memory retrieval. *Human Brain Mapping, 37,* 896–912.

Wheelwright, P. (1940/1967). On the semantics of poetry. In S. Chatman & S. R. Levin (Eds.), *Essays on the language of literature* (pp. 250–263). Boston: Houghton Mifflin.

Wheelwright, P. (1968). *The burning fountain: A study in the language of symbolism.* Bloomington: Indiana University Press.

Wilson, E. (1929). Yeats' guide to the soul. *The New Republic,* January 16, pp. 249–251. http://www.yeatsvision.com/AllReviews.html#CB527.

Wilson, F. (2008). *The ballad of Dorothy Wordsworth.* London: Faber and Faber.

Wimsatt, W. K., Jr., & Brooks, C. (1957). *Literary criticism: A short history.* New York: Knopf.

Wisniewski, E. J., & Bassok, B. (1999). What makes a man similar to a tie? Stimulus compatibility with similarity and integration. *Cognitive Psychology, 39,* 208–238.

Wisniewski, E. J., & Gentner, D. (1991). On the combinatorial semantics of noun pairs: Minor and major adjustments to meaning. In G. B. Simpson (Ed.), *Understanding word and sentence* (pp. 241–284). Amsterdam: North Holland.

Wisniewski, E. J., & Love, B. C. (1998). Relations versus properties in conceptual combination. *Journal of Memory and Language, 38,* 177–202.

Wittgenstein, L. (1922). *Tractatus logico-philosophicus* (C. K. Ogden & F. P. Ramsey, Trans.). Edinburgh: Edinburgh Press. http://www.gutenberg.org/ebooks/5740.

Wolff, P., & Gentner, D. (2000). Evidence for role-neutral initial processing of metaphors. *Journal of Experimental Psychology: Learning, Memory, and Cognition*, 26, 529–541.

Woon, K. (2013). *Water chasing water*. Los Angeles: Kaya Press.

Xie, M. (1999). *Ezra Pound and the appropriation of Chinese poetry: Cathay, translation, and imagism*. New York: Routledge.

Yeats, W. B. (1903). *Ideas of good and evil*. New York: Macmillan.

Yeats, W. B. (1925). *A vision*. London: T. Werner Laurie.

Zaki, J. (2017). Moving beyond stereotypes of empathy. *Trends in Cognitive Sciences*, 21, 59–60.

Zanto, T. P., & Gazzaley, A. (2013). Fronto-parietal network: Flexible hub of cognitive control. *Trends in Cognitive Sciences*, 17, 602–603.

Zeeman, A., Milton, F., Smith, A., & Rylance, R. (2013). By heart: An fMRI study of brain activation by poetry and prose. *Journal of Consciousness Studies*, 20, 132–158.

Zeki, S. (2004). The neurology of ambiguity. *Consciousness and Cognition*, 13, 173–196.

Index

p. 2 poetry engages mind-body w/ rhythm

C + 4 coleridge

p. 204 note 17 on literal language Kitty

p. 22 e.g. of schema vs. literal language

p. 22 plath's 9 syllables 9 ono

p. 24 local M vs extended

3 ul   Frost says poetry is "just made
             of M"
             > perhaps not · M is one part
                of narrative, image, rhythm, tie

p. 35 Coleridge & the creative mind contemplates
       "not only things but the relations
        of things."

36   "words correspond to thoughts"

p. 37-38   IA Richards & New Critics
              as divorced from author....
           > a view influences CMT theory
                poorly

p. 38   Richards wrote "Coleridge on Imagination"

   39   Black as analogies

p. 53 Holyoak emphasizes analogy
          + "coherence theory" from psychology